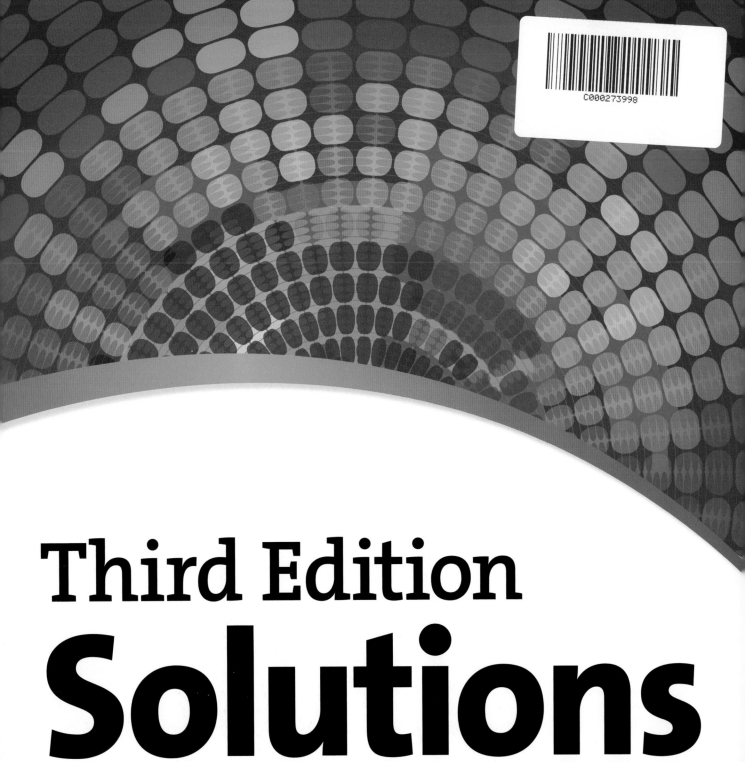

# Third Edition
# Solutions

## Pre-Intermediate

### Student's Book

Tim Falla    Paul A Davies

OXFORD
UNIVERSITY PRESS

# I

# Introduction

## Likes and dislikes

*I can talk about likes and dislikes.*

**1 SPEAKING** Describe the photo. Where are the people? What are they doing?

**2** 🎧 **1.02** Read and listen to the dialogue. Find the names of the people in the photo.

**Ryan** Hi, Izzy. Can I sit here?

**Izzy** Yes, of course. This is Becky. She's new.

**Ryan** Hi, Becky. I'm Ryan, Izzy's brother.

**Becky** Hi. Nice to meet you!

**Ryan** Where are you from, Becky?

**Becky** I'm from London. I moved here two weeks ago.

**Ryan** I love London. I've got friends there. I sometimes visit them and we go skateboarding.

**Izzy** Do you like skateboarding, Becky?

**Becky** Not really. But I like ice skating.

**Izzy** Me too! Let's go ice skating after school.

**Becky** Great idea!

**Ryan** I'm not very keen on ice skating. What do you think of bowling?

**Becky** Bowling? I hate it.

**Ryan** Oh. Actually, I don't mind ice skating ...

**Izzy** There's the bell. I've got maths, then history.

**Becky** I've got PE now. I love PE! See you after school, Izzy!

**Izzy** Bye, Becky.

**Ryan** Yeah ... Bye ...

**3** Are the sentences true or false? Write T or F.

1 This is the first time Izzy and Ryan meet. ___
2 This is the first time Becky and Ryan meet. ___
3 Ryan sometimes goes skateboarding in London. ___
4 Becky does not like skateboarding or bowling. ___
5 Ryan and Becky agree to go ice skating after school. ___
6 Izzy and Becky have got PE next. ___

**4 VOCABULARY** Add three words from the dialogue in exercise 2 to each list.

**Sports and hobbies**
board games
drawing
_____
_____
_____

**School subjects**
drama
IT (information technology)
_____
_____
_____

**5** Work in pairs. How many more words can you add to the lists in exercise 4 in three minutes? Use the pictures below and your own ideas.

**Subjects**

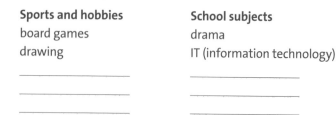

**Hobbies**

➡ **Vocabulary Builder** Sports and hobbies: page 117

**6 KEY PHRASES** Label the phrases below A (*like*), B (*OK*) or C (*don't like*). Which phrases are in the dialogue in exercise 2?

| Likes and dislikes | | |
| --- | --- | --- |
| I can't stand ... ___ | I love ... ___ | ... isn't bad. ___ |
| I don't mind ... ___ | I (quite) like ... ___ | ... is great. ___ |
| I hate ... ___ | I'm really keen on ... ___ | ... is terrible. ___ |

**7 SPEAKING** Work in pairs, taking turns to be A and B.

**Student A:** Find out your partner's opinion of school subjects. Put them into groups A, B and C from exercise 6.

**Student B:** Answer A's questions using phrases from exercise 6.

> What do you think of PE?

> I don't mind it.

**8 SPEAKING** Work in pairs. Try to find three sports or hobbies which you and your partner both like.

> Do you like drawing?

> No, I don't. But I like board games.

> Me too! Do you like ... ?

## Grammar
# Contrast: present simple and present continuous
*I can distinguish the use of the present simple and present continuous.*

Hi, Adam. I'm in the park with some friends. Do you want to join us?

What are you doing?

At the moment, we're listening to Sue. She's playing the guitar.

Is she good?

She's OK. She's getting better. She has guitar lessons every week. So are you coming?

I don't know. We're moving house next weekend, so I need to help my parents. We're packing boxes today.

That's a shame. We're playing volleyball later.

I love volleyball! Maybe just for an hour …

Sure. A game of volleyball doesn't take long. See you later! ☺

**1** **Describe the photo. What are the people doing? Use the verbs below.**

laugh   play   sit   smile   wear

*The girl on the left is playing the guitar.*

**2** **Read the messages above. Why does Adam change his mind about going to the park?**

**LEARN THIS!** Present tense contrast

We use:

a the ¹present simple for something that happens regularly, always or never.

b the ²_____ for something happening at this moment.

c the ³_____ for something happening around this time.

d the ⁴_____ for stating a fact.

e the ⁵_____ with certain verbs that we do not usually use in continuous tenses: *believe, know, like, love, need, understand, want*, etc.

f the ⁶_____ for future arrangements.

**3** **Find examples of the present simple and present continuous in the messages in exercise 2. Then read the Learn this! box and complete the rules.**

**4** **Match each example you found in the messages with the correct rule (a–f) in the Learn this! box.**

**5** **Work in pairs. Explain the difference between sentences a and b in each pair.**

1 a I'm doing my homework after school.
  b I do my homework after school.
2 a Joe is learning to drive.
  b Many teenagers learn to drive when they are seventeen.
3 a Mark plays the guitar.
  b Mark is playing the guitar.
4 a We aren't going on holiday in August.
  b We don't go on holiday in August.

➡ Grammar Builder IB   page 122

**6** **🎧1.03** **Complete the phone dialogue. Use the correct present simple or present continuous form of the verbs in brackets. Then listen and check.**

Toby  Hi!
Leia  Hi, Toby. What ¹*are you doing* (you / do)?
Toby  I'm at the sports centre. I ²_____ (wait) for Tom.
Leia  ³_____ (you / go) swimming?
Toby  No, we ⁴_____ (play) table tennis. We ⁵_____ (play) every Saturday morning. But he's really late!
Leia  What ⁶_____ (he / do)?
Toby  I ⁷_____ (not know). He ⁸_____ (not answer) his phone. Anyway, where are you?
Leia  I'm at the shopping centre, but I ⁹_____ (not buy) anything today. I ¹⁰_____ just _____ (look).
Toby  ¹¹_____ (you / like) table tennis? ¹²_____ (you / want) to play?
Leia  Sure! But I ¹³_____ (not wear) sports clothes.
Toby  ¹⁴_____ (you / wear) trainers?
Leia  Yes, I am – with jeans and a T-shirt.
Toby  That's fine. You ¹⁵_____ (not need) sports clothes. See you soon!

**7** **SPEAKING** **Work in pairs. Ask and answer questions 1–6. Use the activities below or your own ideas.**

**Everyday activities**   do [my] homework   go shopping   go for a walk / a bike ride   have a picnic   listen to music   play football / tennis / video games   read a book   visit friends / relatives   watch a film / TV

1 What do you usually do after school?
2 What are you doing after school today?
3 What do you usually do at the weekend?
4 What are you doing this weekend?
5 What do you usually do during the school holidays?
6 What are you doing next school holiday?

What do you usually do after school?

I listen to music at home.

# 1C Vocabulary
## Describing people
*I can describe people's appearance.*

**1** Look at the photos of famous film characters. Match them with the names below. What films do they appear in? Do you know who the actors are?

James Bond ___     Edward Cullen ___     Galadriel ___
Black Widow ___    Javert ___            Katniss Everdeen ___

**2** Match the sentence beginnings (1–4) with the endings (a–d). Then match the descriptions with four of the characters in exercise 1.

1 _____ has got long brown hair. She's wearing ___
2 _____ has got long wavy red hair. She's wearing ___
3 _____ has got short dark hair. He's wearing ___
4 _____ has got a beard and moustache. He's wearing ___

a a black jacket and black trousers.
b a brown jacket and a black T-shirt.
c a coat and a hat.
d a grey coat, a blue shirt and dark jeans.

**3** **VOCABULARY** Add the adjectives below to the table. Note the order of the adjectives.

**Describing hair**  black  brown  fair  red  long  medium-length  straight  wavy

|  | length | style | colour |  |
|---|---|---|---|---|
| He/She's got | short | curly | dark | hair. |
|  |  |  |  |  |
|  |  |  |  |  |

**4** Work in pairs. How many different items of clothing can you write down? Include all the ones in exercise 2. Put them into groups A and B below.

**A** Top half      jacket, shirt, …
**B** Bottom half   trousers, shoes, …

➤➤ **Vocabulary Builder** Clothes: page 117

**5** In your notebook, write a description of the other two characters in exercise 1.

*Galadriel has got …  She's wearing …*
*James Bond has got …  He's …*

**6** **SPEAKING** Tell your partner what clothes you usually wear when:

a you are at school.
b you go out with friends.
c you are relaxing at home.
d you do sport.

> When I'm at school, I usually wear …

**7** **SPEAKING** Work in pairs. Describe someone in the class. Can your partner guess who it is?

> She's got curly fair hair and blue eyes. She's wearing a red sweatshirt, jeans and black trainers.

> Is it Anna?

# ID Grammar

# Articles

*I can correctly use* a / an *and the* with nouns.

Good morning, children.

This is a classroom in a primary school in South Korea. The classroom is very high-tech. There are some students on the floor. They are playing with a robot dog. Is there a teacher? Yes, there is, but the teacher is a robot! It is difficult to find English teachers in South Korea, so they are starting to use robots instead. The robot can speak, and correct pronunciation. Are the robots popular with the students? Chung Cha, the girl on the right, says, 'The robots are fun, but I think a real teacher is better. I hope robots don't replace teachers because I want to study languages at university and be an English teacher one day!'

**1** Look at the photo of the classroom. What is unusual about it?

**2** Read the text and check your ideas. Would you like to learn English in a classroom like this? Why? / Why not?

> **LEARN THIS!** Articles
>
> **a** We use ¹_____ to talk about something for the first time.
>   There's an interactive whiteboard in our classroom.
>
> **b** We use ²_____ when we mention something again.
>   Our teacher often uses the interactive whiteboard.
>
> **c** We use ³_____ when it is clear what we are talking about, or when there is only one of something.
>   We play basketball in the gym. (The gym at school)
>   The sun is shining.
>
> **d** We use ⁴_____ to say what someone's job is.
>   My mum's a teacher.
>
> **e** Note these set phrases.
>   • ⁵_____: listen to the radio, go to the cinema, play the guitar
>   • ⁶_____: watch TV, listen to music, in / to bed, to / at / from school, at home / work, in hospital

**3** Read the Learn this! box. Complete the rules with *a / an, the,* or *no article* (–).

**4** Read the text in exercise 2 again. Match each of the highlighted words with a rule in the Learn this! box.

**5** Complete the dialogue. Use *a / an* or *the*. Explain your choices.

| Martha | I go to school near ¹the city centre. |
| Jake | Really? What's ²_____ name of ³_____ school? |
| Martha | St Mark's. It's ⁴_____ private school. |
| Jake | I know ⁵_____ girl who goes there. Alice Smith. |
| Martha | There's ⁶_____ Alice Smith in my class. I wonder if it's ⁷_____ same one. |
| Jake | She's got blue eyes, long wavy hair and ⁸_____ nice smile. |
| Martha | That's her! Which school do you go to? |
| Jake | Hadfield College. |
| Martha | Oh. My dad's ⁹_____ maths teacher there: John Chapman. |
| Jake | You're joking! He's my teacher! |

> **LOOK OUT!**
> We do not use *the* when we make generalisations.
> I don't like history. (~~the history~~ ✗)
> I like playing basketball at school. (~~the basketball~~ ✗)

**6** Read the Look out! box. Are the sentences below generalisations or not? Circle the correct words.

1 **Dogs** / **The dogs** are more intelligent than **cats** / **the cats**.
2 **Weather** / **The weather** is nice today.
3 **Football** / **The football** is more fun than **volleyball** / **the volleyball**.

➽ Grammar Builder ID page 122

**7** Read the Learn this! box and complete the rules with *is* or *are*. Find one example of *there is* and one example of *there are* in the text in exercise 2.

> **LEARN THIS!** *There is / are*
>
> **a** We use *There* ¹_____ with singular nouns.
>   There is a book on the desk.
>
> **b** We use *There* ²_____ with plural nouns.
>   There are twenty children in the class.
>
> **c** The short form of *There* ³_____ is *There's. There* ⁴_____ does not have a short form.

**8** **VOCABULARY** Check the meaning of the words below. Which ones are in your classroom?

**In school** canteen classroom computer corridor desk gym hall interactive whiteboard laptop noticeboard playing field reception staff room textbook whiteboard

**9** **SPEAKING** Imagine you are describing your school to a visitor. Talk about some of the places and things in exercise 8. Use *There is / are* and articles correctly.

> There's a canteen and a gym. There are …

# 1 Feelings

## 1A Vocabulary

# How do you feel?

*I can describe how people are feeling.*

**1 SPEAKING** Look at the photos and answer the questions. Use the words below to help you answer question 2.

1 How do you think these people are feeling?
2 What is making them feel that way?

**Photo A** watch  match  team  lose
**Photo B** exam results  pass  marks
**Photo C** plane  late  luggage
**Photo D** school work  difficult  boring

**2 🎧1.04 VOCABULARY** Check the meaning of all the adjectives below. Can you match any of them with the photos in exercise 1?

**Adjectives to describe feelings** anxious  ashamed  bored  confused  cross  delighted  disappointed  embarrassed  envious  excited  frightened  proud  relieved  shocked  suspicious  upset
*The people in photo A look …*

**3** Work in pairs. Put the adjectives in exercise 2 into categories A and B below. Do you know any other adjectives you could add to the categories?

| A Positive feelings | B Negative feelings |
|---|---|
|  |  |
|  |  |

**4** In pairs, do the test below. Then check the answers at the bottom of the page. How many did you get right?

# Can you read people's emotions?

For each photo, choose the adjective (a–c) that matches how the person is feeling.

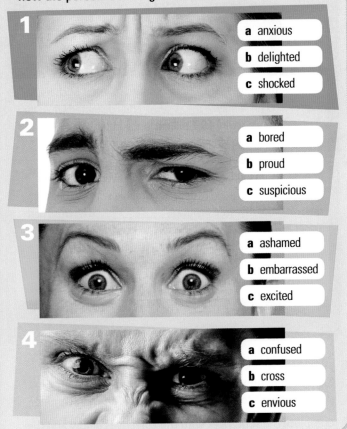

**1**
- **a** anxious
- **b** delighted
- **c** shocked

**2**
- **a** bored
- **b** proud
- **c** suspicious

**3**
- **a** ashamed
- **b** embarrassed
- **c** excited

**4**
- **a** confused
- **b** cross
- **c** envious

**5** Read the tweets and complete the hashtags with adjectives from exercise 2. Then compare your answers in pairs. More than one answer may be possible.

**Tweets**

**1 Stella P** @StellaP02 — 1 min
Jules has got that new phone that I really want … #envious

**2 Amy Price** @Priceyone — 9 mins
There's nothing to do here. #_____

**3 Student Voice** @1234student — 23 mins
It's our end-of-term party tonight!!
#_____

**4 MaryGG** @MaryGG — 1hr
Our English teacher is away so we haven't got a test :D #_____

**5 Music Mad** @mad4music — 2hr
My new MP3 player doesn't work.
#_____

**6 Dan B** @DanB25 — 2hr
Oops! Dropped a plate of food in the school canteen. #_____

**6** 🎧 **1.05** Listen to five speakers. Match one adjective from the list below with each speaker (1–5). There are three extra adjectives.

anxious   cross   confused   disappointed
excited   embarrassed   proud   suspicious

1 _____   2 _____   3 _____   4 _____   5 _____

> **RECYCLE!  Present continuous**
>
> We use the present continuous for things happening as we speak.
>
> *Grace is making dinner (at this moment).*
>
> However, with verbs not used in continuous tenses (*believe, belong, hate, know, seem,* etc.), we use the present simple even for things happening now.
>
> *Look! Jack seems cross (at this moment).*

**7** 🎧 **1.05** Read the Recycle! box. Then listen again and complete the sentences (a–e) with speakers 1–5 and the correct present tense form of the verbs in brackets.

- **a** Speaker ___ _____ (not know) that a friend's exam result is bad.
- **b** Speaker ___ _____ (not understand) why there aren't any buses.
- **c** Speaker ___ _____ (lie) in bed at night and can hear voices.
- **d** Speaker ___ _____ (have) a ticket for a really good concert.
- **e** Speaker ___ _____ (make) a birthday cake for a friend who won't like it.

> How does Speaker 1 feel and why?

> He feels … because he …

**8** In pairs, check your answers to exercises 6 and 7.

**9** VOCABULARY Read the modifying adverbs below. Number them in order from weakest to strongest.

**Modifying adverbs**   a bit ___   a little bit 1   extremely ___
rather ___   very ___

**10** Write notes about how you usually feel in these situations. Sometimes you might need more than one adjective. Include modifying adverbs from exercise 9.

How do you feel when …
1 you have an exam in ten minutes?
2 your exam finishes?
3 you see a large spider in your bedroom?
4 friends or family members are arguing?
5 you arrive at a party?
6 you can't sleep?

**11** SPEAKING In pairs, take turns to ask and answer the questions in exercise 10.

> How do you feel when … ?

> I feel excited, but a little bit anxious too.

1a 2c 3c 4b

# Past simple (affirmative)

*I can use the past simple affirmative.*

**1** Is there a lottery in your country? Do you think it is a good idea to buy tickets? Why? / Why not?

**2** Read the text. Are all lottery winners happy?

Last weekend, somebody bought a lottery ticket, chose all the correct numbers and won millions. How lucky! Or maybe not. In the 1970s, scientists at the University of Illinois studied lottery winners and compared their levels of happiness with other people. The results were interesting. The winners felt delighted for a short time, but after that, their happiness returned to normal levels. A similar study by the University of California in 2008 gave the same results. They looked at lottery winners six months after their win and found completely normal levels of happiness. And for a few unlucky people, a huge lottery win was the start of major problems. Alex Toth, for example, won $13 million in 1990. He stopped working, spent the money quickly and had terrible arguments with his family and friends.

**3** Read the Learn this! box. Find all the past simple forms in the text in exercise 2. Match them with rules a–d in the Learn this! box.

> **LEARN THIS!** Past simple (affirmative)
>
> **a** We form the past simple form of regular verbs by adding *-ed* to the infinitive.
> *want – wanted   talk – talked*
>
> **b** There are some rules about spelling changes.
> **1** *drop – dropped*  **2** *marry – married*  **3** *move – moved*
>
> **c** Some verbs have irregular past simple forms.
> *go – went   begin – began   leave – left   take – took*
>
> **d** The past simple of the verb *be* has two forms, singular and plural.
> *be – was / were*

➡ **Grammar Builder 1B** page 124

**4** Complete the sentences with regular and irregular past simple forms from exercise 3.

1 She won millions of dollars on the lottery. She _____ all the money in only three years.
2 I _____ my keys in the street. Luckily, I _____ them later.
3 Our cousin _____ to university when he was only fifteen years old. He _____ maths there.
4 My grandfather _____ my grandmother in 1965 and they _____ together until she died last year.
5 I _____ home when I was nineteen and _____ to London.

**5** 🎧 1.06 Complete the text with the past simple form of the verbs in brackets. Then listen and check.

In 2002, nineteen-year-old British refuse collector Michael Carroll and his family ¹_____ (be) delighted when he ²_____ (win) £9.7 million in the lottery. He ³_____ (give) millions of pounds to charity and to friends and relatives. He also ⁴_____ (spend) thousands on loud, all-night parties, and over the next few years, he ⁵_____ (get) into trouble with the police several times. His wife Sandra ⁶_____ (be) cross and upset and ⁷_____ (decide) to leave. Soon, he ⁸_____ (have) no money left, and in 2010, he ⁹_____ (begin) work as a refuse collector again. 'I'm just glad it's over,' he ¹⁰_____ (say).

**6** SPEAKING Work in pairs. What is your opinion of what happened to Alex Toth and Michael Carroll? Are their stories difficult to believe? Are they sad, funny, a warning?

**7** Complete the sentences with the adjectives below and the past simple form of the verbs in brackets.

bored   delighted   disappointed   embarrassed
relieved   suspicious   ~~upset~~

1 Sandra Carroll felt (feel) upset when Michael spent (spend) all his money on parties.
2 Spencer _____ (be) _____ when he _____ (drop) all his money on the floor of the shop.
3 Bess _____ (be) _____ when she _____ (win) the essay competition.
4 I _____ (feel) a bit _____ when the man _____ (say) he was a millionaire.
5 We _____ (be) very _____ when the music _____ (stop) and everyone _____ (leave) the party.
6 I _____ (get) a bit _____ because Dan _____ (talk) about his new girlfriend all evening.
7 You _____ (be) extremely _____ when we _____ (find) your mobile phone behind the sofa.

**8** SPEAKING Tell your partner about a time when you had these feelings. Use the past simple.

1 anxious        3 cross        5 shocked
2 confused       4 excited      6 upset

> I was anxious because I had a music exam.

**Listening**
# Problems, problems!
*I can listen for gist.*

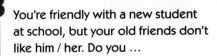

**1 SPEAKING** Describe the photo. What are the girls doing? How are they feeling? What do you think they are saying?

**2 SPEAKING** In pairs, take turns to ask and answer the questions in the questionnaire. Are your answers the same?

**1** You borrowed a DVD from your friend but now you can't find it. Do you …
a tell your friend the truth as soon as possible?
b say nothing and hope your friend forgets about it?
c secretly buy a new copy of the DVD?
d keep looking for the DVD but say nothing yet?

**2** Your friend has stopped speaking to you and you don't know why. Do you …
a send a message asking what the problem is?
b ask your other friends about it?
c insist on talking face-to-face with your friend?
d wait and see if the problem goes away?

**3** You're friendly with a new student at school, but your old friends don't like him / her. Do you …
a stop spending time with the new student?
b tell your old friends they aren't behaving well?
c invite them all to your house so they can get to know one another?
d continue to see them all, but separately?

**Listening Strategy**
You do not have to understand every word in a listening task. Focus on the general meaning and try not to be distracted by words you do not understand.

**3** 🎧 **1.07** Read the Listening Strategy above and the three summaries of a dialogue below. Then listen to the dialogue. Which is the best summary?

a Zak refuses to go out with Tom because he's disappointed about his exam results.
b Zak is anxious about his exams and decides not to go out with Tom.
c Zak is relieved that his exams are six weeks away, and agrees to go out with Tom.

**LEARN THIS!** *should*
a We often use *I think* … + *should*.
   I think she should speak to her friend.
b For the negative, we use *I don't think* … + *should* (NOT ~~I think + shouldn't~~).
   I don't think we should borrow more money.

**4 SPEAKING** Read the Learn this! box. Then say what Zak should do. Use *I (don't) think* … and the phrases below.

calm down    finish his revision plan    stop revising
go out with Tom    revise tomorrow    phone Tom soon

I think / don't think Zak should calm down.

**5** 🎧 **1.08** Listen to four dialogues. Match the dialogues (A–D) with the sentences below. There is one sentence that you do not need.

The person with a problem:
1 accepts an offer of help. ___
2 does not follow the advice. ___
3 is embarrassed to ask for advice. ___
4 feels bad because a friend is cross. ___
5 refuses an offer of help. ___

**6** 🎧 **1.09** Listen again to dialogues B, C and D. Complete the collocations (1–8) with the verbs below.

give    have    make    ~~make~~    ~~take~~    take    tell    tell

**Dialogue A**
1 *make* a plan
2 *take* a break

**Dialogue B**
3 _____ offence
4 _____ somebody a call

**Dialogue C**
5 _____ the truth
6 _____ a word (with somebody)

**Dialogue D**
7 _____ an excuse
8 _____ a lie

**7 SPEAKING** In pairs, plan a dialogue using the prompts below. Choose a problem and two suggestions from exercise 2 or use your own ideas.

A Say hello. Ask how B is.

B Tell A your problem.

A Say what B should do, in your opinion.

B Reject A's suggestion.

A Make another suggestion.

B Agree and thank A for the advice.

**8 SPEAKING** Act out your dialogue to the class.

Hi! How are you?    I'm OK. But I'm worried about something …

## 1D Grammar

# Past simple (negative and interrogative)

*I can use the past simple to describe events.*

**1 SPEAKING** Work in pairs. Say what you did last night.

**2** 🎧 **1.10** Read and listen to the video chat. Why did Anna not enjoy her evening at the cinema?

| | |
|---|---|
| **Sam** | Hi, Anna! Did you go out last night? |
| **Anna** | Yes, I went to the cinema. |
| **Sam** | Oh, really? Who did you go with? |
| **Anna** | My sister. |
| **Sam** | What did you see? |
| **Anna** | The new Jennifer Lawrence film. |
| **Sam** | Did you enjoy it? |
| **Anna** | No, it wasn't great. And I couldn't see the screen very well. The man in front of me was really tall, and he didn't stop talking to his girlfriend! |
| **Sam** | I hate that! |
| **Anna** | And that's not all. I lost my mobile! I think I dropped it in the cinema. |

**3** Read the Learn this! box. Complete the rules.

> **LEARN THIS!** Past simple (negative and interrogative)
> **a** We form the negative form of the past simple with
> ¹_____ and the infinitive without *to*.
> *I didn't go out last night.*
> **b** We form the interrogative form of the past simple with
> ²_____ and the infinitive without *to*.
> *Did Harry text you? Yes, he did. / No, he didn't.*
> **c** We do not use *did / didn't* with the verbs ³_____ or ⁴_____.
> *Was Joe late for school? Yes, he was.*
> *Could you read when you were three? No, I couldn't.*

➡ Grammar Builder 1D page 124

**4** Make the sentences negative.

1 I went shopping on Saturday.
   *I didn't go shopping on Saturday.*
2 I could walk when I was one year old.
3 I walked home from school yesterday.
4 My teacher gave us lots of homework last weekend.
5 It was hot and sunny yesterday.
6 I got up before seven o'clock this morning.

**5** 🎧 **1.11** Complete the second part of the dialogue. Use the past simple affirmative, negative or interrogative form of the verbs in brackets. Then listen and check.

| | |
|---|---|
| **Sam** | You ¹_____ (not leave) your mobile at the cinema. You ²_____ (lend) it to me, remember? I ³_____ (not give) it back to you. |
| **Anna** | Yes, of course! Can you bring it to school tomorrow? |
| **Sam** | I'm really sorry, but I ⁴_____ (leave) it on the bus yesterday evening. |
| **Anna** | Oh no! What ⁵_____ (you / do)? ⁶_____ (you / ring) the bus company? |
| **Sam** | Yes, I did, but they ⁷_____ (not can) find it. It ⁸_____ (not be) on the bus. Don't worry. I ⁹_____ (phone) your number ... |
| **Anna** | ¹⁰_____ (anyone / answer)? |
| **Sam** | Yes! Lucy, from our class. |
| **Anna** | Why ¹¹_____ (she / have) my phone? ¹²_____ (she / be) on the bus with you? |
| **Sam** | Yes. She ¹³_____ (pick) it up by mistake. She's bringing it to school tomorrow! |

> **LEARN THIS!** Question words
> *which why when where how how much / many / often*
> When a *Wh-* question includes a preposition, the preposition usually goes at the end.
> *What are you listening to?*

**6** Read the Learn this! box and copy the list of question words into your notebook. Find two more question words in the dialogue in exercise 2 and add them to your list. Find a question with a preposition at the end.

**7** Complete the *yes / no* questions about your weekend. Use the past simple interrogative form of the verbs below. Then complete the follow-up questions using the question words.

do   do   go   play   see   ~~watch~~

1 Did you watch TV? What *did you watch*?
2 _____ out on Friday or Saturday evening?
   Where _____?
3 _____ anyone on Saturday or Sunday?
   Who _____?
4 _____ any homework? When _____?
5 _____ computer games? Which _____?
6 _____ any sport? What _____?

**8 SPEAKING** Work in pairs. Take turns to ask and answer the questions in exercise 7.

> Did you watch TV?

> Yes, I did.

> What did you watch?

> I watched a basketball match on Saturday night.

➡ Grammar Builder 1D page 124

# Adjective endings
*I can use different adjective endings.*

**1 SPEAKING** Look at the title of the text and the photo. What do you think the story is about?

**2** Read the text. Who replied to Zoe's message? When did they reply, and from where?

# Message in a bottle

In 1990, Zoe Lemon was on a ferry, sailing from Hull in England to Germany. She was going on holiday with her family. The journey was long and tiring and ten-year-old Zoe soon got bored. To pass the time, she decided to write a message in a bottle and drop it into the sea. 'It will be interesting if someone finds it,' she thought. Then she forgot about the bottle completely.

Twenty-three years later, she was amazed to get a reply from someone in the Netherlands. A man was walking on the beach and was surprised to find Zoe's bottle in the sand. He wrote to the address on the message, where Zoe's parents still live. Zoe was delighted, but it was also very moving for her to see her message again after twenty-three years, and she cried when she read it. 'It's astonishing that the bottle didn't break,' said Zoe. Her five-year-old son thinks it is all very exciting and wants to put a message in a bottle himself!

**3 SPEAKING** Work in pairs. Imagine you are going to put a message in a bottle and drop it into the sea. What would you write? Tell the class.

**LEARN THIS!** *-ed / -ing* adjectives

**a** Many adjectives ending in ¹_____ describe how people feel. Adjectives ending in ²_____ describe something which makes them feel that way. Pairs of *-ed / -ing* adjectives like these are formed from verbs, e.g. *disappoint*.
I'm disappointed. My exam result is disappointing.

**b** Sometimes the spelling changes.
*worry* (verb) – *worried, worrying*  *bore* (verb) – *bored, boring*

**c** Not all *-ed* adjectives have *-ing* equivalents, e.g. *delighted, ashamed*.

**4 DICTIONARY WORK** Read the dictionary entries and the Learn this! box. Complete rule a using *-ed* and *-ing*.

> exhausted /ɪgˈzɔːstɪd/ *adj* very tired
> exhausting /ɪgˈzɔːstɪŋ/ *adj* making sb very tired:
> *Teaching young children is exhausting work.*

**5** Find all the *-ed* and *-ing* adjectives in the text in exercise 2. Which of the *-ed* adjectives does not have an *-ing* equivalent?

**6 DICTIONARY WORK** Use a dictionary to find *-ed* and *-ing* adjectives formed from the verbs below. Make a list in your notebook. Which verb does not form an *-ing* adjective?

annoy  worry  disgust  exhaust  relieve
satisfy  surprise

**7** Circle the correct forms to complete the sentences.

1 I don't like this film. It's **bored / boring**.
2 I don't find computer games very **excited / exciting**.
3 Don't be **frightened / frightening**. The dog won't bite.
4 I was **shocked / shocking** when I heard the news.
5 It's really **annoyed / annoying** when you interrupt.
6 Why are you looking so **worried / worrying**?

**8** Complete each pair of sentences with *-ed* and *-ing* adjectives formed from the verbs in brackets.

1 **a** I don't understand this map. It's very _____ . (confuse)
  **b** Can you help me with my maths? I'm _____ . (confuse)
2 **a** I was _____ when I fell over. (embarrass)
  **b** I hate it when my dad dances. It's so _____ ! (embarrass)
3 **a** That journey was very _____ . (tire)
  **b** I was _____ after a long day at school. (tire)
4 **a** Are you _____ in photography? (interest)
  **b** Which is the most _____ lesson in this unit? (interest)
5 **a** Yuck! This cheese smells _____ ! (disgust)
  **b** She was _____ by his bad behaviour. (disgust)

**LEARN THIS!** *How* + adjective

We often react to things we hear or see with *How* + adjective.
How boring! How disgusting! How wonderful!

**9 SPEAKING** Read the Learn this! box. Then work in pairs.

**Student A:** Make a sentence using the past simple and the words below. Add your own ideas.
**Student B:** React to the sentence using *How* + an *-ing* adjective.

1 I / drop / phone / and it / break
2 My dad / dance / my birthday party
3 My favourite football team / lose / the weekend
4 I / get full marks / English exam
5 I / see / a car crash / town centre

I dropped my phone and it broke.    How annoying!

## 1F Reading

# Painless

*I can understand a text about an unusual medical condition.*

**1 SPEAKING** Look at the title of the text and the four warning signs (A–D). What is the connection? What do you think the text will be about?

> **Reading Strategy**
>
> When you do a matching task, follow these steps:
>
> **1** Read the text to get a general idea of the meaning. Do not worry if you do not understand every word.
>
> **2** Read the task and all the options carefully.
>
> **3** Read the paragraphs of the text carefully one by one and match them to the correct option.
>
> **4** Check that the extra options do not match with any of the paragraphs.

**2** Read the Reading Strategy. Then read the text quickly to get a general idea of the meaning. Were your ideas in exercise 1 correct?

**3** Read the text again. Match the questions below with paragraphs A–E of the text. There are two extra questions.

In which paragraph does the writer tell us …
1 when doctors realised Ashlyn had a medical problem? ___
2 what causes her condition? ___
3 what happened when she burned her hands? ___
4 what scientists are doing to find a cure? ___
5 why some people die from this condition? ___
6 what treatment Ashlyn receives every day for her problem? ___
7 how school life for Ashlyn was unusual? ___

**4 SPEAKING** Work in pairs. Talk about information in the text that you found surprising or interesting.

> I found it surprising that …

> I found it interesting that …

**5** Complete the questions using the question words below. Then take turns to ask and answer the questions in pairs.

~~How~~   How many   When   What   Who   Why

1 How did Ashlyn burn her hands?
2 _____ was the doctor shocked when he saw Ashlyn's eye injury?
3 _____ people are born with this medical condition in the USA each year?
4 _____ watched Ashlyn carefully in the playground at school?
5 _____ did Ashlyn's story first appear in newspapers?
6 _____ is the cause of Ashlyn's medical condition?

> How did Ashlyn burn her hands?

> She put her hands on a hot engine.

**6 VOCABULARY** Find the words in the text to do with accidents and injuries and complete them below.

> **Accidents and injuries**
> **Verbs**
> burn / cut / hurt / [1]in___ ___ ___e yourself / your hand, etc.
> fall / [2]tr___p / slip over   [3]b___ ___k your arm / finger, etc.
> bleed   sprain your ankle / wrist   hurt (e.g. *my leg hurts*)
> **Nouns and phrases**
> [4]bl___ ___d   a broken arm / finger, etc.   [5]a b___ ___se
> [6]a b___ ___n   a cut   [7]an in___ ___ ___y   a sprain   pain

**7** Match eight of the verbs from exercise 6 with the past simple affirmative forms below. Are they regular or irregular?

a bled   *bleed (irregular)*
b broke _____
c burned _____
d cut _____
e fell over _____
f hurt _____
g injured _____
h sprained _____

**8 SPEAKING** Work in pairs. Tell your partner about a time when you hurt or injured yourself. Use vocabulary from exercise 6.

> I broke my arm when I was six years old.

**A** WARNING THIS WIRE FENCE IS **ELECTRIFIED** BY A Hotline ELECTRIC FENCER

**B** CAUTION **HOT!** Premium Roast Coffee  Milk/Lait  Tea/The

**C** **MIND YOUR HEAD**

# A life without pain

🎧 1.12

**A** All children hurt themselves from time to time. But when thirteen-year-old Ashlyn Blocker was younger, she had more accidents and injuries than her friends. For example, she once put her hands on a very hot engine and got a serious burn. She
5  only knew about it when she looked at her skin. She showed her parents and they took her straight to hospital. Ashlyn simply did not know when she injured herself.

**B** When Ashlyn was a baby, her parents knew she was different: she didn't cry. Then, when she was eight months old, they
10 noticed there was some blood in her eye, so they took her to see a doctor. The doctor was shocked and confused when he looked at Ashlyn's eye: there was a serious cut. So why wasn't the baby girl upset? Why didn't she cry? The eye injury soon got better, but doctors realised that Ashlyn had a very unusual medical
15 condition: she couldn't feel any pain.

**C** This condition is very rare: only about a hundred people a year in the USA are born with it, and many of them die because of it. Pain is a natural warning: when you're ill or injured, your body hurts and this tells you there's a problem. People who
20 can't feel pain often die young because when they break a bone or have a problem with their heart, they just don't realise.

**D** The first few years of Ashlyn's life were very difficult. She often tripped and injured herself. Once, she broke her ankle and didn't know, so she didn't stop running. At school, Ashlyn needed a lot of attention
25 to keep her safe. For example, in the playground, one teacher watched Ashlyn all the time. When other children fell over, the teachers could ask, 'Does it hurt?' But of course, with Ashlyn, it was not so simple, and the teachers had to search for cuts, bruises or other injuries.

**E** When she was five, Ashlyn's story appeared in newspapers. Then
30 she had invitations to appear on TV shows and became well known. Scientists studied the causes of her condition and found it was a genetic disorder. For some reason, pain signals do not reach her brain. Unfortunately, at the moment, there is no hope of a cure. And as Ashlyn knows, a life without pain is both difficult and dangerous.

SWIMMING POOL

# Narrating events
*I can relate and react to past events.*

**1** Look at the photo. Do you know this sport? How do you think it feels to do it?

**2** Complete the dialogue with the correct affirmative or negative past simple form of the verbs below.

be   get   learn   leave   love   spend   watch

**Kirstie** Hi, Laurie. How are you? Tell me about your summer holiday!

**Laurie** Well, for the first three weeks, I was at a summer camp in Cornwall.

**Kirstie** Really? That sounds like fun!

**Laurie** Yes, it was. I **¹**_____ a new sport – bodyboarding.

**Kirstie** Wow! That sounds great!

**Laurie** Yes, I **²**_____ it. It was really exciting – and a bit frightening too!

**Kirstie** I bet! What else did you get up to over the summer?

**Laurie** Well, the second half of the holiday **³**_____ so good. I **⁴**_____ a stomach bug and **⁵**_____ nearly a week on the sofa.

**Kirstie** Oh dear! How awful!

**Laurie** I **⁶**_____ the house for days. I just **⁷**_____ DVDs. I was so bored!

**3** 🎧 **1.13** Listen and check your answers to exercise 2. Does the photo go with the first or second half of the dialogue? How do you know?

**4** 🎧 **1.14** Listen to four girls talking about events over the summer. Match each speaker (1–4) with an event (a–e) and then circle the correct adjective to describe how she felt about it. There is one extra event.

a Speaker ___ got sunburned.
 She felt **depressed / embarrassed / worried**.

b Speaker ___ ran a half marathon.
 She felt **exhausted / proud / surprised**.

c Speaker ___ got her exam results.
 She felt **disappointed / relieved / upset**.

d Speaker ___ took part in a dance competition.
 She felt **bored / relaxed / suspicious**.

e Speaker ___ visited her friend's new house.
 She felt **envious / interested / shocked**.

---

**Speaking Strategy**

Follow a simple structure for narrating events, for example:

**1** set the scene (where? when? who?)

**2** say what happened

**3** say how you (and / or others) felt about it

---

**5** 🎧 **1.14** Read the Speaking Strategy. Then listen to speakers 1–4 again. Do they all follow the suggested structure?

**6** **KEY PHRASES** Read the phrases for reacting and showing interest. Then find three more in the dialogue in exercise 2.

> Reacting and showing interest
> You're joking / kidding!
> How boring / funny / frustrating / exciting / upsetting!
> That's amazing / exciting / worrying / shocking!
> That sounds great / terrible / annoying / terrifying!
> What a cool thing to do!
> Really? I'm so envious!
> Really? What a relief!
> That sounds like a nightmare!
> Oh no! What a disaster / shame!

**7** **SPEAKING** Work in pairs. Take turns to say a sentence from the list below using the correct past simple form of the verbs in brackets. Your partner reacts with a suitable phrase from exercise 6.

**1** I finally (finish) my science project.
**2** I (learn) to play a new song on the guitar.
**3** I (break) a bone in my foot.
**4** I (drop) my dad's laptop.
**5** I (fall) asleep at my cousin's wedding.

> I finally finished my science project.

> Really? What a relief!

➼ **Vocabulary Builder** *get*: page 117

**8** Make notes about an event from the summer using points 1–3 below. You can use real information or your own ideas.

**1** Set the scene (where? when? who?).

**2** What happened?

**3** How did you (and / or other people) feel?

**9** **SPEAKING** Work in pairs. Use your notes from exercise 8 to take turns to tell your partner about the summer. When your partner is narrating, use phrases from exercise 6 to react appropriately.

## Writing

# A description of an event

*I can describe an event.*

**1 SPEAKING** Describe the photo. What is the boy planning to do? Use the words below to help you.

bathroom   fake spider   play a prank   put   scare

**2** Read the descriptions of two events and check your ideas for exercise 1. What do you think of each prank? Use the adjectives below or your own ideas.

childish   clever   cruel   funny   predictable

Teen Forums > General Chat > Pranks!

▌ Monday 2nd 11:31 AM

**Sarah_B**
Moderator

Tell us about pranks you played on friends or family members!

**Dave338**

When I was about nine years old, I bought an enormous plastic spider from a joke shop. It looked very real and had really long legs. I couldn't wait to play a prank on my sister with it. One morning, I put it in the shower just before my big sister went into the bathroom. I waited outside the door. I heard a really loud scream and my sister ran out of the bathroom. I thought it was really funny, but for her it was a terrifying experience! When she found out that I put the spider there, she was really cross and chased me round the house. I feel bad about it now, because I didn't realise just how afraid of spiders my sister is. It took her ages to get over it because she was so shocked!

**Kate44**

Last February, I sent my brother a Valentine's card. He's quite shy and he didn't have a girlfriend. In the card, I wrote 'Be my Valentine! With love from ???' and I tried to disguise my handwriting. When he opened it, he looked carefully at the writing, and I thought for a moment he realised it was from me. But there was a girl in his class who he liked, and he thought the card was from her. He seemed really pleased about the card. In fact, he decided to ask her out, and now they're going out! Eventually, he mentioned the card to her and she said she didn't send it. He immediately suspected me, so I owned up. He was a bit cross, but he forgave me because of the happy ending.

---

**3** Read the Writing Strategy. Match the adjectives below with people in the stories (A–D). Say when and why they felt that way.

amused   angry (2 people)   anxious
frightened   guilty   pleased (2 people)

**A** Dave _____

**B** Dave's big sister _____

**C** Kate _____

**D** Kate's brother _____

**LEARN THIS!   Phrasal verbs and register**

**a** Phrasal verbs consist of a verb + one or two particles (e.g. *at, down, in, on,* etc.).

**b** Phrasal verbs are usually less formal than verbs with a similar meaning.
*request – ask for   discuss – talk about   replace – put back*

**4 VOCABULARY** Read the Learn this! box. Find four phrasal verbs in the forum posts that mean the same as words a–d.

Phrasal verbs and register

**a** discover _____

**b** recover from _____

**c** examine _____

**d** confess _____

➤➤ **Vocabulary Builder** Phrasal verbs and register: page 117

You played a prank on a friend or family member. Write a forum post for an internet forum called 'Own Up!'
- Give a short description of the prank.
- Say how your friend or family member reacted.
- Describe your feelings at the time.
- Say whether you feel bad about it now, and why / why not.

**5** Read the task above. Make notes using one of the ideas below, real information or your own ideas.
- put salt on someone's ice cream
- put a fake mouse in a kitchen cupboard
- glue some coins to the classroom floor

**6** Write your forum post.

 **CHECK YOUR WORK**

Have you ...
- used adjectives to describe how people felt?
- checked the spelling and grammar?

# 2

# Adventure

## 2A Vocabulary

# Landscapes
*I can describe landscapes.*

**1 SPEAKING** Look at the photos (A–E). Would you enjoy these activities? Why? / Why not?

**2** 🎧 **1.15 VOCABULARY** Match two or more of the nouns below with each photo (A–E). Then listen to the descriptions and check your answers.

**Landscape: features** cave cliff desert forest hill lake mountain ocean river rocks shore stream valley volcano waterfall

A _____   D _____
B _____   E _____
C _____

**3 VOCABULARY** Check the meanings of the adjectives below. Find three pairs of opposites.

**Landscape: adjectives** dark deep icy low narrow rocky shallow steep tall wide

**4** Work in pairs. Match each adjective in exercise 3 with two or more nouns from exercise 2.

*dark forest, dark cave, dark valley; deep …*

**5** 🎧 **1.16** **Listen to four adverts. Match three of them with photos A–E.**

1 ___   2 ___   3 ___   4 ___

**6** 🎧 **1.16** **Listen again. Complete the extracts (1–8) from the adverts using the prepositions below, nouns from exercise 2 and adjectives from exercise 3.**

~~across~~   along   behind   beside   down   inside
near   through   under

1 Kayak *across* icy *lakes* and *shallow* rivers.
2 Your journey _____ _____ mountains and deep _____.
3 Explore the _____ caves _____ the coast of Mexico.
4 After three days _____ the caves, the boat leaves the steep _____.
5 Stand _____ Lake Pinatubo, a lake _____ a _____.
6 A _____ lake formed, which soon became _____.
7 Kayak _____ narrow rivers _____ the trees.
8 Find dark _____ _____ tall _____.

> **RECYCLE!** *There is* and *There are*
> We use *There's ...* for singular countable nouns and uncountable nouns. We use *There are ...* for plural nouns.
> There's a forest.   There are trees.   There's (some) snow.

**7** **Read the Recycle! box. Complete the sentences below with *There's* or *There are* and match them with photos A–E. There is one extra photo.**

1 _____ clear, blue water all around. ___
2 _____ grass in the valley and _____ also some trees. ___
3 _____ trees and bushes on both sides of the river. ___
4 _____ snow on the tops of the mountains. ___

**8** **SPEAKING** **Work in pairs. Describe a typical landscape in your country. Use as much vocabulary from this lesson as you can, and remember to use *There's / There are* correctly. Your partner guesses the landscape you are describing.**

> There's a tall mountain ...

C

D

E

# Past continuous

*I can use the past continuous.*

**1** Read the opening paragraph of a story. Why does the narrator notice the tall man?

With my backpack in my hands, I stepped off the train onto the crowded platform. It was 7.30 in the evening. People were hurrying home. A mother and her two young children were sitting on a bench. The mother was talking to the boy, but he wasn't looking at her. The girl was singing quietly and playing with a toy. Around them, travellers were shouting greetings, waving goodbye, carrying heavy bags or running to catch trains. A very tall man was standing completely still near the exit. Why was he wearing summer clothes in this weather? And why was he looking straight at me?

**2** Read the Learn this! box. Then find all the examples of the past continuous in the text in exercise 1.

> **LEARN THIS! Past continuous**
>
> **a** We often use the past continuous to set the scene.
> It was snowing. Two men were walking towards the house.
>
> **b** We use the past continuous to talk about an action that was in progress at a particular time.
> At midnight, I was doing my homework.
>
> **c** When we use the past continuous with two or more actions, we do not need to repeat the subject (*I*, *we*, etc.) or *was/were* if the subject is the same.
> We were sitting on the sofa and eating pizza.

➤ Grammar Builder 2B page 120

**3** Complete the paragraph below with the past continuous form of the verbs in brackets. Do not repeat the subject or *was / were* if they are not necessary.

I left the hotel early the next morning. Already, the sun
¹_____ (shine) brightly and the temperature
²_____ (rise). In the square, café owners
³_____ (carry) tables outside. A dog ⁴_____
(lie) on the pavement nearby, but it ⁵_____ (not sleep).
Two teenage girls ⁶_____ (sit) on a bench
⁷_____ (share) headphones. What ⁸_____
(they / listen) to?

**4** SPEAKING Work in pairs. Ask and answer questions about the people in the texts in exercises 1 and 3.

What were they doing?
1 the mother
2 the boy
3 the girl
4 the other travellers
5 the tall man
6 the café owners
7 the dog
8 the teenage girls

> What was the mother doing?

> She was ...

**5** Imagine that yesterday you arrived in the centre of a new city. Write sentences in the past continuous to describe the scene. Use the words below or your own ideas.

*A tourist was reading a book.*

| | |
|---|---|
| a tourist | stand / sit |
| some birds | argue / fight |
| two taxi drivers | take photos |
| a street vendor | eat / drink |
| a police officer | talk on the phone |
| some schoolchildren | read a book / magazine |
| a shop owner | laugh / smile / sing |
| some workmen | walk / run / ride a bike |
| some shoppers | |

**6** Work in pairs. Swap the sentences you wrote in exercise 5. Choose three of your partner's sentences and write a question about each one using the past continuous.

*A tourist was reading a book.*
*What book was the tourist reading?*

**7** SPEAKING Ask and answer the questions you wrote in exercise 6.

> What book was the tourist reading?

> A travel guide to the city.

**8** Write the opening paragraph of a story. Use your ideas from exercise 5 and include the extra information from exercise 7.

**9** SPEAKING Read your paragraph to the class. The class decides which is the best opening and why.

# Adrenaline junkies
*I can listen for key words and antonyms.*

**1 VOCABULARY** Put the adjectives below into three groups: describing a) people, b) extreme sports and c) landscapes. Some adjectives can go into more than one group.

**Adjectives to describe adventure**  athletic  brave  impressive  remote  risky  spectacular  strong  terrifying  thrilling

**2 SPEAKING** Describe the photo above. Where are the people? What are they doing? What kind of people do you think they are? Use adjectives from exercise 1 and words from lesson 2A on page 18.

> **Listening Strategy**
>
> The information that you need to understand in the recorded text may be expressed differently in the task.
>
> • Listen out for synonyms of key words in the task. Key words are content words such as adjectives, nouns and verbs.
>
> • Listen out, too, for ways in which words with the opposite meaning, or negative verbs, correspond with key words in the task.
>
> *It's rather cold today.* ≫ *It isn't very warm today.*
> *We won the match.* ≫ *We didn't lose the match.*

**3** 🎧**1.17** Read the Listening Strategy. Then listen to six people talking about BASE jumping. Write the synonyms or words with the opposite meaning that they use for the underlined words.

1 Fred loves being in wild, <u>far-away</u> places. *remote*
2 Sally says BASE jumping isn't popular with <u>older</u> people. _____
3 Chris doesn't consider himself a <u>courageous</u> person. _____
4 Celina says people who aren't strong and <u>fit</u> shouldn't try BASE jumping. _____
5 For Shelley, the appeal of BASE jumping is the <u>breathtaking</u> landscapes where you do it. _____
6 Martin really <u>didn't enjoy</u> BASE jumping. _____

**4** Read the sentences. Can you think of synonyms for any of the underlined words? Write them in your notebook.

1 Tanya <u>likes</u> extreme sports because they're <u>dangerous</u>. ___
2 A friend <u>told</u> Tanya to try BASE jumping. ___
3 Tanya <u>didn't enjoy</u> her first experience of BASE jumping. ___
4 The cliffs in Tonsai, Thailand are the perfect <u>venue</u> for BASE jumping, in Tanya's opinion. ___
5 Tanya thinks the <u>dangers</u> of BASE jumping make women unwilling to try it. ___
6 In Tanya's opinion, Roberta Mancino is a <u>great sportswoman</u>. ___

**5** 🎧**1.18** Listen. Are the sentences in exercise 4 true or false? Write T or F.

**6** 🎧**1.18** Listen again. Did you hear any of the synonyms you wrote down in exercise 4? How did they help you to do the task?

**7 SPEAKING** Work in pairs. Explain why you would or would not like to try BASE jumping. Give three reasons. Use the adjectives in exercise 1 and ideas from exercise 3 to help you.

**8 INTERNET RESEARCH** Use the internet to find out about another extreme sport. Research:

• when and where it began.
• where you can do it and what equipment you need.
• whether there are competitions.

# Contrast: past simple and past continuous

*I can distinguish the use of the past simple and the past continuous.*

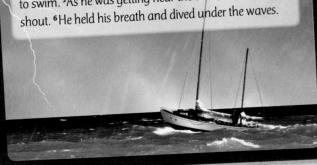

¹A cold wind was blowing and large dark clouds were moving across the sky. ²A hundred metres from the cliffs, the boat was rising and falling with the waves. ³Harry took off his jacket and his jeans and put them behind a rock. ⁴Then he climbed down into the water and began to swim. ⁵As he was getting near the boat, he heard a shout. ⁶He held his breath and dived under the waves.

**1** Read a short extract from a story. Where is Harry at the start of the paragraph? Where is he at the end?

**LEARN THIS!**  Contrast: past simple and past continuous

**a** We use the past simple for a sequence of events in the past. The events happened one after another.
*We had lunch. Then we put on our coats and left.*

**b** We use the past continuous to describe a scene in the past. The events were in progress at the same time.
*It was raining. People were wearing raincoats and carrying umbrellas.*

**c** We use the past simple and the past continuous together for a single event that interrupted a longer event in the past.
*As I was getting dressed, my friend phoned.*

    longer event        interruption

**2** Read the Learn this! box. Match sentences 1–6 from the extract in exercise 1 with rules a–c.

1 __    2 __    3 __    4 __    5 __    6 __

**3** Complete the sentences. Use the past continuous or past simple form of the verbs in brackets.

**a** While he _____ (listen) to their argument, the boat's engines _____ (start).
**b** Someone _____ (fall) into the water. Harry _____ (realise) who it was and _____ (jump) in too.
**c** Still underwater, he _____ (swim) close to the boat, then _____ (come) up silently. Three people _____ (argue) loudly.
**d** The boat _____ (begin) to move away. As he _____ (decide) what to do, he _____ (hear) a scream.
**e** Before it started moving, Harry quickly _____ (climb) onto the back of the boat and _____ (hide).

**4** 🎧1.19 Put the sentences from exercise 3 in the correct order to continue the story. Then listen and check.

1 c, 2 …

➡ **Grammar Builder 2D** page 126

> **LOOK OUT!**
>
> When a single event interrupts a longer event, we can use either *while / as* with the past continuous, or *when* with the past simple.
>
> *While / As I was walking along the beach, I found a gold coin.*
> *I was walking along the beach when I found a gold coin.*

**5** Read the Look out! box. Then find all the sentences in exercises 1 and 3 which begin with *While* or *As*. Rewrite them using *when* before the past simple.

*He was getting near the boat when …*

**6** Choose an interruption from box B for each activity in box A. Then write five sentences using the past simple and past continuous. Use *while / as* or *when*.

*As they were fighting, Harry heard a helicopter.*

**A  activities**
fight    climb back onto the boat    help    hide
put on dry clothes    swim to the shore    talk

**B  interruptions**
call for help    feel ill    find a note    see a shark
find a case of money    hear gunshots
remember something important    hear / see a helicopter

**7** SPEAKING  Work in pairs. What do you think happened next in Harry's story? Discuss your ideas and make notes. Use the questions below and your sentences from exercise 6 to help you.

1 Did Harry know the person who fell into the water?
2 Did they fight or help each other?
3 What happened to the boat?
4 Did Harry return to the shore or get on the boat?
5 What happened next?

**8** SPEAKING  In pairs, write five or six more sentences of the story using your notes from exercise 7. Then read your sentences to the class. The class votes for the best ideas.

**9** 🎧1.20 Listen to the end of the story. Compare it with your ideas from exercise 8. How is it different?

*In my ending … , but in the actual story …*

# Word building

*I can understand parts of speech and dictionary entries.*

**1** Read the text. Find the name of the person in the photo. Do you agree with the theory at the end? Why? / Why not?

**adventure-blog.com**

## *exploration*

Yesterday, sixteen-year-old Hector Turner began his attempt to become the youngest Briton to complete a 242 km 'ultra-marathon' across the Sahara Desert. On the same day, Geordie Stewart, a twenty-year-old university student, set off for Everest. He wanted to be the youngest Briton to achieve the 'Seven Summits' challenge – climbing the highest mountain on each continent. Last year, Mike Perham circumnavigated the world alone by boat at the age of seventeen.

Why do today's teenagers feel this need for exploration and adventure? Why do they want to have wild experiences? Mike Perham has a theory: 'Kids dream more than adults.'

**2** Complete the table with words from the text in exercise 1.

| noun | verb |
|------|------|
| 1 | attempt |
| completion | 2 |
| achievement | 3 |
| 4 | need |
| 5 | explore |
| 6 | experience |
| dream | 7 |

**3** Read the Learn this! box. Which different noun suffixes can you find in the text in exercise 1? Which nouns do not have a suffix?

**LEARN THIS!  Related verbs and nouns**

**a** Some nouns are formed by adding a suffix (e.g. -(at)ion, -ment, -ure) to a verb. Other spelling changes may be necessary.
*argue* (v) – *argument* (n)   *fail* (v) – *failure* (n)
*translate* (v) – *translation* (n)

**b** Some nouns and verbs are identical.
*thunder* (v) – *thunder* (n)   *fall* (v) – *fall* (n)

**c** In dictionaries, related nouns and verbs sometimes appear under the same entry.

**4** **DICTIONARY WORK** Study the dictionary entries. Then answer the questions.

> **attempt** /ə'tempt/ *verb* to try ▶ **attempt** *noun* [C]

> **circumnavigate** /ˌsɜːkəm'nævɪgeɪt/ *verb* to go around something: *circumnavigate the globe/world*
> ▶ **circumnavigation** *noun*

> **thunder**[1] /'θʌndə(r)/ *noun* [U]  the loud noise in the sky that you can hear when there is a storm: *a clap/crash/roll of thunder* ▶ note at **storm** ▶ look at **lightning**
> **thunder**[2] /'θʌndə(r)/ *verb* **1** [used with *it*] to make a loud noise in the sky during a storm: *The rain poured down and it started to thunder.* **2** to make a loud deep noise like thunder: *Traffic thundered across the bridge.*

**1** Which noun is spelled differently from the verb but is under the same entry?
**2** Are the noun and verb forms of *thunder* pronounced differently or the same?
**3** Which entry does not contain any examples?
**4** Which noun is marked as countable? Which is marked as uncountable? Which is not marked?

**5** **DICTIONARY WORK** Work in pairs. Using a dictionary, find the nouns related to the verbs below. Check their meanings.

entertain _____      motivate _____
erupt _____      relax _____
examine _____      rescue _____

**6** Complete sentence b in each pair with the correct noun formed from the underlined verb in sentence a. Use a dictionary to help you if necessary.

**1 a** Teenagers who go on adventures should be proud of what they <u>accomplish</u>.
 **b** Teenagers who go on adventures should be proud of their _____ .
**2 a** Companies will want to <u>employ</u> them.
 **b** Companies will want to offer them _____ .
**3 a** <u>Preparing</u> for the trips is the most difficult part.
 **b** The most difficult part of the trips is the _____ .
**4 a** Teenagers shouldn't be allowed to <u>risk</u> their lives.
 **b** Teenagers shouldn't be allowed to put their lives at _____ .
**5 a** These trips are a great way to <u>develop</u> personal skills.
 **b** These trips are great for the _____ of personal skills.
**6 a** Young people want to go on these adventures because they aren't able to <u>imagine</u> the dangers.
 **b** Young people want to go on these adventures because they don't have enough _____ to understand the dangers.
**7 a** Most teenagers <u>dream</u> of becoming famous.
 **b** The _____ of most teenagers is to become famous.

**7** **SPEAKING** Check your answers to exercise 6 in pairs. Then discuss whether you agree or disagree with the sentences.

# Lost at sea

*I can understand a survival story.*

1 Look at the photos. What do you think the text is about? Choose from headlines a, b and c.

a **TOURISTS' FISHING TRIP DISASTER**

b `How to protect sea creatures`

c **Fish rescues sailors**

2 Read the first paragraph of the text. Did you choose correctly in exercise 1? How do you know?

**Reading Strategy**

When you do a task with gapped sentences in a narrative text, look carefully at the sentence before each gap and think about what is likely to happen next. Then look at the options and see which of the sentences matches your ideas. Finally, check that the text reads smoothly with your chosen sentence in place.

3 Read the Reading Strategy. Then read the text, focusing on each gap and thinking about what might happen next.

🎧 1.21

A dream holiday turned into a nightmare for an American brother and sister called Dan and Kate Suski. They were enjoying a fishing trip in the Caribbean, near the stunning island of
5 St Lucia, when their boat sank, leaving them and their captain to fight for their lives.

The fishing trip began well enough. The weather wasn't brilliant, but Dan wasn't complaining: he had a huge fish on his line!
10 He was trying to pull it onto the boat and Kate was helping him.

But then, the captain realised there was a problem. Water was coming into the cabin and the boat was sinking fast. The captain used
15 his radio to send a message for help. Then he shouted to the Suskis, 'Jump out! Jump out!'
¹___ They were about 15 km from land.

The captain told the Suskis to wait with him in the water. Help was coming. The weather was
20 now awful, but they were wearing life jackets. After an hour, the captain and the Suskis lost each other, and there was no sign of rescue.
²___ They were both thinking the same terrifying thought: sharks!

25 A plane and a helicopter appeared in the sky, but nobody saw Dan and Kate in the water. Hours passed and night came. The Suskis swam for fourteen hours. Then, in the moonlight, they saw some cliffs. They were only a few metres from land!
30 ³___ The waves were breaking against sharp rocks; it was too dangerous. So Kate and Dan swam past the cliffs. By now, they were exhausted. Eventually, they reached a sandy beach. ⁴___

Then they started to look for a town or village. On the
35 way, they picked and ate green bananas. Dan said later that it was the worst – and best – food of his life! After three hours, they met a young farm worker. ⁵___ He also gave them some tragic news: the captain was lost at sea.

40 Dan and Kate Suski spent a few days in hospital. Their story appeared in news programmes around the world. And there was one final piece of astonishing news: the captain also survived. A rescue boat
45 found him after 23 hours in the water!

**4** Match sentences A–G with gaps 1–5 in the text. There are two extra sentences. Do any of the sentences match your ideas from exercise 3?

**A** So Dan and Kate started to swim as fast as they could towards land.

**B** The captain helped them as they climbed onto dry land.

**C** He gave them water and food, and stayed with them until the police arrived.

**D** So they did, and a few minutes later, the boat disappeared under the waves.

**E** Out of the water at last, they lay down and rested.

**F** But the sharks swam away after a few minutes.

**G** But they couldn't get out of the water here.

**5** Explain why the extra sentences in exercise 4 do not make sense in any of the gaps.

**6** Read the text again. Are the sentences true or false? Write T or F.

**1** When Dan and Kate were fishing, the weather was brilliant. ___

**2** Dan was the first person to see that there was a problem with the boat. ___

**3** The boat sank before Dan and Kate could jump into the water. ___

**4** A helicopter saw Dan and Kate in the sea, but it couldn't rescue them. ___

**5** When Dan and Kate reached land, they couldn't get out of the water at first. ___

**6** There was nobody on the beach when Dan and Kate got out of the sea. ___

**7** The captain swam to the beach a few hours after Dan and Kate. ___

---

**LEARN THIS!** Extreme adjectives

**a** Some adjectives are extreme equivalents of simpler adjectives.

delicious = very tasty       filthy = very ²_____

disgusting = very unpleasant      starving = very ³_____

fantastic = very ¹_____      tiny = very ⁴_____

**b** Very common adjectives often have more than one extreme equivalent.

enormous, massive, gigantic, giant, immense = very big

---

**7** Read the Learn this! box and complete it with the adjectives below.

small    good    hungry    dirty

**8 VOCABULARY** Match the extreme adjectives highlighted in the text with the simpler adjectives below.

Extreme adjectives

**1** very bad _____

**2** very good _____

**3** very beautiful _____

**4** very big _____

**5** very surprising _____

**6** very sad _____

**7** very frightening _____

**8** very tired _____

**9** Explain this sentence from the text in your own words. Try to include two extreme adjectives from the Learn this! box in your explanation.

Dan said later that it was the worst – and best – food of his life!

**10 SPEAKING** Work in pairs. Prepare an interview with Dan or Kate.

**Student A:** You are the interviewer. Write six questions using the prompts below and / or your own ideas.

**Student B:** You are Dan or Kate. Prepare your answers to Student A's questions. Use as much information from the text as you can.

**1** what / weather / like / that day?

**2** what / you / doing?

**3** what / happened / boat?

**4** why / you / start / swimming?

**5** how / you / feel?

**6** how / you / reach safety?

**11 SPEAKING** Work in pairs. Act out your interview.

What was the weather like that day?

# Photo description

*I can describe and speculate about a photo.*

**1 VOCABULARY** Match two or more of the pieces of equipment below with each photo (A–C).

**Sports equipment** boots helmet dinghy life jacket paddles poles rope rucksack safety harness

A _____

B _____

C _____

➡ **Vocabulary Builder** Sports clothing and equipment: page 118

> **Speaking Strategy**
> Make sure your photo description has a simple structure. Start by saying what the photo shows in general (Who? What? Where?). Then mention interesting details. You can finish with a personal comment or some speculation.

**2** 🎧**1.22** Read the Speaking Strategy. Then listen to two students describing photos A and B. Who follows the strategy better, in your opinion?

**3** 🎧**1.22** **KEY PHRASES** Complete the phrases for describing a photo with the words below. You need to use some words more than once. Then listen again and check.

at in looks on seems shows

> **Describing a photo**
> The photo ¹_____ …
> ²_____ the foreground / background
> ³_____ the top left corner / bottom right corner
> ⁴_____ the top / bottom
> ⁵_____ the left / right
> ⁶_____ the centre
> It ⁷_____ like a …
> It ⁸_____ as if they're …
> She ⁹_____ to be …

**4 SPEAKING** In pairs, describe photos A and B. Follow the advice in the Speaking Strategy and use phrases from exercise 3.

**5 KEY PHRASES** Work in pairs. How do you think the people in photos A and B are feeling? Use the words below or other adjectives from lesson 1A on page 8.

angry bored calm excited nervous relaxed scared shocked

> **Speculating about feelings**
> She's probably feeling … and …
> I expect they're feeling … , but maybe a bit …
> Judging by her expression, I'd say …
> To me, they look as if they're feeling …

**6** 🎧**1.23** Listen to the second student answering the teacher's questions about photo B. Which adjectives from exercise 5 does she use?

**7** 🎧**1.23** Listen again. Complete the phrases at the beginning of extracts 1–6. Then translate the phrases.

1 *Well, basically,* you can see it in their faces.
2 _____ , no, I wouldn't.
3 _____ , the worst thing would be that I couldn't stop.
4 _____ , I went on a bike ride with a friend of mine.
5 _____ , it was a really good day out .
6 _____ that's the last time I did an outdoor activity.

**8 SPEAKING** Describe photo C using words and phrases from this lesson. Then ask and answer these questions.

1 Do you think the person is enjoying himself? Why do you think that?
2 Would you like to try this activity? Why? / Why not?
3 Can you tell me about the last time you did an outdoor activity?

# An invitation

*I can write an invitation and a reply.*

**1 VOCABULARY** Match two of the words below with the photos. Then describe the photos.

**Outdoor activities** abseiling  jet-skiing  kayaking  mountain biking  orienteering  paintballing  quad biking  rock climbing  kite surfing

A _____ B _____

➡ **Vocabulary Builder** Outdoor activities: page 118

**2** Answer the questions about the activities in exercise 1.

1 Which outdoor activities from the list would you like to do? Why?
2 Which would you dislike? Why?

**3** Read two invitations and a reply. Which invitation does the reply match? Write the missing names.

To: harry@email.com

Dear Harry,

It's my birthday at the end of August and I'm planning a party at an outdoor activity centre. It offers lots of activities (e.g. rock climbing, abseiling, etc.).

The party is on Saturday 26 August. We're meeting at my house at 8:30 a.m. and driving to the activity centre in a minibus.

I really hope you can make it, but don't worry if you can't. A lot of people are away or busy that weekend.

Paddy

RSVP by text or email

To: bess@email.com

Hi Bess,

I'm having a party on the beach to celebrate the end of term. It's on Sunday 20 July and starts at 3 p.m.

In the afternoon, we're going to try two different water-sports: jet-skiing and kite surfing. It's going to be a lot of fun!

In the evening, we're having a BBQ on the beach, with loads of food and music too. Please let me know if you can come.

Lisa

PS My dad is doing the BBQ, so you don't have to bring anything.

Dear ¹ _____,

Thank you so much for your invitation. It sounds like a great way to celebrate the start of the school holidays. Unfortunately, I can't make it because I'm going to be in France with my parents.

We get back on 27 July. It would be nice to meet up some time. Why don't we go to the cinema?

I hope you enjoy the party!

² _____

**4 KEY PHRASES** Look at the phrases below. Find two more in the reply in exercise 3.

Making suggestions
Shall we (do something)?
Let's (do something)
Do you fancy (doing something)?
How / What about (doing something)?
We could always (do something)

¹ _____
² _____

**5 SPEAKING** Work in pairs. Take turns to be A and B. Use different expressions from exercise 4 to make suggestions.

**Student A:** Suggest doing one of the activities from the list below.
**Student B:** Say 'I'd rather not' and then suggest a different activity.

do homework  go for a bike ride  go shopping  go swimming  have lunch in a café  play tennis  watch a DVD

**Writing Strategy**
In an informal text, you can use common abbreviations like *e.g.* and *etc.* You should use short forms like *I'm* and *don't*, not full forms (*I am* and *do not*).

**6** Read the Writing Strategy. Find these abbreviations in the invitations in exercise 3. What do they mean? Do you know any other common abbreviations?

a.m.  BBQ  p.m.  e.g.  etc.

**7** Write an invitation to a party that includes outdoor activities. Remember to include:

- the reason for the party (birthday, end of exams, etc.).
- the date, time and place of the party.
- any instructions (what the person should bring, wear, etc.).

**8** Work in pairs. Swap your invitations from exercise 7. Then write a reply. In your reply, you should:

- thank your partner for the invitation.
- say why you cannot come to the party.
- suggest doing something another time.

**CHECK YOUR WORK**
Have you ...
- covered all the points in exercises 7 and 8?
- used short forms rather than full forms?
- used a phrase from exercise 4 in your reply?
- checked the spelling and grammar?

# Exam Skills Trainer

## Reading

> **Strategy**
>
> Some questions are about the whole text, so you need to have a general idea of what the text is about. Read the text quickly before you look at the questions and ask yourself:
>
> **1** Who or what is the text about?
>
> **2** What kind of text is it?
>
> **3** Where might you read the text?
>
> **4** Why has the writer written it?

**1** Read the Strategy and decide which question (1–5) in the task is about the whole text. Then read the text quickly and answer the four gist questions in the Strategy.

**2** Read the text and answer the questions (1–5). Circle the correct answer (A–D).

### Lost in Australia

When eighteen-year-old British student Sam Woodhead left college, he dreamed of joining the army – but he decided to have a gap year and go travelling first. Sam was already a keen long-distance runner and was very fit and healthy, but he thought backpacking in Australia was great training for his future.

In December 2012, Sam arrived in Central Queensland and found a job on a cattle farm. The farm was in the middle of the countryside, and Sam was enjoying his life there. One Tuesday morning, only eight days after his arrival, he decided to go for a run. But Sam made some mistakes. He took a heavy backpack but only one bottle of water. He also didn't have a route, and he didn't know the landscape. After only two hours, he finished his water and realised he was lost. The temperature was close to 40°C and he was soon exhausted. After four or five hours, he decided to stop and spend the night in the outback.

The next morning, Sam didn't report for work. His employers checked his room. His backpack and running shoes were gone, but his mobile and wallet were there. They called the rescue services and then they called Sam's family in England. The rescue services sent helicopters to the area to try to find Sam, but there were a lot of trees and plants in the area so it was difficult for the pilots to see a person on the ground.

Meanwhile, Sam was trying to find his way back. He made an SOS emergency signal on the ground from all the clothes in his backpack, including a pair of colourful shorts. Then, on Friday morning, Sam heard two helicopters flying over him. He shouted and waved his arms, but of course they didn't see him, and they couldn't hear him because their engines were too noisy. Then, in the afternoon, a third helicopter flew right over the SOS signal. At first, the pilot didn't see anything, but the wind from the helicopter's engine picked up Sam's shorts, and the pilot suddenly spotted them. He searched the area again, and at last he found the missing student only four or five kilometres from the cattle farm. Sam went to a hospital in the nearby town, Longreach, to recover. He was lucky to be alive!

**1** Sam went backpacking because
   **A** he didn't know what to do with his life.
   **B** he didn't like being a student.
   **C** he wanted to become fit.
   **D** he thought it would be good for his career plans.

**2** Sam got lost because
   **A** he didn't prepare well.
   **B** his map was incorrect.
   **C** the weather suddenly changed.
   **D** he wasn't well.

**3** Sam's employers realised Sam was lost when
   **A** he called them from his mobile.
   **B** they saw that all his money was gone.
   **C** his family rang to speak to him.
   **D** some of his things were missing.

**4** The rescue services found Sam after they
   **A** heard him shouting.
   **B** saw him moving about.
   **C** noticed his signal.
   **D** decided to land.

**5** In the article, the author
   **A** gives advice on survival.
   **B** describes an adventure that went wrong.
   **C** advertises a rescue centre.
   **D** tells the story of Sam's career.

## Listening

> **Strategy**
>
> In some listening tasks, the recordings you hear are connected by one topic. It helps to look at typical topics for a listening task and brainstorm vocabulary related to them.

**3** Read the Strategy. Put the words below in the correct categories (A–D).

boat   bored   burn   canoe   cave   cliffs   climbing   condition   confused   cure   cut   delighted   diving   embarrassed   injury   kayaking   landscape   ocean   ~~proud~~   stream

**A** Feelings   *proud, ...*      **C** Nature
**B** Sport                      **D** Health

**4** 🎧 **1.24** Listen to six people talking about sport. Match sentences A–G with speakers 1–6. There is one extra sentence.

**A** We learn how a new sport developed. _____
**B** We find out about a new sporting venue. _____
**C** The speaker is talking to holiday guests. _____
**D** The speaker is talking about the different benefits of sport. _____
**E** The speaker is describing a personal experience of a sport. _____
**F** The speaker is advertising sports activities. _____
**G** The speaker is explaining the advantages of extreme sports. _____

# Exam Skills Trainer

## Use of English

**5** Read the Strategy. Complete the text with one word in each gap.

### Why do people travel?

Do you enjoy travelling, or do you prefer to stay at home? Some people go on holiday in their own country with ¹_____ family or friends, and spend time on beaches or sightseeing in cities. They're more interested in relaxing than doing anything else. However, there are some people who love to travel all ²_____ time. They give up their normal lives and have adventures such ³_____ going to Australia for a year, or travelling around Africa. They live with local people and explore deserts, rainforests and other amazing places. If they run out of money, ⁴_____ find work in bars and restaurants, or they teach English to local people. They don't care about having careers at home or earning lots ⁵_____ money. They only want ⁶_____ have the experience of travelling. Often, young people go travelling before or after they go to university. Travelling is also popular with older people who want to take a break from work. So why do people love travelling so ⁷_____? If you're travelling alone, it's ⁸_____ great way to meet new and interesting people. You can learn ⁹_____ different cultures, eat new food and practise a new language. More ¹⁰_____ anything, travel gives you memories that you have forever.

## Speaking

**6** Read the Strategy and look at the photo. Then look at phrases 1–5. Which can we use to speculate? Can you think of any other phrases?

1 He could be …
2 It's clear that …
3 He's probably …
4 You can see that …
5 Maybe he is …

**7** Describe the photo.

**8** Answer questions 1–3.

1 Why is this person smiling?
2 Would you like to try something like this? Why? / Why not?
3 Talk about a situation when you or someone you know did something really enjoyable or exciting.

## Writing

**9** You are going to write an invitation to a friend asking him / her to come on a camping weekend with you and a few other friends. Read the Strategy. Then use some of the phrases below to write sentences suggesting things you might do.

Shall we … ?    How / What about … ?    We could always …
Do you fancy … ?    Let's …

**10** Write a short email invitation to a friend, asking them to come on a camping weekend with you and a few other friends. Remember to include:

- the date, time and place of the weekend.
- suggestions for things to do.
- a request for your friend to bring something (e.g. tent, sleeping bag, cooking equipment).

# 3

# On screen

## Unit map

● **Vocabulary**
Films and TV programmes
Adjectives to describe films
and TV programmes
Aspects of films
Collocations: verb + noun
Social activities

● **Word Skills**
Negative adjective prefixes

● **Grammar**
Quantity
*must, mustn't* and *needn't / don't
have to*

● **Listening** Advertising

● **Reading** Video games and
health

● **Speaking** Reaching an
agreement

● **Writing** An informal letter

● **Culture 3** Screen exports

● **Vocabulary Builder** page 118

● **Grammar Builder** page 128

● **Grammar Reference** page 129

## 3A Vocabulary

# Films and TV programmes
*I can talk about films and TV programmes.*

1 **SPEAKING** Look at photos A–D. Do you know any of these films or TV programmes? Can you name any of the actors or characters?

2 🎧**1.25** **VOCABULARY** Match four of the words below with photos A–D. Then listen to the wordlist and check your answers.

**Films and TV programmes** action film   animation   chat show   comedy
documentary   fantasy film   game show   horror film   musical   news bulletin
period drama   reality show   romantic comedy   science fiction film
sitcom   soap opera   talent show   thriller   war film   weather forecast   western

A _____   B _____   C _____   D _____

3 🎧**1.26** Listen to six short excerpts. Match each excerpt with a type of film or TV programme from exercise 2.

1 _____   2 _____   3 _____
4 _____   5 _____   6 _____

4 **VOCABULARY** Work in pairs. Talk about which types of TV programmes and films you and your partner like and dislike. Give reasons using the adjectives below.

**Adjectives to describe films and TV programmes**   boring   confusing
convincing   embarrassing   exciting   funny   gripping   imaginative
interesting   moving   scary   spectacular   unrealistic   violent

> I think horror films are really exciting. What about you?

> I'm not a fan of horror films. They're really violent. But I like …

5 🎧**1.27** Listen to four dialogues. Does each pair of speakers agree or disagree, in general?

1 _____   2 _____   3 _____   4 _____

6 🎧**1.27** **VOCABULARY** Listen again. Complete the sentences from the dialogues with the words below.

**Aspects of films**   acting   characters   ending   plot   scenes   script
soundtrack   special effects

1 The _____ was quite moving.
2 Animations don't usually make me laugh, but there were some really funny _____ .
3 I found the _____ really confusing.
4 The _____ were spectacular.
5 The _____ was totally convincing.
6 I'm not a fan of romantic comedies, but I found the _____ really interesting.
7 The _____ was really cool.
8 The _____ was really unnatural in places.

**7** Read the Recycle! box. Find two examples in exercise 6 of a general comment without the definite article.

**8** **SPEAKING** Work in pairs. Tell your partner your opinion of a film your saw recently. Use the language in exercise 6 to help you.

*I recently saw a really exciting action film. The special effects were amazing!*

**9** **SPEAKING** Complete the film and TV quiz below with words from exercises 2 and 6. Then work in pairs or small groups and do the quiz. Check your answers at the bottom of the page.

---

**RECYCLE!** Articles

Remember: we omit the article when we make general comments.

I don't enjoy <u>violence</u> in films.

However, we use the article when we are being specific.

I didn't enjoy <u>the violence</u> in that film.

---

# Film and TV Quiz

## Round 1 True or false?

**1** For two years, pop star Kylie Minogue was in a well-known s__ p o_ _ _ a.
**True / False**

**2** The TV r_ _ _ _ _ _ y sh_w *Big Brother* was originally a German programme.
**True / False**

**3** Pop groups Little Mix, Girls Aloud and One Direction all became famous after being on t_ _ _ _ t sh_ _ s. **True / False**

## Round 2 Odd one out

**1** Which of these ch_ _ _ _ _ _ _ rs is the odd one out? Why?
**a** Willy Wonka **b** the Mad Hatter
**c** Bilbo Baggins **d** Jack Sparrow

**2** Which of these f_ _ _ _ _ _ y f_ _ _ s is the odd one out? Why?
**a** *New Moon* **b** *Catching Fire*
**c** *Breaking Dawn* **d** *Eclipse*

**3** Which of these is not an a_ _ _ _ _ _ _ _ n?
**a** *Turbo* **b** *Shrek* **c** *Rango* **d** *Belle*

## Round 3 Matching

**1** Match the films with the genres.
1 *The Woman in Black*     **a** a_ _ _ _ _ _ _ _ n
2 *Wall-E*                 **b** m_ _ _ _ _ _ l
3 *Gravity*               **c** h_ _ _ _ _ r f_ _ m
4 *Annie*                 **d** t_ _ _ _ _ _ _ r

**2** Match the actors with the characters they play in these a_ _ _ _ _ n f_ _ _ s.
1 Robert Downey Jr   **a** Batman
2 Ben Affleck        **b** Iron Man
3 Andrew Garfield    **c** Superman
4 Henry Cavill       **d** Spider-Man

**3** Match the two halves to make titles of r_ _ _ _ _ _ ic c_ _ _ _ _ ies.
1 *Mr & Mrs*          **a** *Woman*
2 *When Harry Met*    **b** *Smith*
3 *Pretty*            **c** *Polly*
4 *Along Came*        **d** *Sally*

# Quantity

*I can talk about quantities.*

**1 SPEAKING** Work in pairs. Which of these different kinds of video games do you prefer? Give an example of each kind. If you do not like any kind, say why.

adventure games    city-building games
combat games    puzzle games    racing games
role-playing games    sports games

**2** Read the text. Does the game sound interesting to you? Why? / Why not?

*Anno 2070* is a video game set in the year 2070. Many cities are now under the ocean. There aren't any countries or continents, but there are a lot of islands. Players have to build new cities. There are two main groups of characters: the Tycoons and the Ecos. As a player, you can choose to be in either group. *Anno 2070* is not a combat game, but there are a few conflicts between the two groups and there are some important differences between them. The Tycoons build cities quickly and earn a lot of money. But their lifestyle causes a lot of pollution, and there are not many trees or plants on their islands. In contrast, the Ecos build 'green' cities but their progress is slow. They don't use any coal or oil so there is not much pollution on their islands. The inhabitants eat healthy food and even have a little time for some hobbies, like listening to music. The aim of the game is to create your own world. How many cities can you build? How much energy do they all need? Can you grow any food? Can you complete any special missions? It depends how well you play the game!

**3** Find two examples of *some* and four examples of *any* in the text in exercise 2. Then complete the rules in the Learn this! box.

> **LEARN THIS!** *some* and *any*
>
> We use *some* and *any* with uncountable and plural countable nouns.
>
> **a** We use _____ in affirmative sentences.
> **b** We use _____ in negative sentences and questions.

**4** Complete the sentences with *some* or *any*.

1 This game doesn't contain _____ violence at all.
2 I spent _____ time choosing a good game for my sister.
3 There are _____ well-known sports games, like the FIFA series.
4 Racing games often include _____ amazing special effects.
5 Twenty-five years ago, there weren't _____ 3D graphics.
6 Do you play _____ role-playing games?

**5** Find the phrases below in the text in exercise 2, paying attention to the nouns which follow them. Then complete the rules in the Learn this! box.

a few    a little    a lot of    how many
how much    not many    not much

> **LEARN THIS!** *not much, not many, a lot of, a little, a few*
>
> **a** We use _____ or _____ + uncountable noun for a small quantity of something.
> **b** We use _____ or _____ + plural noun for a small number of something.
> **c** We use *much* + uncountable noun for a large quantity of something.
> **d** We use *many* + plural noun for a large number of something.
> **e** We use _____ + uncountable or plural noun for a large quantity or number of something.
> **f** We use _____ … ? + uncountable noun or _____ … ? + plural noun for questions about quantity or number.

➤➤ **Grammar Builder 3B** page 128

> **LOOK OUT!**
>
> In affirmative sentences, *much* and *many* often sound very formal. In everyday English, we use *a lot of*.

**6** 🎧 **1.28** Read the Look out! box above and the dialogue below. Circle the correct words to complete the dialogue. Then listen and check.

**Jack** Look, there's a building with ¹**many / some** people outside. Turn left just before you get there.
**Evie** I can't see ²**any / some** people. There isn't ³**many / much** light. Hey! What's that noise?
**Jack** Nothing. There was ⁴**any / some** rubbish in the road.
**Evie** I hate this part of town. There aren't ⁵**a few / many** nice areas. Let's go north.
**Jack** How ⁶**many / much** fuel have we got? Only ⁷**a few / a little** litres.
**Evie** Oh no, listen. The police are chasing us now.
**Jack** Let me drive. I know ⁸**a few / a little** tricks.
**Mum** Jack, are you doing ⁹**any / many** homework in there?
**Jack** Er … Yes. We're doing ¹⁰**a little / much** IT homework.
**Evie** Jack! That's not true …
**Jack** Well, we're spending ¹¹**a lot of / a few** time on the computer!
**Evie** But we aren't doing ¹²**some / any** work!

**7** Work in pairs. Prepare a description of the setting of a video game, real or invented. Use phrases from exercise 5 and the words below and / or your own ideas.

buildings    cafés    cars    characters    cinemas
countryside    crime    islands    money    parks    pollution
roads    rubbish    shops    traffic    trees    wildlife

**8 SPEAKING** Present your description to the class.

# 3C Listening
## Advertising
*I can predict what I'm going to hear.*

AS SEEN ON TV...

## Slogans quiz
**Can you match these TV advertising slogans with their products (a–h)?**

1 **The ultimate driving machine.**
2 **Because I'm worth it.**
3 **Finger lickin' good.**
4 **JUST DO IT.**
5 **DON'T LEAVE HOME WITHOUT IT.**
6 *It's good to talk.*
7 Melts in your mouth, not in your hands.
8 **Think different.**

a sports clothes
b a car
c a computer
d a credit card
e a phone network
f hair products
g sweets
h fast food

**1 SPEAKING** Work in pairs. Do the slogans quiz. Then decide which slogan is the best, in your opinion. Say why.

> **Listening Strategy**
> In listening tasks, the instructions and questions usually give you some idea of the kind of topic and the type of language you are going to hear. Reading them carefully before you listen will help you to 'tune in'.

**2** Read the Listening Strategy. You are going to hear an advertisement for bread. What kind of language do you think you will hear? Choose one from the list below.

Language for:
a agreeing and disagreeing
b giving directions
c narrating events
d complaining
e persuading

**3** 🎧 **1.29** Listen to the advert and complete these phrases. Write one to three words for each gap. Do the phrases support your answer to exercise 2?

1 _____ Hathaway's new organic bread?
2 _____ for sandwiches and toast.
3 _____ Hathaway's organic wholemeal.
4 _____ the day with Hathaway.

**4 SPEAKING** In pairs, take turns to ask and answer the questions below about the advert in exercise 3.

1 Is it a good advert, in your opinion? Why? / Why not?
2 Is it aimed at children or adults?
3 Which extract from exercise 3 do you think is the slogan?

**5** Read situations 1–4 below. What kind of language from exercise 2 (a–e) would you expect to hear in each situation?

1 a customer talking to a sales assistant in a shop
2 an advertising executive in a business meeting
3 somebody telling a friend what happened earlier
4 somebody trying to follow a satnav

**6** 🎧 **1.30** Now listen to the four situations. Match them with sentences A–E below. There is one extra sentence.

A Not everyone is happy with the final decision. ___
B One of the speakers was very unlucky. ___
C This person finds it impossible to make a decision. ___
D This person gets confused and cross. ___
E Somebody needs help to solve the problem. ___

**7** 🎧 **1.30** Listen again. Complete the adjectives with the ending that you hear, *-ed* or *-ing*.

1 annoy_____
2 disappoint_____
3 confus_____
4 exhaust_____
5 bor_____
6 amus_____
7 satisf_____
8 shock_____

**8 SPEAKING** Work in pairs. Do the questionnaire about advertising. Do you agree or disagree with your partner? Give reasons.

**1** Which word best describes your attitude to TV adverts?
a annoying    b boring    c entertaining

**2** How often do you click on adverts online?
a never    b sometimes    c usually or always

**3** Which products should never have adverts on TV? (Choose any number.)
• sugary drinks    • violent video games
• children's toys    • junk food
• cigarettes

**4** What is your view of celebrities who take part in adverts?
a It's fine – it's just part of their job.
b It's sometimes OK, but they need to choose the adverts carefully.
c It's wrong – celebrities shouldn't be in adverts.

**9 PROJECT** Write and perform your own TV advert in groups. Choose from the products below or use your own ideas. Think of five adjectives to describe the product and make up a good slogan.

computer game    electric car    fruit snack
online language course    smartphone    sports club    trainers

## 3D Grammar
# *must, mustn't* and *needn't / don't have to*
*I can talk about prohibition and necessity.*

**1** Do you know the game show in the photo? What happens on the show? What is the correct answer to the question?

In the sitcom *How I Met your Mother*, what is Ted Mosby's job?

A lawyer          C architect

B designer        D reporter

**2** 🎧**1.31** Read and listen to the dialogue and circle the correct verbs.

**Host** This question is for £125,000. Jill, in the sitcom *How I Met your Mother*, what is Ted Mosby's job? Is it A, lawyer, B, designer, C, architect, or D, reporter?

**Jill** Um ... I'd like to ask the audience, please.

**Host** OK. Audience, you ¹**must / mustn't** answer A, B, C or D on your keypads ... now! ... OK, 30% think it's B and 50% think it's C. But you ²**mustn't / needn't** take their advice.

**Jill** Mmm, I think I'll phone my friend Danny.

**Host** OK, let's ring Danny. ... Hello, Danny. Jill has a question worth £125,000. You ³**must / needn't** answer within thirty seconds. OK?

**Jill** Hi, Danny. In the sitcom *How I Met your Mother*, what is Ted Mosby's job? Is it A, lawyer, B, designer, C, architect, or D, reporter?

**Danny** Um, I think it's B ... or maybe C ... No, it's D. ...

**Host** Sorry, you're out of time. But you ⁴**don't have to / must** answer the question. You can walk away with £64,000.

**Jill** I'm going to answer C.

**Host** Final answer?

**Jill** No. Yes. No.

**Host** You ⁵**don't have to / mustn't** change your mind!

**Jill** The answer is B. Final answer.

**Host** Oh, Jill, the answer is C, architect. You've just lost £32,000!

> **LEARN THIS!** *must, mustn't* and *needn't / don't have to*
>
> **a** We use ¹_____ to say that something is necessary or very important to do.
>
> **b** We use ²_____ and ³_____ to say that something is not necessary.
>
> **c** We use ⁴_____ to say that something is prohibited (a negative order).

**3** Read the Learn this! box and complete the rules. Use *must, mustn't, needn't* and *don't have to*. Use your answers to exercise 2 to help you.

➡ **Grammar Builder 3D** page 128

**4** What are the rules for using mobiles at your school? Write sentences with *must, mustn't* and *needn't* and the phrases below. If you can, add ideas of your own.

Using mobiles
bring our mobiles to school
leave them in our bags
turn our mobiles off at the start of the lesson
put them on our desk during lessons
keep them on silent all day
send texts during lessons
give them to the teacher at the beginning of the lesson

*We needn't bring our mobiles to school.*

> **LOOK OUT!**
>
> **a** *must* and *have to* are very similar. However, *must* often expresses the feelings of the speaker.
> *You must do more exercise.* (That's my strong opinion.)
> *have to* often expresses an external obligation.
> *You have to wear a helmet.* (It's the law.)
>
> **b** *mustn't* and *don't have to* do NOT have the same meaning. *don't have to = needn't*, but *mustn't* means 'it is prohibited'.

**5** Read the Look out! box. Then, using the words in brackets, rewrite the sentences so that they have the same meaning.

1 It isn't necessary for you to help me. (needn't)
   *You needn't help me.*
2 It's compulsory for us to wear school uniform. (have to)
3 You aren't allowed to talk in the exam. (mustn't)
4 It's important that I'm not late. (mustn't)
5 It's important that you listen to me. (must)
6 We are obliged to study maths at school. (have to)
7 You needn't write the answer. (have to)
8 It's important for Jake to revise hard for his exams. (must)

**6** Work in pairs. Make notes about the rules of a game show that you know. Use *must, mustn't* and *needn't / don't have to*.

*You must answer as quickly as possible. Your partner mustn't help you.*

**7** **SPEAKING** Work in pairs. Ask and answer about the rules of your game. Can your partner guess the name of your game?

> Can my partner help me?

> No, your partner mustn't help you.

**Word Skills**

# Negative adjective prefixes

*I can form and use adjectives with negative prefixes.*

**1** Read the notices. What are they warning you not to do?

**PIRACY IT'S A CRIME**

**2** Read the views of some teenagers. Who thinks illegally downloading things is not a problem? Who thinks it is as serious as any other crime?

## To download or not to download?

DVDs and computer games are so expensive. It's unsurprising that people download them illegally. But it's unfair on the small, independent companies. **Mark**

It's the same as stealing from a shop. It's simply dishonest and unacceptable. **Samantha**

You're very unlikely to get caught. That's why people do it. **Harry**

It's like an invisible crime. You can't see the victim. That's why many people don't feel bad about it. **Joe**

I have no sympathy for the big film and music companies – they make a lot of money, so I think illegal downloading is OK. **Hannah**

**LEARN THIS!** Negative prefixes: *un-, in-, im-, ir-, il-* and *dis-*
The prefixes *un-, in-, im-, ir-, il-* and *dis-* are negative. When they come before an adjective, they make its meaning opposite.

*certain – uncertain   patient – impatient*
*honest – dishonest   responsible – irresponsible*

**3** Read the Learn this! box. Then find the opposites of the adjectives below in the text in exercise 2.

| | |
|---|---|
| acceptable _____ | legal _____ |
| dependent _____ | likely _____ |
| fair _____ | surprising _____ |
| honest _____ | visible _____ |

**Dictionary Skills Strategy**
You can often find synonyms (words with the same meaning) and antonyms (words with the opposite meaning) of adjectives in a learner's dictionary.

**4** **DICTIONARY WORK** Read the Dictionary Strategy. Then study the dictionary entry. What synonym and antonym of *loyal* are given? How are they indicated?

loyal /ˈlɔɪəl/ *adj* [used about a person] not changing in your friendship or beliefs: *a loyal friend/supporter* SYN **faithful** OPP **disloyal** ▶ **loyally** *adv* ▶ **loyalty** /ˈlɔɪəlti/ *noun* [C,U] (*pl* **loyalties**)

**5** Rewrite the sentences using the adjectives in brackets with a negative prefix. You can use a dictionary to help you.

1 Her bedroom is in a mess. (tidy)
   *Her bedroom is untidy.*
2 That answer is wrong. (correct)
3 It isn't nice to tease your little sister. (kind)
4 He was very rude to me! (polite)
5 Don't use that old microwave. It's dangerous. (safe)
6 I'm unhappy with my exam results. (satisfied)
7 I don't believe that story. (believable)
8 I can't do this exercise! (possible)

**6** Complete the sentences with adjectives with the opposite meaning.

1 Is your handwriting legible or _____ ?
2 Are you generally honest or _____ ?
3 Do you think teenagers are generally responsible or _____ ?
4 Are you generally patient or _____ ?
5 Is smoking in public places legal or _____ in your country?
6 Do you think that reversing climate change is possible or _____ ?

**7** **SPEAKING** In pairs, take turns to ask and answer the questions in exercise 6.

> Is your handwriting legible or illegible?

> My handwriting is legible.

**8** **SPEAKING** Do you agree with the views expressed in exercise 2? Why? / Why not? Use these phrases to help you.

*I agree / disagree with (Mark) that ...*

**1 SPEAKING** Look at the headlines. Do you think playing computer games is bad for your health? Why? / Why not?

**2** Read the text. How many different video games does the writer mention by name? What are they?

> **Teenager dies after playing video game for 40 hours without eating or sleeping** (Daily Mirror)

> **Playing computer games encourages obesity** (Daily Mail)

> **Overload of screen time 'causes depression in children'** (Independent)

# Why video games are good for your health

**🎧 1.32** Many people assume that video games have a negative effect on young people. A lot of time in front of a screen is bad for the mind and the body, they believe. Newspaper headlines often express
5 the same opinion – and combat games cause the most concern because of the violence. But is there any evidence for this view? According to a report in *American Psychologist*, the truth is not so simple. Playing video games is sometimes good for children's
10 education, health and social skills.

Research shows that video games can actually improve certain mental skills. This is especially true for combat games. These games teach players to think about objects in three dimensions and this
15 makes them better at studying science, technology, engineering and maths. Other types of video game do not usually provide these benefits.

However, other types of video game can have other positive effects. In 2013, scientists did some research
20 into the effect of role-playing games (RPGs) on children. The research showed that when children spend a lot of time playing RPGs, they get better grades at school than children who do not play them. Other research showed that playing any kind of video
25 game, including violent games, improves children's creativity. But using a computer or smartphone for emails or other tasks does not provide this benefit.

Quick and simple games like *Angry Birds* can improve players' mood and prevent them from
30 feeling anxious. This emotional benefit is important, the report suggests. Feeling relaxed and happy is good for your health. The report also describes another emotional benefit of video games: they teach children how to react well to failure. In video games,
35 players continually fail and try again. This makes them emotionally strong in real life.

Video games can improve social skills too, the report says. More than 70% of gamers play with a friend, not alone, and millions of people take part in huge online
40 games like *Minecraft* and *Farmville*. The players learn useful social skills: how to lead a group, how to work together and how to make decisions. Overall, the report does not deny that some video games can have negative effects; but it is important to think
45 about the benefits too. And remember: you mustn't believe everything you read in the newspapers!

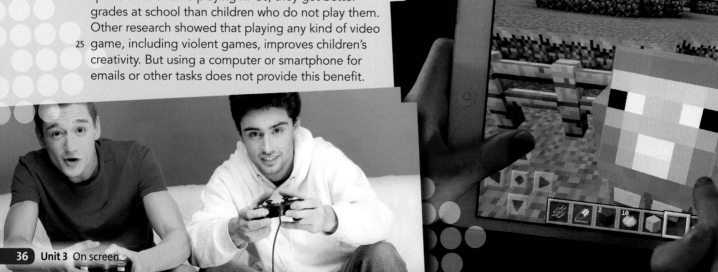

**Reading Strategy**

When you do a multiple-choice task, decide whether each question is about the whole text or a specific part. If it is about a specific part, find the relevant sentences and underline them.

**3** Read the Reading Strategy and questions 1–5 in exercise 4 below. Decide which question is about the whole text. Then find the relevant sentences in the text for the other questions.

**4** Circle the correct answers (a–d).

1 Newspaper headlines about video games
   a only talk about violent games.
   b always present the same view.
   c do not tell the truth.
   d usually present a negative view.

2 You learn to think about things in three dimensions when you
   a play combat games.
   b play any kind of video game.
   c study engineering or maths.
   d do scientific studies.

3 Research shows that role-playing games
   a are the only games that make children more creative.
   b do not provide as many benefits as violent games.
   c help children to do well at school.
   d help children to learn how to use computers.

4 The report also suggests that video gamers
   a spend a lot of time on their own.
   b learn some useful skills by playing with others.
   c usually fail in other areas of their lives.
   d spend a lot of time feeling anxious.

5 According to the report, the effect of video games on children
   a is mostly good.
   b is mostly bad.
   c is not known.
   d is not very important.

**5** Look back at the question in exercise 1. Has the text changed your opinion at all? If so, how?

**6** VOCABULARY Complete these verb + noun collocations from the text using the words below.

cause   do   express   get   have   make   provide   take part in   use

| Collocations: verb + noun |
| --- |
| 1 _____ a positive / negative effect |
| 2 _____ an opinion |
| 3 _____ concern |
| 4 _____ a benefit |
| 5 _____ research |
| 6 _____ (good) grades at school |
| 7 _____ a computer / smartphone |
| 8 _____ online games |
| 9 _____ a decision |

**7** Answer the questions using information from the text.

1 What do many people assume about the effects of video games on young people?
2 What kinds of skills can combat games improve?
3 What can simple games like *Angry Birds* prevent?
4 What kind of game helps children to get better grades at school, according to a 2013 report?
5 What kind of game teaches children how to work together?

**8** SPEAKING Work in pairs. Complete the questions with *How much* or *How many*. Then ask and answer.

1 _____ different types of screen do you use regularly? (phone, computer, tablet, TV, etc.)
2 _____ time do you spend watching TV or DVDs each day?
3 _____ different video games do you play?
4 _____ different people do you play video games with?
5 _____ different tasks do you use a computer for? (games, emails, homework, etc.)
6 _____ time do you spend in total each week in front of a screen?

> How many different types of screen do you use regularly?

> I use ...

# Reaching an agreement

*I can discuss and agree on an activity.*

**1** **SPEAKING** Work in pairs. Look at the posters. What genres of film are they? Which genre do you like most? Why?

> **Speaking Strategy**
> In the exam, you will have about one minute to read the task. Use this time to 'think in English', identifying key words and phrases that you could use in the conversation.

**2** Read the Speaking Strategy and the task below. Think of three nouns and three adjectives that you could use in your answer.

> Your British friend is coming to visit you and you are proposing to take him / her to the cinema. Decide together which of the films in the posters you will see, where and when to meet, and whether to invite any other people.

**3** **1.33** Read the questions. Then listen to a student doing the exam task and answer them.

1 Which film a) does the student want to see, b) does the examiner want to see, and c) do they agree on?
2 Did they use any of the words you chose in exercise 2?
3 When and where do they decide to meet?
4 What reason does the examiner give for not wanting to invite Donna?
5 Do they decide to invite someone else, or not?

**4** **KEY PHRASES** Complete the phrases using the words below.

agree   agreed   better   fan   fancy   idea
keen   prefer   rather   settle   stand

> **Expressing likes and dislikes**
> I quite ¹_____ ... / I don't really fancy ...
> I'm / I'm not a big ²_____ of ...
> I'm / I'm not ³_____ on ...
> I adore ... / I can't ⁴_____ ...
> **Expressing a preference**
> I'd ⁵_____ ... I'd ⁶_____ (to) ...
> I think ... will be ⁷_____ / more fun, etc.
> **Reaching an agreement**
> Shall we ⁸_____ on ... ?
> OK, I ⁹_____ .
> That's ¹⁰_____ then.
> That's a great ¹¹_____ .

➡ **Vocabulary Builder** Expressing likes and dislikes: page 118

**5** **1.33** Listen again and check your answers in exercise 4. Which phrases in exercise 4 does the student use?

**6** Work in pairs. Read the task below and prepare your dialogue. Make notes in the chart below.

> You and a group of friends are deciding what to do on the Saturday night after your last exam. Decide on an activity, the type of food you will eat, and where and when you will meet.

| Possible activities: |
| --- |
| what? _____ |
| when? _____ |
| where? _____ |
| cost? _____ |
| **Food:** |
| type? _____ |
| cost? _____ |
| where? _____ |
| **Meet:** |
| where? _____ |
| when? _____ |

**7** **SPEAKING** Work in pairs. Act out your dialogue to the class. Use phrases from exercise 4.

**Writing**

# An informal letter
*I can write an informal letter.*

**1 SPEAKING** Look at the photo. Do you know this film? Can you name the actor?

**2** Read the task below and the letter on the right. Find the parts of the letter that match elements 1–4 of the task.

> You and a friend went to see a film at the cinema recently. Write a letter to another friend in which you:
> 1 say what film you saw and who you went with.
> 2 give your personal opinion of the film.
> 3 mention what you did after the film.
> 4 invite your friend to do an activity with you soon.

**3** Look at parts of the letter you identified in exercise 2. Does each part simply mention the element in the task or does it provide extra information? Give examples.

**4** Look at the part of the letter where Andy mentions his personal opinion and read the aspects of the film below. Which ones does he mention?

acting  characters  ending  plot  scenes
script  soundtrack  special effects

---

**Writing Strategy**

When you write a letter to a friend or relative:

- Start with: Dear [*Jake*],
- Begin the main part of the letter with a short introduction. You can use phrases like: *How are you? Sorry I didn't reply sooner. Thanks for your letter.*
- Write in paragraphs.
- Do not use very formal language in your letter.
- Use contractions (*it's, there's*, etc).
- Finish the main part of the letter with a short paragraph. You can use phrases like: *That's all for now. I'd better go now. Write again soon.*
- End the letter with *Love,* or *Best wishes,* and your first name.

---

**5** Read the Writing Strategy. Then answer the questions.

1 What phrase(s) does Andy include in his introduction?
2 How many paragraphs does he write?
3 Does he use any very formal language?
4 What contractions does he use?
5 What phrase(s) does Andy include in the final paragraph?

**6** Read the Learn this! box and complete it with the phrase Andy uses for making his invitation.

---

**LEARN THIS! Invitations**

*Would you like* + infinitive?

*Why don't you / we* + infinitive without *to*?

*How about* + *-ing* form?

_____ + *-ing* form?

---

> Dear Jake,
>
> Thanks for your letter and sorry I didn't reply sooner.
>
> I went to see a great film at the cinema last weekend – Iron Man 3. I went with my friend Paddy because he loves the Iron Man films. It isn't a new film, but it was definitely worth seeing again. The special effects are amazing and it also has a clever plot with lots of twists. There are some funny lines in the script too.
>
> After the film, we met some other friends at a noodle bar in town. It was fun, but I didn't really like the food. It was very spicy!
>
> Do you fancy going to the cinema next week? They're having a season of action films, including all the Batman series. Let me know and I'll book the tickets!
>
> Anyway, I'd better go now. Ring me and let me know about the cinema.
>
> Love,
>
> Andy

**7 SPEAKING** Work in pairs. Take turns to make invitations using phrases from the Learn this! box and the ideas below.

**Social activities** go for a bike ride  go shopping
have a coffee  listen to music  meet friends in town
play basketball  play table tennis

> Why don't we go for a bike ride?

> OK! / Good idea! / Sorry, I can't.

 **Vocabulary Builder** Social activities: page 118

**8** You are going to do the task in exercise 2. Plan your letter using the prompts below and your own ideas. Remember to include extra information for each element of the task.

1 Title of film, who you went with
2 Your opinion
3 Later activity
4 A suggestion to do something

**9** Write your letter using your plan from exercise 8.

---

**CHECK YOUR WORK**

Have you ...

- mentioned and developed each element of the task?
- followed the advice in the Writing Strategy?
- checked the spelling and grammar?

---

# 4
# Our planet

## Unit map

● **Vocabulary**
Weather
Describing temperature
Natural disasters
Verbs of movement
In the street
Climate change

● **Word Skills**
Phrasal verbs

● **Grammar**
Comparative adjectives
Superlative adjectives
*too / enough*

● **Listening**  Eyewitness

● **Reading**  Gliders in the storm

● **Speaking**  Photo comparison

● **Writing**  An article

● **Culture 4**  The English language

---

## 4A  Vocabulary
### Weather
*I can describe the weather.*

**1**  Do the weather quiz in pairs. Then check your answers at the bottom of the page.

# Weather QUIZ

**1**  What shape is a raindrop before it starts falling?

**a**     **b**      **c**

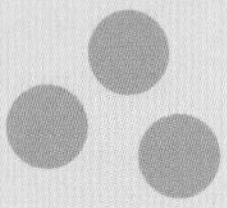

**2**  What makes the sound of thunder?
  **a**  a cloud    **b**  rain    **c**  lightning

**3**  You see lightning and then hear thunder six seconds later. How far away is the storm?
  **a**  2 km    **b**  3 km    **c**  6 km

**4**  You only get foggy weather when
  **a**  the air is cold.
  **b**  it is rainy.
  **c**  you are near the ocean.

**5**  You only get hail when
  **a**  it is windy.    **b**  there are storm clouds.    **c**  there is no sunshine.

**6**  In what direction does an 'east wind' blow?
  **a**  towards the east →    **b**  towards the west ←

**7**  What is the maximum time a snowflake takes to reach the ground?
  **a**  a minute
  **b**  five minutes
  **c**  twenty minutes
  **d**  an hour

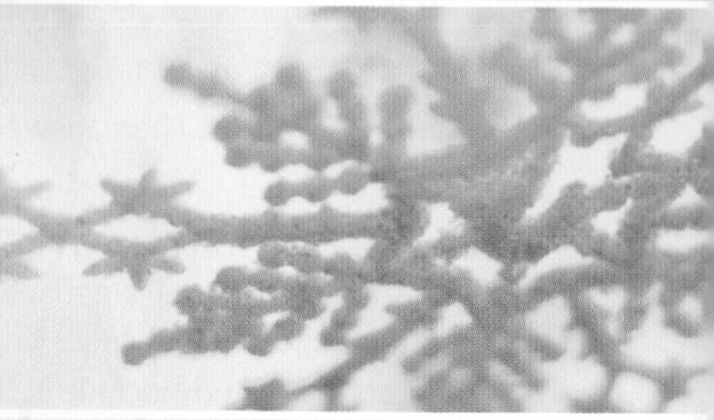

**8**  When you are facing a rainbow, the sun is always
  **a**  in front of you.    **b**  behind you.    **c**  to one side.

Answers: 1a 2c 3a 4a 5b 6b 7d 8b

**2 VOCABULARY** Complete the table with the highlighted words from the quiz in exercise 1. What do you notice about the way the adjectives are formed?

| Weather | | | |
|---|---|---|---|
| Noun | Adjective | Verb | Related words and phrases |
| 1 | cloudy | | rain clouds 2 |
| fog | 3 | | |
| frost | frosty | | frostbite |
| 4 | | hail | hail storm |
| ice | icy | | |
| 5 | | | flash of lightning |
| mist | misty | | |
| 6 | 7 | rain | 8 |
| shower | showery | | rain shower |
| snow | snowy | snow | 9 |
| 10 | stormy | | thunderstorm |
| 11 | sunny | (the sun) shines | 12 |
| 13 | thundery | to thunder | clap / crash of thunder |
| 14 | 15 | (the wind) blows | |

**3 SPEAKING** In pairs, ask and answer the questions (1–4) below. Use words and phrases from exercise 2 and the words below.

**Describing temperature**

It's minus ten.    It's 35 degrees (Celsius).    It's below zero.
It's freezing / cold / cool / mild / warm / hot / sweltering.

1 What is the weather like today?
2 What is it usually like in December?
3 What is it usually like in August?
4 Do you prefer rainy, snowy or icy weather? Why?

**4** 🎧1.34 Listen to five weather reports (1–5). Match three of them with the photos (A–C).

1 ___    2 ___    3 ___    4 ___    5 ___

**RECYCLE!** *a few, a little, not much / many, a lot of*

Remember: we use *a few, not many* or *a lot of* with plural (countable) nouns.

*a few thunderstorms*

We use *a little, not much* or *a lot of* with uncountable nouns.

*a little snow*

**5** 🎧1.34 Read the Recycle! box. Then listen again and complete these sentences from the weather reports.

**Report 1**
1 It's –10°C and there's _____ everywhere.
2 We're expecting _____ this afternoon.

**Report 2**
3 There is _____ on the ground.
4 There isn't _____ but the wind is blowing the snow into my face.

**Report 3**
5 There's _____ on the grass after a cold night.
6 There aren't _____ in the sky.

**Report 4**
7 There's _____ in people's gardens.
8 There's _____ on the pavements.

**Report 5**
9 There were _____ and it was windy too.
10 Now there's _____ and the wind is extremely strong.

**6** In pairs, invent a weather report. Use the prompts below to help you plan it.

- What type of weather?
- Temperature?
- What can you see? (snow, ice, clouds, etc.)

**7 SPEAKING** Present your weather report to the class.

Here in Birmingham, there's a strong wind blowing from the north.

# Comparison

*I can make comparisons.*

**1 SPEAKING** Work in pairs. Do you know what a shooting star is? Compare your ideas.

**2** Read part 1 of the text. Check your ideas from exercise 1.

**3** Complete the table with comparative adjectives from part 1 of the text.

| Short adjective | Comparative | Rule |
|---|---|---|
| small | 1 | + -er |
| large | 2 | + -r |
| early | 3 | -y → -ier |
| big | 4 | double consonant + -er |
| **Long adjective** | **Comparative** | **Rule** |
| powerful | 5 | *more* + adjective |
| **Irregular adjective** | **Comparative** | |
| far | 6 | |
| good | better | (no rules) |
| bad | worse | |

**4** Read the Learn this! box. Then find examples of each rule (a–d) in part 1 of the text.

> **LEARN THIS! Comparative forms**
>
> **a** We use *than* to make comparisons.
>   Greece is hotter than the UK.
>
> **b** We use *not as ... as* to make negative comparisons.
>   It isn't as warm as yesterday.
>
> **c** We use *as ... as* to say two things are equal.
>   Yesterday, London was as hot as Athens.
>
> **d** We use *far* or *much* to make a comparison stronger.
>   Libya is far / much hotter than Canada.

**5** Read the Look out! box. Complete part 2 of the text with the comparative form of the words in brackets.

➡ **Grammar Builder 4B** page 130

> **LOOK OUT!** *little – less*
> Some quantifiers also have comparative forms.
> *few – fewer  much / many – more*

**6** Complete the sentences with the correct form of the words in brackets.

1 My brothers often fight, but Tom is much stronger than Nathan (Tom / much / strong / Nathan) so he usually wins.
2 Delhi is bigger than Mexico City but _____ (it / not as / large) Tokyo.
3 The Chelyabinsk explosion _____ (much / small) than the Tunguska Event.
4 Occasionally, hail stones can _____ (be / big / as) tennis balls!
5 A hurricane _____ (much / powerful) an ordinary storm.

## Part 1

On a clear night, you can often see meteors – space rocks – as they fall towards the Earth. Each rock is smaller than an apple, but they look as bright as stars in the night sky, so people call them 'shooting stars'. Larger meteors are much rarer, but their effects are far more spectacular. In 2013, a meteor exploded in the sky above the city of Chelyabinsk in Russia. The explosion was more powerful than the 1945 Hiroshima atomic bomb, but its effect was not as devastating as the bomb because the meteor exploded much further from the ground. Scientists compared the Chelyabinsk meteor to an earlier – and far bigger – explosion: the Tunguska Event.

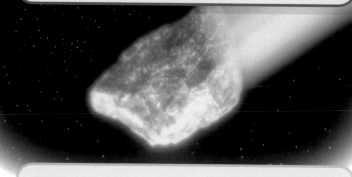

## Part 2

The Tunguska Event of 1908 was ¹_____ (far) from a city so ²_____ (few) people saw it, but it was much ³_____ (powerful) than the one in Chelyabinsk. It destroyed more than 80 million trees in the Siberian forest, so it's lucky it was not ⁴_____ (close) to a town or city. The night sky became ⁵_____ (bright) than normal for a few days, and people a hundred kilometres away could read a newspaper outdoors even at midnight. Most scientists believe it was a meteor explosion, but there are some ⁶_____ (unusual) theories too. Perhaps it was a UFO!

**7** Write questions beginning *Which ... ?* Use the comparative form of the adjectives.

1 dangerous / a blizzard / a thunderstorm / ?
   *Which is more dangerous, a blizzard or a thunderstorm?*
2 beautiful / snowflake / rainbow / ?
3 holiday venue / good / the mountains / the beach / ?
4 city / get / little snow / Warsaw / Moscow / ?
5 for you personally / temperature / bad / –5°C / 35°C / ?
6 type of weather / frightening / hail / lightning / ?
7 country / rainy / Spain / England / ?
8 in your country / month / hot / July / August / ?

**8 SPEAKING** Work in pairs. Ask and answer the questions in exercise 7. Do you agree with your partner?

> Which is more dangerous, a blizzard or a thunderstorm?

> I think a blizzard is more dangerous. What about you?

> I agree. / I don't agree. I think a thunderstorm is more dangerous.

# Eyewitness

*I can identify the context of a dialogue or monologue.*

**1** 🎧 **1.35** SPEAKING **How observant are you? Look at the photo for 30 seconds and remember as much detail as you can. Then cover the photo and listen to the description. What mistakes do you notice in the description?**

> **Listening Strategy**
>
> It is important to be able to identify the context of the listening, i.e. who is speaking, where and when they are speaking, and what the situation is. This is not always obvious so listen carefully for clues to help you.

**2** 🎧 **1.36** **Read the** Listening Strategy. **Then listen to three dialogues and answer questions 1–3 below for each one. Give reasons for your answers.**

1 Who is speaking?
2 When are they speaking?
3 Where are they?

**3** 🎧 **1.37** **Listen and match each dialogue with a photo of a natural disaster (A–E).**

1 \_\_\_   2 \_\_\_   3 \_\_\_   4 \_\_\_   5 \_\_\_

**4** 🎧 **1.37** Listen again and circle the correct answers (a–c).

1 The interview is taking place
  a in the man's house.
  b in the street outside the man's house.
  c in a church hall.
2 The speaker
  a works for a charity.
  b is a politician.
  c raises funds for a charity.
3 The people who started the fire
  a did it intentionally.
  b were cooking.
  c left without phoning the fire service.
4 The volcanic eruption
  a happened last year.
  b has just finished.
  c is still happening now.
5 When the wave reached the boat, the boat was
  a close to the shore.
  b moving away from the shore.
  c in the port.

**5** VOCABULARY **Check the meaning of all the natural disasters below in your dictionary.**

**Natural disasters** avalanche drought earthquake epidemic famine flood forest fire mudslide tornado tsunami volcanic eruption

**6** **Work in pairs. Write a dialogue between a journalist and a witness to a natural disaster (real or imaginary). Include some of this information.**

1 Where was the witness? (at home, in the street, in a car)
2 What did they see and do? (helped children / old people, found family members, ran away, phoned the emergency services)
3 How did they feel? (terrified, upset, shocked, worried, helpless)
4 Was anyone injured? (people died / were injured / were taken to hospital, doctors helped people)

**7** SPEAKING **Act out your dialogue to the class.**

# Superlative adjectives, *too* and *enough*

*I can use different structures to make comparisons.*

**1 SPEAKING** Describe the photo. What do you think happened? Use the words below to help you.

carry   dry land   leave   lift (v)   tsunami   wave (n)

**2** Read the text and check your answers from exercise 1.

The Tohoku earthquake in 2011 was the most powerful earthquake ever in Japan and the fifth most powerful in the world. The earthquake happened 70 km from the coast, but it caused one of the biggest tsunamis ever recorded. The wave was over 40 m high and was large enough to travel 10 km inland in some places. The worst damage was in coastal towns where the land was flat. Some people managed to go to places high enough to be safe, but others weren't so lucky and didn't have enough time to escape. More than 18,000 people lost their lives. The wave also damaged the nuclear power station at Fukushima. Some people say that the power station was too close to the sea. The Prime Minister of Japan said, 'In the 65 years since the end of World War II, this is the toughest and the most difficult crisis for Japan.'

**3** Read the Learn this! box. Then study the highlighted superlative forms in the text and find:

1 a short adjective without a spelling change.
2 a short adjective with a spelling change.
3 two long adjectives.
4 an irregular adjective.
5 a superlative adjective followed by *in* and a place.

**LEARN THIS!  Superlative adjectives**

**a** We add *-est* to short adjectives.
*rich – richer – the richest   slow – slower – the slowest*

**b** Sometimes the spelling changes.
*foggy – foggier – the foggiest   hot – hotter – the hottest*

**c** We put *the most* before long adjectives.
*dangerous – more dangerous – the most dangerous*

**d** There are a few irregular comparative forms.
*good – better – the best   bad – worse – the worst*
*far – further – the furthest*

**e** We can use *of* after superlative adjectives.
*the sunniest day of the week*

**f** We use *in* (not *of*) with nouns for groups or places.
*the tallest boy in the class   the biggest lake in the world*

**4** Complete these earthquake facts using the superlative form of the adjectives in brackets.

1 The largest (large) earthquake ever recorded was in Chile in 1960 (magnitude 9.5).
2 _____ (early) recorded earthquake was in China in 1177 BC.
3 _____ (deadly) earthquake happened in 1556 in China. About 830,000 people died.
4 _____ (deep) earthquake recorded occurred 450 km below the surface of the Earth.
5 Antarctica is the continent with _____ (small) number of earthquakes.
6 The _____ (destructive) earthquake ever recorded was in 1906 in San Francisco.

➜ Grammar Builder 4D (Part 1)  page 130

**5** Study the underlined examples of *too* and *enough* in the text in exercise 2. Complete the Learn this! box with *after* and *before*.

**LEARN THIS!  *too* and *enough***

**a** *too* comes [1]_____ an adjective.  *too small*
**b** *enough* comes [2]_____ an adjective.  *not small enough*
**c** *enough* comes [3]_____ a noun.  (*not*) *enough money*
**d** We often use an infinitive with *to* after *too* + adjective or adjective + *enough*.
*He's too young / old enough to join the army.*

➜ Grammar Builder 4D (Part 2)  page 130

**6** Rewrite the sentences using the adjective in brackets and *too* or *enough*.

1 He isn't tall enough to reach the shelf. (short)
*He's too short to reach the shelf.*
2 Skiing holidays aren't cheap enough for me. (expensive)
3 My dad's old car is too dangerous to drive. (safe)
4 The storm was too weak to cause much damage. (strong)
5 My shoes aren't clean enough to wear to the party. (dirty)
6 The sky's too cloudy to see the moon. (clear)

**7** Write questions using the superlative form of the adjectives.

1 what / interesting subject / at school / ?
*What's the most interesting subject at school?*
2 who / attractive actor / in the world / ?
3 what / funny comedy / on TV / ?
4 what / interesting city / in your country / ?
5 who / bad singer / in the world / ?
6 what / dangerous animal / in the world / ?

**8 SPEAKING** Work in pairs. Ask and answer the questions in exercise 7.

In your opinion, what's the most interesting subject at school?

**Word Skills**

# Phrasal verbs

*I can understand and use a variety of phrasal verbs.*

**1 SPEAKING** Describe the photo. Use the words below to help you.

**nouns** chimney   factory   pollution   smoke
**verbs** breathe   pollute   pour out

**2** 🎧 **1.38** Complete the compound nouns in the fact file with the words below. Use a dictionary to help you. Then listen and check your answers.

climate   fossil   global   greenhouse   ice   rain   renewable
sea   surface

## GLOBAL WARMING
### FACT FILE

> The Earth is heating up. The average ¹_____ temperature is 0.75°C higher now than it was 100 years ago.

> When we burn ²_____ fuels, they give off ³_____ gases like carbon dioxide ($CO_2$). This causes ⁴_____ warming.

> We have cut down over 50% of the Earth's ⁵_____ forests in the last 60 years. These are important because they remove $CO_2$ from the atmosphere and add oxygen. They are also home to over half of the world's plant and animal species.

> Some scientists believe that by 2050, about 35% of all plant and animal species could die out because of ⁶_____ change.

> ⁷_____ levels are rising and the polar ⁸_____ caps are melting.

> Scientists say that fossil fuels like coal and gas may run out by the year 3000. So we need to develop alternatives, such as ⁹_____ energy and nuclear energy.

---

**LEARN THIS!** Phrasal verbs

**a** Some phrasal verbs have a meaning which is similar to the meaning of the main verb (e.g. *to use up = to use all of something*).

**b** Other phrasal verbs have a meaning which is completely different from the meaning of the main verb (e.g. *to carry on = to continue*).

---

**3** Read the Learn this! box. Find five phrasal verbs in the fact file. Which have a similar meaning to the main verb and which have a completely different meaning?

**4** Read what two students say about global warming and climate change. Who is more worried about the situation?

**5** Find nine phrasal verbs in the texts in exercise 4. Match five of them with the definitions below. Check the meaning of the others in the dictionary. Are the meanings similar to the main verbs or different?

1 continue _____
2 delay _____
3 stop using or doing sth _____
4 take care of _____
5 think of _____

**6** Complete the phrasal verbs in the sentences with the words below. All the verbs are in the texts in exercises 2 and 4.

cut   down   looked   out   up   up   used

1 Internet cafés are dying ____ because people use smartphones instead.
2 My dad ____ down the tree in the front garden.
3 Kate gave ____ chocolate because she wants to be healthier.
4 Supermarkets are causing small shops to close ____ .
5 We've ____ up all the bread. Can you buy some more?
6 You can heat ____ the soup in the microwave.
7 I ____ after my little brother while Mum was out.

**7 KEY PHRASES** Complete the useful phrases with the words below.

believe   disagree   honest   opinion
see   seems   true   wrong

| Expressing opinions |
| --- |
| I think / I don't think that …   In my ¹_____ , … |
| I ²_____ that …   It ³_____ to me that … |
| To be ⁴_____ , …   As I ⁵_____ it, … |
| **Agreeing and disagreeing** |
| I agree / ⁶_____ with (Emma) that … |
| (Tom) is right / ⁷_____ to say that … because … |
| It's ⁸_____ that … (but …) |

**8 SPEAKING** Do you agree more with Emma or Tom? Why? Use the phrases in exercise 7 to help you.

---

Emma

We are using up fossil fuels like coal and gas very fast. If we carry on like this for much longer, we will have no fuel left and it will be impossible to stop climate change. We must change the way we live and start looking after the environment. Politicians must wake up and take action! We can't put it off!

Tom

It's impossible to come up with a solution that everyone is happy with. We can't just close down all the coal and gas power stations. We rely on fossil fuels for most of our energy. And it's difficult to persuade people to change the way they live. How many people will give up their cars? Not many! We should just learn to live with climate change, not try to stop it.

# Gliders in the storm

*I can understand a text about a paraglider.*

1 **SPEAKING** Work in pairs. Look at the title and the photos, read the *I can …* statement for this lesson and predict what happens in the text. Tell the class your ideas.

2 Read the text, ignoring the gaps. How accurate were your predictions?

3 Read the Reading Strategy. Then look at the gaps in the text. Which gaps begin with a verb in the past simple?

**Reading Strategy**

To help you decide which phrases fit which gaps, think about the grammar of each sentence. For example, is first word in the gap a verb, or is a different kind of word needed?

4 Match the phrases (A–K) with gaps 1–10 in the text. Use your answers to exercise 3 to help you. There is one extra phrase which you will not need.

A flew higher and higher
B to keep away from some dark clouds
C which was spinning above her head
D seemed certain
E came together and trapped her
F where she took off
G to spend more time on the ground
H were getting ready to take off
I she got away with it
J lost consciousness
K became worse

# A bumpy ride

🎧 1.39

In February 2007, about two hundred paragliders were in Australia for a few days to prepare for the World Championship. They included Ewa Wiśnierska, a German
5 paragliding champion. One morning, as the competitors ¹___ , they noticed that a thunderstorm was approaching. However, they decided to carry on. After all, these were the best paragliders in the world; they
10 were certainly skilful enough ²___ . Or so they thought.

Unfortunately, as the competitors took off, the weather quickly ³___ .That was the start of the most terrifying and dangerous
15 experience of her life. Ewa tried to get away from the storm, but two enormous clouds ⁴___ .

The clouds pulled Ewa up inside the storm like a leaf in the wind. She ⁵___ , with
20 lightning and hail all around her. 'I was shaking,' she told reporters afterwards. 'The last thing I remember, it was dark. I could hear lightning all around me.' She rose to an altitude of nearly 10,000 m –
25 that's higher than the top of Mount Everest – and then ⁶___ . At that height, the temperature was about -40°C and there was very little oxygen. Death ⁷___

**5 VOCABULARY** Match the six highlighted verbs of movement in the text with the definitions below. Write the infinitives.

Verbs of movement

1 to go round and round quickly _____
2 to go up from the ground _____
3 to come down to the ground _____
4 to move nearer _____
5 to arrive at a certain place _____
6 to move in an certain direction _____

**6 SPEAKING** Work in pairs. Prepare an interview with Ewa.

**Student A:** You are the interviewer. Prepare six questions using the prompts below and / or your own ideas.
**Student B:** You are Ewa. Prepare your answers to Student A's questions. Use as much information from the text as you can.

1 what / you / do / in Australia?
2 what / weather / like / that morning?
3 why / you / take off?
4 what / can / remember / about the storm?
5 what / most terrifying part / experience?
6 how / you / feel / afterwards?

**7 SPEAKING** Act out your interview.

> What were you doing in Australia?

> I was preparing ...

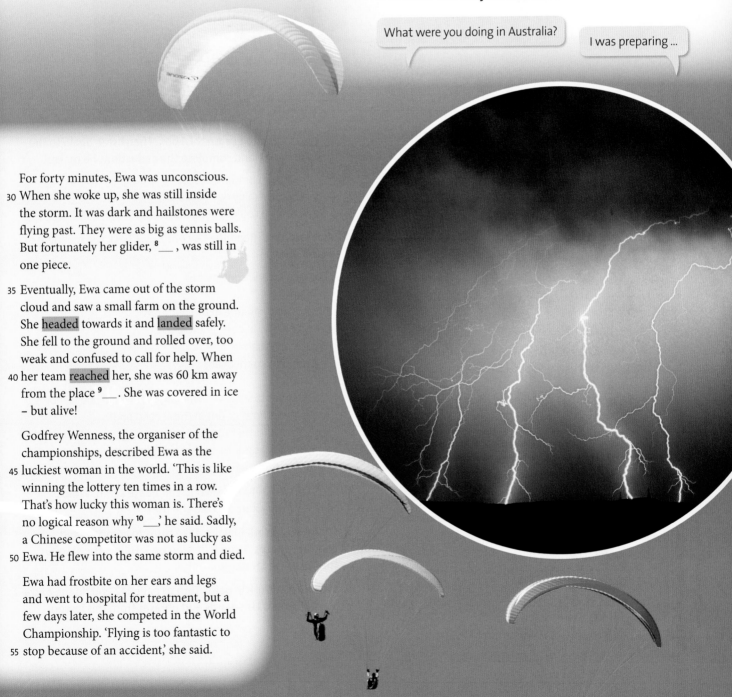

For forty minutes, Ewa was unconscious.
30 When she woke up, she was still inside the storm. It was dark and hailstones were flying past. They were as big as tennis balls. But fortunately her glider, [8]___ , was still in one piece.

35 Eventually, Ewa came out of the storm cloud and saw a small farm on the ground. She headed towards it and landed safely. She fell to the ground and rolled over, too weak and confused to call for help. When
40 her team reached her, she was 60 km away from the place [9]___ . She was covered in ice – but alive!

Godfrey Wenness, the organiser of the championships, described Ewa as the
45 luckiest woman in the world. 'This is like winning the lottery ten times in a row. That's how lucky this woman is. There's no logical reason why [10]___,' he said. Sadly, a Chinese competitor was not as lucky as
50 Ewa. He flew into the same storm and died.

Ewa had frostbite on her ears and legs and went to hospital for treatment, but a few days later, she competed in the World Championship. 'Flying is too fantastic to
55 stop because of an accident,' she said.

# Photo comparison

*I can describe, compare and contrast photos.*

**1** Look at the photos. Match them with the events below.

music festival    parade    street market

**2** **VOCABULARY** Find five of the things in the list below in photo C.

In the street  bus stop   lamp post  pavement
pedestrian crossing   road sign   shop sign   traffic light

➜ Vocabulary Builder  In the street: page 119

**Speaking Strategy**

When you do a photo comparison task, follow these steps.

**1** Describe each photo in general (e.g. mention the people, where they are, speculate about what is happening, etc.)

**2** Describe any obvious differences or similarities between the photos.

**3** Speculate about how the people in the photos are feeling, or what they are thinking or saying.

**3** 🎧 **2.02** Read the Speaking Strategy. Then listen to two candidates comparing the photos. Answer the questions.

1 Which two photos does each student compare?
2 Do they both follow all of the advice?

**LEARN THIS!**

You can use *must be* to talk about things which you can deduce are true.

They're wearing T-shirts, so the weather must be warm.

You can use *can't be* to talk about things which you can deduce are not the case.

It can't be a British city because the flags are all American.

**4** 🎧 **2.02** Read the Learn this! box. Then listen again to the first candidate and complete the deductions he makes.

1 It can't be in Britain because _____
2 It must be a rainy day because _____
3 It must be a cold night because _____

**5** **KEY PHRASES** Read the key phrases. Check the meaning of all the phrases.

Comparing and contrasting
**Similarities**
The common theme in the photos is …
You can see … in both photos.
Both photos show …
In both photos there are …
**Differences**
The first photo shows … , whereas the second photo shows …
In the first photo … , but in the second photo …
One obvious difference is (that) …
Unlike the first photo, the second photo shows …
In contrast to the first photo, the second photo …

**6** 🎧 **2.03** Listen to the second candidate again. Which phrases from exercise 5 did she use?

**7** **SPEAKING** Work in pairs. Take turns to compare and contrast photos A and C in exercise 1. Follow the steps in the Speaking Strategy.

**8** **SPEAKING** Work in pairs. Turn to page 142 and do the extra speaking task. Use words and phrases from this lesson.

## 4H Writing
# An article
*I can write an article about a global issue.*

**1** Look at the article below. Do you agree or disagree with the statement in the debate? Give reasons for your opinion.

**2** Read the article. Do you agree with Ben? Does he mention any of the reasons you gave in exercise 1?

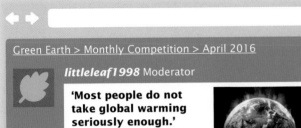

Green Earth > Monthly Competition > April 2016

 **littleleaf1998** Moderator

**'Most people do not take global warming seriously enough.'**
**Do you agree?**

Join the debate. A prize for the best article!

**ben_the_climber**

Global warming is probably the most serious threat we face, and we should all be worried about it. And indeed, it seems to me that most people take the issue very seriously. These days, people take a lot of care to recycle plastic, paper, glass and other materials. If recycling bins are available, they use them. What is more, they often choose to walk or cycle somewhere in order to reduce carbon emissions.

There are people who believe that it is normal for the temperature of the Earth to go up and down. They don't believe that humans are causing global warming, so they don't believe that humans need to alter their behaviour. Other people may just be too selfish to lead a green lifestyle. Nevertheless, the majority of people believe the evidence and do whatever they can to combat climate change.

Ben

### Writing Strategy

When you are expressing your opinions and the opinions of others, give your text a clear structure. For example:

- In one paragraph, give your opinion with two or three arguments that support it.
- In another paragraph, give the opposing view with one or two arguments supporting it. You can then say why you disagree with the opposing view (a counter-argument).

**3** Read the Writing Strategy and answer the questions.

1 In paragraph 1 of Ben's article, how many arguments does he give in support of his opinion?
2 In paragraph 2, how many arguments does he give in support of the opposing view?
3 Does he give a counter-argument?

**4** **VOCABULARY** Complete the collocations from the text with the words below.

alter  cause  combat  lead  recycle  reduce

Climate change

1 _____ plastic / paper / glass
2 _____ carbon emissions
3 _____ global warming
4 _____ your behaviour
5 _____ a green lifestyle
6 _____ climate change

➡ **Vocabulary Builder** Climate change: page 119

**5** Read the phrases below. Add the highlighted phrases in Ben's post to the correct group (A–D).

**A Expressing an opinion**
I think / don't think that …  To be honest, …  As I see it, …
I believe / don't believe that …  In my opinion, …
_____

**B Presenting an opposing opinion**
Having said that, …  On the other hand, …
_____

**C Presenting a counter-argument**
However, …  In spite of this, …  _____
**D Making an additional point**
Moreover, …  Furthermore, …  In fact, …  _____

### LEARN THIS!  Zero conditional

We use the zero conditional to talk about things that are generally or always true, especially scientific facts.
*If you heat ice, it melts.*

**6** Read the Learn this! box and find a zero conditional sentence in the forum post.

➡ **Grammar Builder 4H**  page 130

**7** Work in pairs. Read the statement and decide if you agree or disagree. Prepare arguments for and against it. Use the ideas below to help you.

'Global warming is the most significant problem facing us today.' Do you agree?

- **For:** We need to protect the planet / prevent climate change / save endangered species.
- **Against:** There are other problems such as poverty, disease, nuclear war, etc. / Millions of people die every year because of … / A nuclear war could destroy …

**8** Write your article. Use phrases from exercise 5 and your ideas from exercise 7 to help you. Follow the structure suggested in the Writing Strategy.

### CHECK YOUR WORK

 Have you …
- followed the advice in the Writing Strategy?
- included useful phrases from exercise 5?
- checked the spelling and grammar?

## Reading

**1** Read the Strategy. Then read the statements that follow the text and underline the key words. The first one has been done for you.

**2** Read the text. Are the sentences true or false? Write T or F.

### Hurricane in Jamaica

I was staying with my aunt and uncle in Jamaica when the hurricane came. They've lived in Jamaica all their lives so they know about hurricanes. I, on the other hand, was born in Britain because my parents came here when they were first married. They bought a house in London, found work, and my sister and I were born a few years later. Our parents always tell wonderful stories about Jamaica and we go there as often as we can. We love staying with our aunt and uncle in the north of the island. Last year, my sister started university and my parents were busy working, so they said I could go on my own, which meant the visit was even more exciting than usual.

I went in December, because between October and mid-December the weather isn't as hot, but it's still lovely. However, it's also the hurricane season during those months, so you have to watch out for that. Luckily, my aunt and uncle heard the warning on the radio before I arrived, and as a result, there was already lots of extra food and drink in the house. I was glad about that, as one of my favourite things about being in Jamaica is the food!

As soon as we saw the first signs of the hurricane, we closed the windows and the doors, and then we waited. The storm was a Category 1 hurricane, with heavy rain and winds of about 125 km/h. I played games and chatted with my cousins to pass the time, and we ate lots of food. But I remember the sound of the wind crashing around the house, day and night, and I felt quite scared. My aunt told me there was nothing to worry about and that they'd had worse storms than that, so I felt a bit better. While we waited, we listened to the news on the radio; there was some flooding on the roads and on farms, and some damage to buildings. The storm began on Monday, and then by Wednesday it was moving out to sea. So we weren't indoors for very long really, and afterwards, there was sunshine again!

**1** The writer <u>used to live</u> in Jamaica. _____

**2** Her parents are always positive about their home country. _____

**3** The writer was worried about going to Jamaica this time. _____

**4** Most hurricanes in Jamaica take place at the end of the year. _____

**5** The storm surprised the writer and her family. _____

**6** The writer was afraid for the whole time. _____

**7** The rain flooded their house. _____

**8** The hurricane lasted for less than a week. _____

## Listening

**3** Read the Strategy. Then read the questions and answers and predict what the recording is about. Think about words you might connect with this topic.

**4** 🎧 **2.04** Listen to the text and answer the questions. Circle the correct answers (A–C).

**1** When the writer was a child, her parents
  **A** taught her the names of all the stars.
  **B** bought her books about space.
  **C** spent time listening to her talk about the planets.

**2** What is true about the writer at school?
  **A** She liked science best.
  **B** She imagined being a musician one day.
  **C** She was talented at maths.

**3** When did she decide to be a space scientist?
  **A** after a lesson at school about meteoroids
  **B** after she saw a shooting star
  **C** after she watched a film about space travel

**4** What did she do when she first finished her education?
  **A** She worked abroad.
  **B** She went travelling.
  **C** She stayed in Britain.

**5** What is her advice to people who want to be space scientists?
  **A** work hard at university
  **B** get a good science degree
  **C** study different subjects

## Use of English

**5** Read the Strategy. Then read the text and complete gaps 1–8. Circle the correct answer A, B or C.

## The Avengers

Superheroes are very popular: people love films like *The Amazing Spider Man*, *Batman Begins*, *X-Men*, *Thor* and *Captain America*. All of these films are great, but in my opinion *The Avengers* is **¹___** superhero film. I like *The Avengers* because it's different. Superheroes are usually lonely people – they save the world on their own. **²___** isn't how things work in *The Avengers*.

Loki is the bad character in the film, and he's **³___** Thor's brother. The film begins when Loki and his powerful army steal the Tesseract. This is a source of energy, and Loki can use it to destroy the Earth. Nick Fury is the good character, and he's also the leader of an organisation called S.H.I.E.L.D. Nick knows that he isn't strong **⁴___** to fight against Loki – so he creates a team of superheroes. Now Iron Man, the Hulk, Thor, Captain America, Hawkeye and Black Widow are working together! How can they fail?

There are **⁵___** characters in *The Avengers*, but they each have a great story and great scenes to play too. The final battle scene between the superhero team and Loki's army is the **⁶___** scene in the film. The script is very clever too, and there are **⁷___** funny lines for all the characters.

The **⁸___** of putting superheroes together was amazing, and audiences loved it. The film made $1.51 billion worldwide and received many awards.

| | | |
|---|---|---|
| 1 A good | B better | C the best |
| 2 A What | B Then | C This |
| 3 A too | B also | C as well |
| 4 A many | B either | C enough |
| 5 A a lot of | B much | C a little |
| 6 A exciting | B most exciting | C more exciting |
| 7 A any | B some | C much |
| 8 A idea | B opinion | C view |

## Speaking

**6** Read the Strategy and the phrases below. Which of the phrases could be used for talking about similarities (Si), differences (D) and speculation (Sp)? Can you add any more phrases to each category?

1 (It) can't be … because …
2 Both photos show …
3 One obvious difference is …
4 (They) must be … because …
5 In contrast to the first photo, the second photo …
6 The common theme in the photos is …

**7** Compare and contrast the two photos.

**A**

**B**

## Writing

**8** Read the Strategy. Then read the example of a message. Underline three spelling mistakes and two punctuation mistakes.

✉ Hi Luke.

I went to see *Jurassic World* last night. The storie is about a place called Jurassic World which is an artificial dinosaur resort off the coast of Costa Rica. One of the dinosaurs escapes and thats when the trouble starts! It's realy good? I love the speciel effects.

Anyway, while I was at the cinema, I saw an advert for a job. They want people to sell popcorn. I know you're looking for a job, so you should phone them.

See you soon. Ben.

**9** Imagine you went to the cinema last night and are writing to your English friend. Write a message in which you:

- describe the film.
- give your opinion of the film.
- make a suggestion to your friend.

# 5
# Ambition

## Unit map

## 5A Vocabulary

# Jobs
*I can talk about jobs and work.*

1 Look at the photos (A–D). Which job looks the most interesting, in your opinion? Why?

2 🎧 **2.05** VOCABULARY Match four of the words below with photos A–D. Then listen to the wordlist and check your answers. Make sure you understand the meaning of all the words.

**Jobs (1)** architect cleaner dentist engineer farm worker hairdresser paramedic pilot programmer receptionist sales assistant solicitor sports coach travel agent waiter

A _____ B _____ C _____ D _____

3 Work in pairs. Put all the jobs into two groups: the best-paid and the worst-paid. Then compare answers with another pair. Do you agree?

> We think paramedic is one of the best-paid jobs.

> We agree. / We don't agree. We think it's one of the worst-paid.

4 🎧 **2.06** Listen to which jobs are the best-paid and worst-paid in the UK. Do you find any of the information surprising?

5 VOCABULARY Check the meaning of the adjectives below. In pairs, ask and answer questions about the jobs in exercise 2 using the superlative form. Give your own opinions.

**Describing jobs** creative challenging repetitive rewarding stressful tiring varied

> Which job is the most creative?

> In my opinion, it's ... / I think it's probably ...

**6 VOCABULARY** Look at the photos (E–H). What do you think each holiday job involves? Match two or more phrases from the list below with each job.

**Work activities**   answer the phone
be on your feet   be part of a team
deal with the public   earn a lot (of money)
make phone calls   serve customers
travel a lot   use a computer   wear a uniform
work alone   work indoors / outdoors
work with children   work long hours / nine-to-five

*An au pair works with children.*

**7** 🎧 **2.07** Now listen to four teenagers talking about their holiday jobs. Match one adjective from exercise 5 with each speaker's job. Give a reason for your choice.

1 Ellie: *tiring*
2 Tom: _____
3 Katie: _____
4 Fynn: _____

> **RECYCLE!  Past simple affirmative and negative**
> With most verbs, we only use the past simple form (regular or irregular) of the verb for the affirmative. In the negative, we use *didn't* + infinitive without *to*.
> *I got the job. / I didn't get the job.*
> The verb *be* is an exception.
> *The job was / wasn't very challenging.*

**8** Read the Recycle! box. Complete the sentences about the four teenagers from exercise 7 with the past simple affirmative or negative form of the correct verb. Look again at the work activities in exercise 6 to help you.

1 Ellie _____ a lot of money as an au pair.
2 She _____ a lot while she was with the family.
3 Tom _____ long hours as a gardener.
4 He _____ part of a team.
5 Katie _____ with children every day.
6 She _____ long hours most days.
7 Fynn _____ nine-to-five as a charity fundraiser.
8 He _____ phone calls to lots of people.

**9** 🎧 **2.07** Listen again and check. Do any of the descriptions surprise you?

**10 SPEAKING** Work in pairs. Do the questionnaire opposite and write down your partner's answers.

**11 SPEAKING** In pairs, discuss your answers to the questionnaire. Try to find the ideal job for your partner. Choose from the jobs and activities in exercises 2 and 6 or your own ideas.

> You want to earn a lot of money and travel around the world. I think you should be a pilot!

E au pair

F gardener

G sports coach

H charity fundraiser

# Just the job?

**1** Which is more important to you?
a  Doing a challenging and rewarding job.
b  Earning a lot of money.

**2** Which do you prefer?
a  Working indoors.
b  Working outdoors.

**3** Do you want a job that involves travelling a lot?
a Yes.
b No.
c I don't mind.

**4** Which sentence is true for you?
a  I like being part of a team.
b  I prefer working alone.

**5** Do you want a job that involves dealing with the public and/or serving customers?
a Yes.
b No.
c I don't mind.

**6** Which sounds better?
a  Sitting at a desk for most of the day.
b  Being on your feet for most of the day.

**7** Which sentence is true for you?
a  I don't mind working long hours.
b  I want to work nine-to-five.

# 5B Grammar

## *will* and *going to*

*I can make predictions, plans, offers and promises.*

**1** Describe the photo. How do you think the girl is feeling?

**2** 🎧 **2.08** Read and listen to the dialogue.

**Toby** Hi, Mia. Is anyone sitting here?

**Mia** Hi, Toby. No. Sit down, I'll move my bag.

**Toby** Thanks. Are you OK? You look a bit anxious.

**Mia** I've got a job interview in twenty minutes.

**Toby** Oh! I won't chat, then, I promise!

**Mia** It's OK. I'm going to leave soon anyway. I need to walk to Hill Top Road. Is it far?

**Toby** Not really. It'll take about ten minutes.

**Mia** Oh no. Look at that rain! I'm going to get wet!

**Toby** I'll lend you my umbrella.

**Mia** It's OK. I'll call a taxi.

**Toby** There isn't time for that. Here, take it.

**Mia** Thanks. I'll give it back later. Where will you be?

**Toby** I'll wait here for you. Good luck!

**3** Read the Learn this! box. Then find all the examples of *will* and *going to* in the dialogue in exercise 2.

> **LEARN THIS!** *will* and *going to*
>
> **a** For predictions, we use:
>   **1** *going to* when the prediction is based on what we can see or hear.
>     *Look at those clouds! There's going to be a storm.*
>   **2** *will* when the prediction is based on what we know or is just a guess.
>     *I (don't) think the weather will be warmer next month.*
> **b** For plans, we use:
>   **1** *going to* when we have already decided what to do.
>     *I'm going to stay in tonight. I've got the DVD ready!*
>   **2** *will* when we are deciding what to do as we speak.
>     *Somebody's at the door. I'll see who it is.*
> **c** For offers and promises, we use *will*.
>     *I'll phone you later. I won't forget.*

**4** Match each example of *will* and *going to* in the dialogue with a rule in the Learn this! box.

➡️ Grammar Builder 5B page 132

**5** Complete the second part of the dialogue with the correct form of *will* or *going to*. Who do you think will be more successful in the future?

**Mia** Here's your umbrella.

**Toby** Thanks. Well? [1] *Are you going to tell* (you / tell) me about the interview?

**Mia** I got the job! I [2] _____ (start) on 1 August! It's just for the summer.

**Toby** What [3] _____ (you / do) after that?

**Mia** I [4] _____ (study) maths at university. Then I [5] _____ (get) a job in finance. That's the plan.

**Toby** Why finance?

**Mia** It pays well. My salary [6] _____ (be) quite high.

**Toby** Do you think it [7] _____ (be) rewarding?

**Mia** I don't know, Toby. At the moment, I'm more interested in being successful.

**Toby** Me too. That's why I [8] _____ (not do) a degree.

**Mia** I don't think you [9] _____ (get) a very good job without a degree.

**Toby** I [10] _____ (not apply) for a job. I [11] _____ (start) my own business.

**Mia** What kind of business?

**Toby** A web-based marketing company. I predict I [12] _____ (be) a millionaire before I'm 25!

**Mia** Really?

**Toby** It [13] _____ (not be) easy. But I'm confident.

**Mia** Well, good luck!

**6** 🎧 **2.09** Listen and check your answers. How is the word *to* pronounced in *going to*?

> **LOOK OUT!**
>
> We can make predictions and plans more certain or uncertain by adding *definitely* or *probably*. Pay attention to the position of the adverb.
>
> *I'll definitely / probably apply for a summer job.*
> *I definitely / probably won't earn very much.*
> *I'm definitely / probably (not) going to travel.*

**7** Read the Look out! box. Then make notes about your own future. Write down:

- a job you will probably do some time in the future.
- a job you will definitely never do.
- something you're probably going to eat this evening.
- something you're definitely not going to do this evening.
- something you're probably going to buy soon.
- a place you will probably visit this year.

**8** SPEAKING Work in pairs. Talk about your plans and predictions from exercise 7. Use *will* and *going to*.

> I'll probably work in a café some time in the future.

> I'll probably work in my parents' shop.

**Listening**

# Changing jobs

*I can use signpost phrases to predict what I'm going to hear next.*

A

B

C

D

E

**1 VOCABULARY** Match five of the jobs below with photos A–E.

**Jobs (2)** builder   estate agent   gardener
groundskeeper   journalist   locksmith   photographer
pizza delivery man / woman   police officer
stunt performer   surfing instructor   video game developer

A _____   C _____   E _____
B _____   D _____

**2** Answer the questions. Use the jobs and work activites from lesson 5A to help you.

1 Choose two jobs from exercise 1 and describe them.
   *Builders work outdoors. They're on their feet all day. I think it's repetitive work but it is skilled.*

2 Which is the easiest of all the jobs in your opinion? Why?
   *I think the easiest job is . . . . That's because . . . .*

3 Which is the most difficult? Why?

> **Listening Strategy**
> Some words and phrases can help you to predict what is coming next in a listening. For example, if you hear *however*, you know that it will be followed by a contrasting point. Listen out for 'signposts' like these that help you understand the structure of the listening.

**3 KEY PHRASES** Read the Listening Strategy. Match the words below with what they indicate (1–6).

although   that's because   in my opinion   however
what is more   moreover   in other words   what I mean is
as I see it   for example   for instance   such as
not only that   nevertheless   in spite of this
on the other hand   therefore

1 a contrasting point _____
2 an additional point _____
3 an example _____
4 a paraphrase _____
5 an opinion _____
6 a reason _____

**4** 🎧**2.10** Listen to the sentences (A–F). What do you expect to hear next? Choose from items 1–6 in exercise 3.

A 1   B ___   C ___   D ___   E ___   F ___

**5** 🎧**2.11** Listen to the completed sentences and check your answers to exercise 4.

**6** Complete the sentences in your own words. Use the words in brackets to help you.

1 Working in healthcare can be challenging. Nevertheless,
   _____ (rewarding)

2 Waiters have a very stressful job. For instance,
   _____ (work long hours)

3 Having a university degree will help you get a good job.
   Not only that, _____
   (earn more money)

4 I don't think university education should be free. As I see it,
   _____ (parents should pay)

5 I don't want to be a sales assistant. That's because
   _____ (deal with the public)

**7** 🎧**2.12** Listen to an interview with Sean Aiken, who did 52 different jobs in a single year. Make notes about:

a how he got the idea.
b money.
c what he learned from the experience.

**8** 🎧**2.12** Read the sentences below. Then listen again. Are the sentences true or false? Write T or F.

1 After talking to his dad, Sean knew what job he wanted to do. ___
2 An accident outside of work prevented him from returning to his previous job. ___
3 He found the majority of the jobs on the internet. ___
4 He took a few short breaks between the jobs. ___
5 Sean saved a lot of money while he was working. ___
6 He thinks that it's important to work with people who you have a lot in common with. ___

**9 SPEAKING** Work in pairs. Think of five jobs that you would like to try for a week. Tell your partner what you would like about them.

> I'd like to be a dentist for a week because it's a well-paid and challenging job. I'd also like to deal with the public.

## 5D Grammar

# First conditional

*I can talk about a future situation and its consequences.*

**1** Describe the photo. What is the job of the man on the right? Use the words below to help you.

button   doors   floor   lift   close (v)   operate (v)
open (v)   press (v)

**2** Read the text and check your answer to exercise 1. What other jobs do you think might disappear in the future?

A hundred years ago, every lift had an operator who stopped the lift at the different floors, and opened and closed the doors. That job no longer exists because lifts are now automatic. Which jobs that people do today will disappear because of technology? Most people book their holidays online. If this trend continues, travel agents will probably become unnecessary. Self-service check-outs at supermarkets are becoming very common, and so are automated toll booths on motorways. Many people now read the news online. If newspapers disappear entirely, we won't need newsagents. And what will happen if everyone learns online instead of in a classroom? Teachers might disappear!

**3** Look at the highlighted first conditional sentence in the text in exercise 2, and read the Learn this! box below. Complete rule a with *present simple* and *will + verb*. Then find two more examples in the text.

---

**LEARN THIS!** First conditional

**a** We use the first conditional to predict the result of an action. We use the ¹_____ to describe the action, and ²_____ to describe the result.
*If I get the job, I'll have to move to New York.*

**b** The *if* clause can come before or after the main clause. If it comes after, we don't use a comma.
*I won't take the job if it isn't challenging enough.*

---

**4** Match the two halves of the sentences.

1 People will no longer need guidebooks ___
2 If people can find flats and houses online, ___
3 We won't need switchboard operators ___
4 If there aren't any schools, ___
5 Teenagers won't get jobs delivering papers ___

a will we need teachers?
b if they use tourist information websites.
c if all companies use automated telephone systems.
d if newspapers only appear in digital form.
e we won't need estate agents.

➤➤ **Grammar Builder 5D** page 132

**5** Complete the first conditional sentences. Use the present simple or the *will* form of the verbs in brackets.

1 I _____ (quit) my job if I _____ (not get) a pay rise.
2 If you _____ (be) confident, I think you _____ (do) well in the interview.
3 I _____ (look for) a job in finance if I _____ (pass) all my exams.
4 If you _____ (not go) to university, you _____ (not earn) as much money.
5 You _____ (be) much happier if you _____ (find) a less stressful job.
6 If my computer _____ (go) wrong, _____ you _____ (fix) it for me?

**6** Complete the email. Use the correct form of the verbs in brackets.

---

✉ **To:** pierre@email.com

Hi Pierre,

Thanks for your email. I am well, thanks, but very busy at the moment as I have school exams next month. I'm sure I ¹_____ (pass) if I ²_____ (work) hard, but I want to do really well. If I ³_____ (get) top grades, I ⁴_____ (apply) to study science at the University of London. If my marks ⁵_____ (not be) so good, I ⁶_____ (probably / go) to another university – maybe Sheffield.

If I ⁷_____ (have) time, I ⁸_____ (email) you again before the exams. If I ⁹_____ (not have) time, I ¹⁰_____ (be) in touch soon after. Anyway, I still hope to come and see you in Paris in August. If I ¹¹_____ (find) a well-paid summer job, I ¹²_____ (be able to) afford the plane ticket. Fingers crossed!

Love, Emma

---

**7** **SPEAKING** Work in pairs. Ask and answer the questions.

What will you do if …
1 you lose your mobile phone?
2 it rains all day on Saturday?
3 you get good marks in your final exams?
4 you don't feel well tomorrow morning?
5 you forget to do your homework at the weekend?
6 you can't sleep tonight?

> What will you do if you lose your mobile phone?

> I'll buy another one. What will you do?

# 5E Word Skills
## Prefixes
*I can use and understand a range of prefixes.*

**1 SPEAKING** Work in pairs. Think of two advantages of going to university and two advantages of going straight into a job after leaving school. Use the phrases below to help you.

get qualifications   earn money   get into debt
have a good social life   feel pressure   get stressed
be unemployed   have a good time   be independent
learn a lot   gain opportunities

**2** Read the text. Why is Andrew going to the USA?

| Home | Entertainment | Music | Health | Technology | Politics |

# Is university education overvalued?

Eighteen-year-old Andrew Brackin has received $100,000 to go and live in San Francisco, California, for two years. But there is a catch. During that time, he can't go to university or study. Instead, he has to develop his own business, a website that helps charities to raise money.

The money comes from Peter Thiel, multi-millionaire and co-creator of PayPal. Every year, Thiel selects 20 students from thousands of applicants. He only chooses those with the best business ideas. Andrew got through the semi-finals, which involved a Skype call, and then flew to San Francisco for the final. There, he had to present his ideas to an audience of important business people from Silicon Valley.

Thiel is an ex-student himself – he went to the BRIT School in London – and he has strong views on university education. He feels that many young people apply for degree and postgraduate courses without really thinking about what they want to do afterwards. They overestimate the benefits of university education and undervalue the benefits of working in business.

**3** Read the Learn this! box. Then read the text in exercise 2 again and find words with seven of the prefixes in the table.

**LEARN THIS!** Prefixes

Prefixes change the meaning of nouns, adjectives and verbs. Sometimes a hyphen is used with a prefix and sometimes it is not (e.g. *semi-final, semicolon*). You may need to check in a dictionary.

| Prefix | Meaning | Example |
|--------|---------|---------|
| co | with | co-operate |
| ex | former | ex-wife |
| mini | small | miniskirt |
| micro | extremely small | microchip |
| mis | wrongly | misunderstand |
| multi | many | multicoloured |
| over | too much | overcooked |
| post | after | post-war |
| re | again | rewrite |
| semi | half | semicircle |
| under | too little | undercooked |
| sub | under | submarine |

**4 USE OF ENGLISH** Rewrite the sentences, replacing the underlined words with a word starting with the prefix in brackets.

1 I spelled the word wrongly. (mis) I misspelled the word.
2 My mum doesn't get much money for the job she does. (under)
3 Mick slept for too long and missed his bus. (over)
4 We drove to the match in the small school bus. (mini)
5 Please write the sentence again. (re)
6 We live in a society with lots of people of different cultures. (multi)

**5 SPEAKING** Work in pairs. Ask and answer the questions. Give extra information where you can.

1 When did you last use a microwave oven? (What did you cook or reheat?)
2 When did you last re-read a book because you enjoyed it? (What?)
3 Which jobs do you think are overpaid? (Why?)
4 When did you last misunderstand something? (What?)
5 Are you good at multi-tasking? (Give an example.)

> When did you last use a microwave oven?

> Last weekend.

> What did you cook?

> I reheated some pasta.

Reading

# Dream jobs

*I can understand a text about people's ideal jobs.*

**1** **SPEAKING** Look at the photos. What do you think these people's jobs are? Compare ideas in pairs.

**2** Look quickly at texts A–C opposite. Match each text with a photo from exercise 1 (1–3) and one of the titles below. There are two extra titles.

a Duvet tester      Photo ___ Text ___
b Lego sculptor      Photo ___ Text ___
c Costume designer      Photo ___ Text ___
d Film tagger      Photo ___ Text ___
e Special effects designer    Photo ___ Text ___

> **Reading Strategy**
>
> When you complete gap-fill sentences about a text, the words you need to write are in the text. However, the words immediately before or after the gap may be different. Think carefully about the meaning and look for synonyms and paraphrases.

**3** Read the Reading Strategy. Then look at the sentences in exercise 4 below. Find a synonym or paraphrase in the text for each underlined phrase in the sentences.

**4** Complete the sentences with information from the text. Use your answers to exercise 3 to help you.

1 The Lego company <u>was very keen on</u> the _____ that Andrew Johnson sent with his job application. [1 word]
2 Andrew is happy <u>to earn money for</u> something that used to be a _____ . [1 word]
3 Jo Unsworth <u>has a job</u> at a famous British _____ _____ . [2 words]
4 Jo's <u>university qualification</u> helps her to identify _____ _____ when she sees it. [2 words]
5 <u>An advantage of the job is that</u> Joe Mason can _____ when he wants. [1 word]
6 A <u>disadvantage of</u> the job is that Joe can't _____ what programmes to watch. [1 word]

**5** **VOCABULARY** Complete the job-related collocations from the texts using the verbs below.

have   have   join   look   notice   offer   send   take

Collocations: jobs

1 _____ for a job
2 _____ an advertisement
3 _____ in an application
4 _____ somebody a job
5 _____ a team
6 _____ the job of (doing something)
7 _____ a degree (in something)
8 _____ a day off

**6 SPEAKING** Work in pairs. Decide which of the three jobs looks a) most fun and b) most difficult. Explain your decision. Use the words below to help you, and your own ideas.

badly-paid   creative   challenging   repetitive
rewarding   stressful   tiring   varied   well-paid

> As I see it, the job of Lego sculptor would be quite repetitive.

> I don't agree. I think …

**7 INTERNET RESEARCH** Look at online job advertisements. What is the best job you can find? Explain why you think it is the best.

*The best job is … It's a great job because:*
- *it's challenging / rewarding / well-paid, etc.*
- *it isn't …*
- *you can travel / work alone / work outside, etc.*
- *you don't have to …*

# The *best* jobs in the world … probably

🎧 2.13

**A** Back in 2012, Andrew Johnson was near the end of his History & Photography degree in Chicago. He planned to apply to film school after graduation, rather than look for a job. But then his dad noticed an advertisement for a job with toy manufacturer Lego. Andrew, who was already a Lego fan, sent in an application. It included a video of himself making models. The company loved
5 it and invited him to take part in an unusual interview. He had to compete against seven other finalists in a model-building test. Andrew won, and as a result, they offered him a job: he joined the team at Legoland Discovery Centre in Illinois as a Master Model Builder. He meets visitors and helps to give them exciting new ideas. Perhaps one day he'll go to film school, but for now, he's happy. 'Lego was always just a hobby, but now I can do what I love and get paid for it,' said
10 Andrew in an interview.

**B** Do you find it difficult to get out of bed sometimes, especially on frosty winter mornings? Well, imagine having a job where you don't have to. Jo Unsworth works as a duvet tester for John Lewis, a British department store. She has the job of finding the most comfortable duvets in the world to sell in their shops. Jo has a degree in textiles, so she can recognise good quality.
15 But the real test of a duvet is sleeping under it. 'It's probably the only career where it's OK to fall asleep while you're at work,' Jo says. She often can't believe how lucky she is to have her 'dream job'! What is more, she finds it rewarding: 'If I do my job properly, hundreds of other people sleep better. It's brilliant!'

**C** Some film providers like Netflix employ people to watch new films and TV series from the
20 comfort of their own home! Their job is to make a note of what type of film it is (horror, rom-com, etc.) and what age group and type of person might like it. The film provider can then recommend it to their members. Joe Mason finished his degree in film studies about two years ago and didn't know what to do next. Then he read an article about film taggers. 'It sounded like a fantastic job so I did some research online and wrote to Netflix,' said Joe. At first they
25 weren't interested, but when Joe told them he speaks fluent French – his mum is French – they gave him a job. He watches French films and TV programmes. 'It's a great job because I can work when I want. I can take a day off if I like and work at the weekend instead.' The only problem with the job is that Joe can't choose what he wants to watch. 'Sometimes I have to watch 15 episodes of rubbish! But I shouldn't complain really.'

# 5G Speaking
## Choosing a job
*I can compare and contrast different holiday jobs.*

---

**1** **Sales assistant** wanted for busy clothes shop.
Hours: 9.00 a.m. – 5.30 p.m. Mon–Sat. £6.50 an hour.

☆ save job ✉ apply by email

**2** **Fruit-pickers** needed! Get out in the fresh air and come and pick strawberries! The more you pick, the more you earn! You can earn up to £300 a week if you work really hard! Hours: 8 a.m. – 4 p.m.

☆ save job ✉ apply by email

**3** **Dish-washer** needed to join the friendly team in our restaurant kitchen. £8 an hour. 11 a.m. – 4 p.m. and 7 p.m. – 11 p.m.

☆ save job ✉ apply by email

---

**1** Match job adverts 1–3 with photos A–C.

1 ___     2 ___     3 ___

**2** **VOCABULARY** Check the meaning of the words below. Then discuss questions 1–2 in pairs.

**Personal qualities** enthusiastic flexible friendly good at communicating hard-working honest patient physically fit reliable

**1** In your opinion, which three qualities are generally most important at work?

> In any job, it's important to be ... , ... and ... .

**2** Choose one quality that you think is most important for each of the jobs in exercise 1. Give reasons for your opinions.

> Fruit-pickers work long hours outdoors, so they really need to be ...

➡ **Vocabulary Builder** Personal qualities: page 119

**3** 🎧 **2.14** Read the task below. Then listen to a conversation between a candidate and the examiner. Answer the questions.

You want to get a holiday job in order to save some money. Discuss the three job adverts with a member of staff at the job agency. Decide which job you will do and why.

**1** Which job does the candidate choose?
**2** What is her main reason for choosing it?
**3** What are her main reasons for not choosing the other two jobs?

**Speaking Strategy**

When you discuss a topic and give reasons for your opinions, try to include some complex sentences. For example, use words like *although / even though*, *nevertheless* and *however* to make contrasts.

**4** 🎧 **2.14** **KEY PHRASES** Read the Speaking Strategy. Then listen again and complete the phrases using the words below.

choosing hours kitchen long pay tiring well-paid well-paid

**Making contrasts**

Although it's ¹_____ , it will be very ²_____ .
I'm sure I'll enjoy it even though the ³_____ are ⁴_____ .
The job is quite ⁵_____ . However, I really don't want to work in a ⁶_____ .
The ⁷_____ is not very good. Nevertheless, I'm ⁸_____ this job because I'm interested in fashion.

**LOOK OUT!**

We often use *find* + noun + adjective and *find it* + adjective (+ infinitive) to give a personal reaction or opinion.

*I will find the job stressful.*
*I find it difficult to concentrate.*

**5** Read the Look out! box. Then work in pairs and say which job in exercise 1 you would choose and why. Include the structure from the Look out! box.

**6** **SPEAKING** Work in pairs. Turn to page 142 and do the extra speaking task. Use words and phrases from this lesson in your answer.

**Writing**

# An application letter

*I can write a letter applying for a job.*

**1** Read the formal letter. Match elements a–g with parts 1–7 of the letter.

a the address the letter is going to ___
b the writer's name ___
c the writer's address ___
d the date ___
e the writer's signature ___
f the person the letter is going to ___
g the subject line ___

**2** Complete the paragraph plan by matching paragraphs A–E of the letter with descriptions 1–5 below.

1 **Paragraph** D: what you are sending with the letter and when you can start work
2 **Paragraph** ___: what you would like to happen next
3 **Paragraph** ___: what the job is and how you found out about it
4 **Paragraph** ___: why you are interested in the job
5 **Paragraph** ___: why you are the right person for the job

**3** In which paragraph does Grace mention ...

1 her plans and intentions? What are they?
2 her personal qualities? What are they?

---

**Writing Strategy**

When you write a formal letter:

- Start with: *Dear (Mrs White)*, if you know the name of the person, or *Dear Sir or Madam*, if you do not.
- You can include a subject line at the start, similar to the subject line of an email.
- Write in paragraphs. One-sentence paragraphs are fine for opening or closing an application letter.
- Do not use colloquial language or short forms (*I'm, there's*, etc.).
- Finish with *Yours sincerely*, if you used the person's name at the start, or *Yours faithfully*, if you did not.

---

**4** Read the **Writing Strategy**. Answer the questions.

1 What is the subject line in Grace's letter?
2 Does Grace include any one-sentence paragraphs?
3 How does Grace express these things in a more formal way?
  a I really want to ... (paragraph B)
  b I think I've got ... (paragraph C)
  c ... if you ask me to. (paragraph D)
4 Why does Grace end the letter with *Yours faithfully*?

➡ **Vocabulary Builder** Formal language: page 119

---

[1]The Manager
[2]Harleys Department Store
Palace Walk, London

[3]14 Langley Drive
London
[4]30th May 2017

Dear Sir or Madam,

[5]**Application for the role of sales assistant**

**A** I noticed your online advertisement for a sales assistant during the summer and am writing to apply for the post.

**B** In October, I am going to start a degree in design at Brighton University. Until then, I am keen to find a position which suits my interest in fashion.

**C** I have experience of working in retail. Last summer, I spent six weeks as a sales assistant in a clothes shop. Furthermore, I believe I possess all the necessary personal qualities for the post. I am hard-working, honest and reliable.

**D** I am enclosing my CV, including full contact details. I can send references on request. If I pass my exams in June, I will be available to start work in July.

**E** I look forward to hearing from you soon.

Yours faithfully,

[6]*G Browning*

[7]Grace Browning

---

**5** Read the online job advert below and plan an application letter. Follow the paragraph plan you completed in exercise 2.

*Paragraph A: waiter in a hotel – online advertisement*

 **Summer jobs in catering**

JUST ADDED

A busy London hotel is looking for hard-working, polite and reliable waiters for the summer months (July – September). Experience an advantage.

Apply in writing, enclosing your CV, to: The Restaurant Manager, Clarks Hotel, Bond Street, London.

**6** Write your letter. Use your plan from exercise 5.

---

**CHECK YOUR WORK**

 Have you ...
- followed your paragraph plan?
- used appropriately formal language?
- checked the spelling and grammar?

---

# 6 Tourism

## 6A Vocabulary
## Worth a visit
*I can describe visitor attractions.*

1 **SPEAKING** In pairs, look at the photos of visitor attractions (A–G). Do you know which countries they are in? Match them with the countries on the map (1–7).

A ___    B ___    C ___    D ___    E ___    F ___    G ___

2 **VOCABULARY** Match seven of the words below with photos A–G from exercise 1.

**Visitor attractions** aquarium botanical gardens castle cathedral
fountain harbour market mosque museum national park
palace ruins statue temple theme park tower water park

A _____    C _____    E _____    G _____
B _____    D _____    F _____

3 🎧 **2.15** Listen to the words in exercise 2 and check your answers to exercises 1 and 2.

4 **VOCABULARY** Check the meaning of the adjectives below. Then look at the photos in exercise 1 again. Can you match any of the adjectives to the photos?

**Describing visitor attractions** atmospheric beautiful boring
busy cheap crowded disappointing expensive historic
impressive peaceful remote romantic spectacular touristy

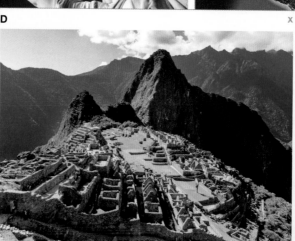

1 USA

2 Peru

**5** Describe three places in your own or another country using adjectives from exercise 4.

> The old market in … is quite cheap.

> I think … is a very peaceful place.

> In my opinion, … is touristy and expensive.

**6** 🎧 **2.16** Listen to a tour guide talking to tourists on a coach. What countries are they going to visit? Write them in order. Choose from the countries below.

Croatia   the Czech Republic   Germany   Greece   Hungary   Italy   Latvia   Lithuania   the Netherlands   Poland   Slovakia   Slovenia   Turkey

*Germany, …*

**7** 🎧 **2.16** Listen again. Match the tourist attractions they will visit with countries from exercise 6. Which adjectives from exercise 4 does the guide use to describe each attraction?

1   Havel's Market *touristy*
2   The Liberty Statue _____
3   The Old Harbour _____
4   The Trevi Fountain _____

> **RECYCLE!**  *will* and *going to*
>
> We use *going to* to talk about plans and intentions.
> *We're going to spend a day in the capital, Prague.*
> We use *will* to make predictions based on our own ideas.
> *It will be very cold!*

**8** Read the Recycle! box. Imagine you are going to visit three places anywhere in the world. Think about the places and why you want to visit them. Use adjectives from exercise 4.

**9** **SPEAKING** In pairs, ask and answer questions about your plans from exercise 8. Use *going to* for plans and *will* for predictions.

> Where are you going to visit first?

> I'm going to visit the Grand Canyon in the USA.

> Why do you want to go there?

> Because I think it will be really spectacular!

E

F

England **3**

France **4**

Turkey **5**

China **7**

Kenya **6**

G

## 6B Grammar

# Present perfect

*I can talk about recent events.*

Dear Jenny,

We've been in Florence for three days. What an amazing city! The weather hasn't been very good, so we've been to a lot of museums and art galleries. I've seen Michelangelo's David and hundreds of beautiful paintings. I've bought you a souvenir. Have you missed me?

Love, Ella

P.S. I had a text from Dylan. He's passed his driving test!

AIR MA

Dear Jenny,

We've been in Florence since Monday. The weather's terrible, so we haven't done much. In fact, we've spent most of our time in museums. I've seen about five hundred paintings and I've had enough! Ella hasn't asked me what I want to do. How long have we been friends? Unbelievable!

Love, Madison

AIR ⋒

**1** Look at the photo. Can you identify the city and / or country?

**2** Read the postcards and find the answer to the question in exercise 1. Who is enjoying the holiday more, Ella or Madison?

---

**LEARN THIS!** Present perfect

We use the present perfect:

**a** to give news, when we do not say exactly when the event happened. *Guess what? I've won a competition!*

**b** to talk about events during a period of time (e.g. a holiday) that is still continuing. *I'm in Paris. I've visited a museum but I haven't seen the Eiffel Tower.*

**c** to ask how long a situation has existed. *How long have you been in Spain?*

**d** with *for* or *since* to say how long a situation has existed. We use *for* with a period of time and *since* to say when it started. *We've been in Spain for a week / since Tuesday.*

---

**3** Read the Learn this! box. Find at least one example of rules a–d in the postcards.

---

**LOOK OUT!**

We often use *been* (instead of *gone*) as the past participle of *go*. It means the person has gone and come back.

*She's been to a museum.* (She's now back at the hotel.)

*She's gone to a museum.* (She's still there.)

---

**4** Read the Look out! box. Then find all the examples of *been* in the postcards and decide whether each one is from the verb *be* or the verb *go*.

➡ Grammar Builder 6B page 134

**5** Complete the phone conversation with the present perfect form of the verbs in brackets.

Ted     Hello?
Molly   Hi Ted, it's Molly.
Ted     Hi, Molly. Are you enjoying your holiday?
Molly   Yes. Backpacking is great! I ¹*'ve met* (meet) some really interesting people.
Ted     How long ² _____ (you / be) away?
Molly   I ³ _____ (be) away for ten days.
Ted     ⁴ _____ (you / reach) Istanbul?
Molly   No. I'm still in Italy. We ⁵ _____ (stop) at some interesting places – Rome, Pisa ... I ⁶ _____ (visit) lots of ruins but I ⁷ _____ (not buy) any souvenirs.
Ted     ⁸ _____ (you / take) many photos?
Molly   Hundreds. But I ⁹ _____ (not put) them on my Facebook page. Is there any news from home?
Ted     Yes. My dad ¹⁰ _____ (break) his ankle. He ¹¹ _____ (be) in hospital since Monday. But the doctors ...
Molly   Oh no! I ¹² _____ (use) all my credit. Bye!

**6** 🎧 **2.17** Listen and check your answers.

**7** Imagine you are on a backpacking holiday. Invent answers to these questions and make notes.

**a** How long have you been away? (Use *for* or *since*.)
**b** Which countries have you visited? (Three countries.)
**c** Which of these things have you done? (Choose two.)

buy souvenirs   meet interesting people   sunbathe
swim in the sea   take lots of photos   watch TV

**8** **SPEAKING** Work in pairs. Role-play a phone call about your holiday, taking turns to be A and B.

**Student A:** You are on holiday. Answer B's questions using your notes from exercise 7.
**Student B:** Your friend, A, is on a backpacking holiday. Find out:
• how long he / she has been away.
• where he / she has visited.
• what activities he / she has done.

How long have you ... ?   Where have you ... ?
Have you swum in the sea? Have you ... ?

## Listening
# Check your ticket!
*I can understand and use emphatic stress.*

**1 SPEAKING** Describe the photo. Where are the people? What are they doing? What do you think they are saying?

**2** 🎧 **2.18** Read and listen to the sentences describing the photo. Correct the information in the sentences.

1 The flight attendant is wearing a ~~blue~~ top. *red*
2 She's handing a meal to the man.
3 The man next to the flight attendant is wearing a white jacket.
4 The woman on the right is wearing a T-shirt.
5 The food is in a cardboard box.
6 We can see a woman in glasses in front of the man in the white shirt.

**3** 🎧 **2.19** Listen and check your answers to exercise 2. Which words are stressed? Read your answers to your partner, stressing the correct words.

**4** 🎧 **2.20** Read and listen to the dialogue. When, where and how did Lydia go on holiday in the summer?

**Tom** Did you go to Spain in July?
**Lydia** No, we went to Portugal. And we went in August.
**Tom** Where did you fly to?
**Lydia** We drove there, actually.

> **Listening Strategy**
> Notice the way that speakers emphasise certain words to stress an alternative or to correct what someone has said:
> 'Would you like a <u>double</u> room or a <u>single</u> room?'
> 'A <u>double</u> room, please.'
> 'Does the plane arrive at <u>nine</u>?' 'No, it arrives at <u>five</u>.'
> 'Dave's in <u>Paris</u>.' 'No, he isn't. He's in <u>Rome</u>.'

**5** 🎧 **2.20** Read the Listening Strategy. Which words in the dialogue in exercise 4 do the speakers stress emphatically? Listen again and check.

**6** 🎧 **2.21** Listen to the sentences. Pay attention to the words that are stressed. Circle the sentence in each pair (a or b) which the speaker is replying to.

1 No, he flew to <u>Italy</u> last summer.
  a Did Sam fly to France last summer?
  b Did Sam fly to Italy last spring?
2 I'd like a black coffee, please.
  a Would you like a drink?
  b Would you like white coffee or black coffee?
3 No, we're meeting at three fifty.
  a Are we meeting at three fifteen?
  b Are we meeting at two fifty?
4 I haven't got a credit card.
  a You can buy the tickets by credit card.
  b Why didn't you buy the tickets online?
5 I'll have a ham sandwich, please.
  a What kind of sandwich would you like?
  b Would you like something to eat?
6 No, I'll be on the 2.15 train.
  a Which train will you arrive on?
  b Will you be on the 2.15 bus?

**7** Look at the photos. Which place would you prefer to go for a holiday? Why?

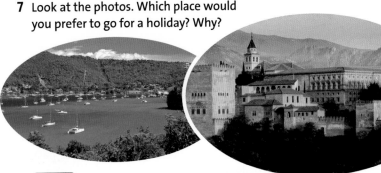

**8** 🎧 **2.22** Listen to a true story about a holiday that went wrong. What was the misunderstanding between Georgina and the travel agent?

**9** 🎧 **2.22** Listen again. Are the sentences true or false? Write T or F.

1 The woman next to Georgina was the first to mention Spain. ___
2 Georgina booked the holiday by phone. ___
3 She discovered her mistake just after the plane took off. ___
4 The flight attendant was kind and helpful. ___
5 The travel agent has given her a free holiday in Australia. ___

**10 SPEAKING** Work in pairs. Prepare an interview with Georgina Hepworth.

**Student A:** Prepare five questions using the prompts below.
**Student B:** Prepare the answers.
1 where / buy your ticket?
2 where / want to go?
3 when / realise your mistake?
4 what / happen / on the plane?
5 you / finally go to Granada?
6 you / get any compensation?

**11 SPEAKING** Act out your interview to the class.

## 6D Grammar

# Contrast: past simple and present perfect

*I can distinguish the use of the past simple and the present perfect.*

**1** Describe the photo in exercise 2. What has happened? Use the words below to help you.

fall over   hurt him / herself   lie   ski (v, n)   snow

**2** 🎧 **2.23** Read and listen to the dialogue. Answer the questions.

1  When did Fred go to Bulgaria?
2  What happened to him while he was there?

**Beth**   Have you ever been to Bulgaria?
**Fred**   Yes, I went there last year with my family. Have you been there?
**Beth**   No, I haven't. What cities did you visit?
**Fred**   We didn't visit any cities. We went skiing.
**Beth**   Sounds great. I've never been skiing, but I'd love to go. Was it good?
**Fred**   Not really. I fell and broke my leg on the first day, so I spent the rest of the holiday in hospital!

**3** Find all the examples of the present perfect and the past simple in the dialogue in exercise 2.

---

**LEARN THIS!** Past simple and present perfect contrast

**a** We use the present perfect to talk about an experience at any time in the past. The exact time of the experience is not stated.
I've read 'The Hobbit' three times.
Have you ever travelled by helicopter?

**b** We use the past simple to talk about a specific occasion in the past.
I watched a good film on TV last night.
Did you go to Newcastle last weekend?

**c** We often use the present perfect to ask and answer questions about an experience, and then use the past simple to give specific information about it.
'Have you ever been to the USA?'
'Yes, I have. I went to New York last winter.'

---

**4** Read the Learn this! box. Why are some verbs in the dialogue in exercise 2 in the past simple and others in the present perfect? Use rules a–c to explain.

➡ **Grammar Builder 6D** page 134

---

**LOOK OUT!**

We use finished-time phrases (e.g. *yesterday, last week, at 2 p.m.*) with the past simple but not with the present perfect.

I went to London last May. ✓

~~I've been to London last May.~~ ✗

---

**5** Read the Look out! box. Circle the correct words to complete the sentences.

1  **I travelled** / **I've travelled** to Paris on the Eurostar last May.
2  Tom loves the *Hunger Games* books. **He read** / **He's read** them all.
3  'Did you ever eat / Have you ever eaten at the Chinese restaurant in town?' 'No, never.'
4  **I bought** / **I've bought** this scarf on Saturday. Do you like it?
5  Where's my maths homework? Oh, no! **I forgot** / **I've forgotten** it!
6  Amy went on holiday to France last week. **She met** / **She's met** some really nice people.

**6** Complete the dialogue with the verbs below. Use the present perfect or the past simple. Remember the difference between *been* and *gone*. (See the Look out! box on page 60.)

be  go  go  not see  spend  take  visit  visit  watch

**A** ¹_____ you ever _____ abroad?
**B** Yes, I ²_____ the USA last summer with my family.
**A** What ³_____ it like? I ⁴_____ never _____ to America.
**B** Really interesting. We ⁵_____ a week in New York. We ⁶_____ a boat trip round Manhattan and we ⁷_____ a basketball game at Madison Square Garden.
**A** Cool! ⁸_____ you _____ the Empire State Building?
**B** Yes, but it was foggy so we ⁹_____ much!

**7** Write questions from the prompts. Use *Have you ever ... ?*

1  travel / on a plane?
   *Have you ever travelled on a plane?*
2  lose / anything while travelling?
3  buy / anything online?
4  eat / food from another country?
5  download / music?
6  miss / a train, bus or plane?
7  forget / to do your homework?
8  go / abroad?

**8** **SPEAKING** Ask and answer the questions in exercise 7. If the answer is 'Yes', ask a follow-up question.

> Have you ever travelled on a plane?

> Yes, I have.

> Where did you fly to?

> I flew to London.

# 6E Word Skills

## Compounds

*I can understand and use a range of compounds related to travel.*

**1 SPEAKING** Describe the photo. Where is the boy? What is happening? Why?

**2** Read the text. Who first realised that the boy did not have a ticket?

a a passport control officer
b a waiter
c a security guard
d a flight attendant
e a police officer

**3 VOCABULARY** Read the text again. Complete the compound nouns.

| At an airport | | |
|---|---|---|
| bag drop | departure ⁴_____ | seat belt |
| ¹_____ carousel | ⁵_____ attendant | ⁷_____ check |
| boarding ²_____ | flight number | security ⁸_____ |
| ³_____ crew | hand luggage | window seat |
| check-in desk | passport ⁶_____ | |

**4** Which items in exercise 3 do you find in an airport terminal? Which five do you find on a plane?

**LEARN THIS! Compound nouns: noun + noun**

a Most compound nouns are formed from two nouns.
b We usually write them as two words (*travel agent*), but sometimes as one word (*whiteboard*) or with a hyphen (*film-maker*). Check in a dictionary.
c The stress is usually on the first noun. *whiteboard*

**5** 🎧 **2.24** Read the Learn this! box. Then listen and repeat the compound nouns in exercise 3.

**6** Complete the text below with compound nouns from exercise 3.

When you arrive at the airport, go to the ¹c_____. The clerk will check in your luggage and might ask if you want an aisle seat or a ²w_____. He or she will give you a ³b_____. Show your passport at ⁴p_____. You will also have to go through a ⁵s_____, where they X-ray your ⁶h_____. Then you reach the ⁷d_____, where there are duty-free shops. You can find your flight on the departures board by looking at the ⁸f_____ or the departure time. When they announce your flight, go to the gate.

## Can I see your boarding pass?

A nine-year-old boy managed to get on a plane without a ticket or boarding pass and fly from Minneapolis to Las Vegas. He didn't have to go through passport control as it was a domestic flight, but he managed to pass all the security checks without any problem.

The previous day, security cameras filmed him stealing suitcases from the baggage carousel in the arrivals hall and then ordering a meal in a restaurant in the terminal building. However, after the meal he told the waiter that he had to go to the toilet, and left the restaurant without paying. The following day he returned to the airport, walked through to the departure lounge and then boarded a plane. Apparently, he stayed close to another family as they passed through airport security.

On the plane, the cabin crew became suspicious of the small boy sitting alone in first class. A flight attendant contacted the Las Vegas police, who met the boy when the plane landed.

**LEARN THIS! Compounds**

We can also form compounds from an adjective and a noun.

*single room   first class   half board   full time   high season   online check-in*

**7** Read the Learn this! box. Find one of the compounds in the text in exercise 2.

**8** 🎧 **2.25** Match the words in A with the words in B to make five more compounds. Then listen and repeat all the compounds in the Learn this! box and below.

A   double   economy   full   low   part
B   board   class   room   season   time

**9** Complete the sentences with compounds from the Learn this! box and exercise 8.

1 I'm travelling alone so I'm going to book a _____ at the hotel.
2 _____ accommodation at a hotel includes breakfast and dinner.
3 There's much less room in _____ than in first class.
4 August is _____, so holidays are much more expensive.
5 My mum is a check-in clerk, but she only works _____.
6 You can use the _____ and print your boarding pass at home.

**10 SPEAKING** Look at the text in exercise 2 for two minutes. Then cover it and retell the story in your own words.

A young boy went to Minneapolis Airport one day …

# Holidays without parents

*I can understand a text about holidays without parents.*

**1** SPEAKING Describe the pictures. Then say which holiday looks more enjoyable, and why.

**2** Look through the texts quickly. Match two of the three texts (A–C) with the pictures (1 and 2).

1 ___    2 ___

**3** Read the texts. Match the three writers (Hilary, Kevin and Terry) with the sentences below.

This writer:
1 had an enjoyable experience with a friend. _____
2 had an experience that friends found amusing. _____
3 had an embarrassing experience with an adult. _____

# Free at last?

🎧 2.26

Have you ever seen travel programmes on TV about teenagers on holiday without parents? They're always having a wild and exciting time. But is it really like that? We asked three writers to tell us their personal experiences …

**A** *Hilary Bradt: co-founder of a travel guide company*

When I was fifteen, I went to stay with my penfriend in north Germany. It was my first trip abroad and the first without my parents, and I hated every minute of it. The worst moment was probably the time when I was alone in the house and
5 somebody rang the doorbell. They rang it again and again – but I ignored it. Then I saw the visitor walking around the house looking through the windows. Frightened, I hid under the dining-room table. That afternoon, Christina's mother came home from work and said, 'I needed to pick up some
10 papers from the house today and I didn't have my key. I rang the bell. But you didn't hear me.' 'Oh, I was in my room, I expect,' I said. 'Sorry!' My face went red, because she knew I was lying. I'm certain she saw me under the table.

**B** *Kevin Rushby: writer*

At sixteen, I hitch-hiked down to Cornwall in the south-west
15 of England with a friend. We spent the holiday walking along the coastal path with a tent and a backpack, staying at campsites on the way. The weather was fantastic and the sea was beautiful. We had almost no money and lived on sandwiches and tea. One of the first things I learned was this:
20 a fire and a mug of tea can make the world seem perfect. The second thing: spending more money does not mean having more fun. What really mattered was talking to people. I had to do lots of chatting, negotiating, discussing and questioning. Strangers could be very helpful and interesting, I discovered.
25 They could also be dangerous, boring and stupid. It was up to me to judge them and decide – and that skill has been useful to me many times since then. I wrote it all down, but I've lost the notebook now, unfortunately.

1

2

**4** Read the Reading Strategy. Then look at questions 1–5 in exercise 5. Find the underlined words in the text and explain why those options are not correct.

**Reading Strategy**

Do not assume that because a multiple-choice option contains words from the text, it is correct. Focus on meaning, not on individual words.

Treat each option as a true or false task in order to find the option that is true.

**C  Terry Alderton: comedian**

My friends and I were nineteen and on holiday in the coolest place in the world: Ibiza. On the first day, I fell asleep on the beach – with no suncream. My friends knew I was getting sunburned, but they didn't wake me up because they thought it was funny. When I woke up, I felt a little sore. Then I took off my sunglasses and my friends all fell on the floor, laughing. I had two clear white rings around my eyes! That night, we all went out dancing and of course I had to keep wearing the same sunglasses because of my sunburn. I wasn't enjoying myself, so I left before my friends. For some reason, I didn't want to wait for a bus back to our hotel, so I walked seven kilometres along busy roads. When I finally arrived, my friends were already there, sitting around the pool. I've never understood how they got there so quickly.

**5** Circle the correct answers (a–d).

1 Hilary went red because her penfriend's mother knew
  a that Hilary didn't hear the <u>doorbell</u>.
  b that Hilary was in her bedroom.
  c that Hilary was not telling the truth.
  d why Hilary did not want to open the door.

2 On Kevin's first holiday without his parents, he
  a walked all the way to the south-west of England.
  b decided to <u>hitch-hike</u> around south-west England.
  c spent the holiday at a campsite in Cornwall.
  d camped at various places along the coast.

3 Meeting lots of different people taught Kevin
  a some useful skills that he later lost.
  b that negotiating with strangers can be <u>dangerous</u>.
  c how to decide what strangers are like.
  d that talking to strangers is usually boring.

4 Terry had circles around his eyes because
  a his friends put lots of <u>suncream</u> on his face.
  b the rest of his face was red from the sun.
  c his eyes were sore from too much sun.
  d he wanted to make his friends laugh.

5 Terry decided to walk back to the hotel because
  a he wanted to get back to the hotel before his friends.
  b he knew there were no more <u>buses</u>.
  c he didn't feel like standing at the bus stop.
  d he knew it was not very far.

**6** **SPEAKING** In pairs, decide which holiday experience was the best and which was the worst. Give reasons. Which holiday (A, B or C) would you prefer to go on?

**7** **VOCABULARY** Form holiday-related compound nouns by matching the words below with words 1–8. All of the compounds are in the texts.

burn  cream  friend  glasses  guide  pack  programme  site

1 travel _____     3 pen_____     5 camp_____     7 sun_____
2 travel _____     4 back_____     6 sun_____     8 sun_____

**RECYCLE!  First conditional**

Remember: we form the first conditional with the present simple in the *if* clause and *will* in the main clause.

If we forget to pack suncream, we'll get sunburned.

**8** Read the Recycle! box. In pairs, imagine you are going on holiday with some friends. What will be the advantages and disadvantages of being without adults? Use the *if* clauses below for ideas.

if we run out of money    if we lose our passports
if we get ill    if we don't want to go sightseeing
if we make some new friends    if we argue with each other

**9** **SPEAKING** Discuss your ideas from exercise 8 with the class. Overall, are holidays without adults a good or a bad idea?

If we become ill, our parents won't be there to look after us.

Yes, but on the other hand, if we don't want to go sightseeing, we won't have to.

# Planning a holiday
*I can discuss and plan a holiday trip.*

**1 SPEAKING** Describe the photo. Where are the people? What are they doing?

**2 VOCABULARY** Check the meaning of the tourist attractions below. Which are places and which are events?

**Tourist attractions**  art gallery   carnival   church
concert   festival   monument   musical   safari park
old town   opera house   park   restaurant
shopping district   square   theatre

**3** 🎧 **2.27** Read the task below. Then listen to a candidate doing the task. Which attractions from exercise 2 do they mention?

> You are planning a trip to London with a friend. Discuss the trip with your friend and agree on:
> • accommodation in London.
> • the tourist attractions you will visit.
> • places to eat.
> • the best way to travel around.

**4 KEY PHRASES** Look at the phrases for making suggestions (1–6) and say what follows them: a) verb + -*ing*, b) infinitive with *to*, c) infinitive without *to*.

> **Making suggestions**
> 1 Shall we ... ?
> 2 Let's ...
> 3 Do you fancy ... ?
> 4 Why don't we ... ?
> 5 What about ... ?
> 6 It would be nice ...
> 7 We could always ...

**5 KEY PHRASES** Complete the phrases with the words below.

both   good   keen   like   mind   not   rather
really   sounds   suggestion   sure   that   think

> **Accepting a suggestion**
> That ¹_____ like a great idea.
> What a ²_____ idea!
> I ³_____ that idea.
> That's a ⁴_____ good plan.
> Yes. Why ⁵_____?
> Let's do ⁶_____.
> **Declining a suggestion**
> I'm not ⁷_____ about that.
> I don't ⁸_____ that's a great idea.
> I'm not very ⁹_____ on that idea.
> I'd ¹⁰_____ not.
> **Expressing no preference**
> I don't ¹¹_____.
> Either ¹²_____ is fine by me.
> They're ¹³_____ good ideas.

**6** 🎧 **2.27** Listen again. Which phrases from exercises 4 and 5 did the speakers use?

**7 SPEAKING** Work in pairs. Take turns to make suggestions using the prompts below. Your partner either accepts the suggestion, or declines it and suggests something else. Use expressions in exercises 4 and 5.

go to an Indian restaurant   get some pizza
stay in an expensive hotel   book the hotel in advance
hire bicycles in the city   visit the science museum
go on an out-of-town excursion   travel by underground

➡ **Vocabulary Builder** City tourism: page 120

> **Speaking Strategy**
> If you don't understand something someone has said, don't panic! Ask for clarification. You can use these phrases:
> • Pardon?
> • Could you repeat that, please?
> • Sorry, did you say ... ?
> • Sorry, what does 'tourist attraction' mean?

**8** 🎧 **2.28** Read the Speaking Strategy. Then listen to another candidate doing the task in exercise 3. How many times does the candidate ask for clarification? Which words did she not understand?

**9** Work in pairs. Read the task below and make notes.

> **Student A:** You are the tourist.
> **Student B:** You live near the famous town.
> You are planning a trip with a friend to a famous town in your country.  Discuss the trip with your friend and agree on:
> • the best way to travel around.
> • the best places to eat.
> • tourist attractions you will visit.
> • out-of-town excursions that you will go on.

**10 SPEAKING** Role-play a conversation to the class.

**Writing**

# A holiday blog

*I can write a holiday blog post.*

## Holiday BLOGSPOT

**8.15 p.m. @Harry445**

Hi, everyone! We arrived safely in Paris on Saturday evening. It was very windy and rainy, so the flight was a bit bumpy. Emma screamed when the plane landed! Hilarious, lol! The weather is much better now. Still cloudy, but it's stopped raining.

We've already been up the Eiffel Tower. We took the lift up, but walked back down the stairs. We've also walked down the Champs Elysées. The shops there are really expensive, so I didn't buy anything!! Yesterday we went on a boat trip on the river Seine and then visited the Louvre art gallery. We saw the Mona Lisa, which was a bit disappointing. It's tiny!

Tomorrow we are going to visit Disneyland. It isn't far from here. Can't wait! Then on Friday we're going shopping (but not on the Champs Elysées!) – I want to buy some souvenirs. Will post another entry tomorrow when we're back from Disneyland.

**9.04 p.m. @Emily99**

Sorry I haven't posted since Friday! Arrived in Snowdonia two days ago with Joanna after a long, tiring journey by coach from London. There were roadworks on the motorway and an accident, so the journey took ten hours instead of six. We're staying in a small, comfortable hotel. It's near a river. The weather is sunny and dry and I can see hills and a beautiful waterfall from my window.

We've already been kayaking on the lake and abseiling on a cliff near the hotel. The kayaking was fun and the abseiling was fantastic, but a bit scary! Tomorrow we're going mountain biking. We're going to hire bikes from a shop in the nearest town. Really looking forward to it! Watch out for more blog entries in the next few days!

**1** Look at the photos. Where would you prefer to go on holiday? Why?

**2** Read the blog posts. Who has already done four things and has another two planned? Who has done two things and has another one planned?

**3** Read the task below. Do both blog posts include all four points?

> You are on holiday with your family. Write a blog post. Include information about:
> - the journey to your holiday destination and where you are staying.
> - the weather.
> - some holiday activities you have done.
> - something you plan to do in the next few days.

**Writing Strategy**

In informal style (e.g. in emails, blogs and postcards) we can omit sentence subjects *I* and *we*.

*Must go now! Wish you were here!*

With the present continuous, we can also omit the auxiliaries *am* and *are*.

*Having a great time in Italy!*

However, only do this once or twice in a text. Do not omit every instance of *I* and *we*.

**4** Read the Writing Strategy. Find sentences where the writers have omitted the subject.

**5** Rewrite the sentences, omitting the subject.

1 We have finally arrived!
2 I am looking forward to seeing you again.
3 I went up the Empire State Building yesterday.
4 We visited the Musée d'Orsay on Friday.
5 We are flying back tomorrow.

**6** In the blog posts, find:

1 five words that describe weather.
2 five landscape features.
3 three outdoor activities.

**7** VOCABULARY Complete the holiday activities below. They are all in the blog posts in exercise 2.

> Holiday activities
> 1 go s_____ / k_____ / a_____ / m_____ b_____
> 2 take a b_____ t_____
> 3 go up a t_____
> 4 visit an a_____
> 5 hire a b_____
> 6 buy s_____

➡ **Vocabulary Builder** Holiday activities: page 120

**8** Read the task in exercise 3 again. Make notes for each of the four points.

**9** Write your blog post.

**CHECK YOUR WORK**

Have you …
- included all four points in the task?
- used an appropriately informal style?
- checked the spelling and grammar?

## Reading

1 Read the Strategy. Then read the text and predict what ideas and pronouns the gapped sentences might contain.

2 Read the text. Match sentences A–I with gaps 1–7 in the text. There are two extra sentences.

### My trip to Delhi

*Saturday*

After two flights, I finally arrived in Delhi. ¹___ It didn't take long, and I was soon driving through the streets to my small hotel. The owner was really kind and friendly. ²___ It was very clean and comfortable. I was really tired, so I read some of my tourist guide to India. ³___

*Sunday*

I got up at about 8 o'clock and went down for breakfast. ⁴___ Afterwards, I went out into Delhi. I found a taxi and went to my first tourist spot: the Shri Lakshmi Narain Temple. ⁵___ Inside, I found a guide and learned a lot about the history of the beautiful building. After this, I went to Raj Ghat. This is the last resting place of Mahatma Gandhi. The gardens were very green and there were lots of trees, but the fountains were dry because of the heat. After this I was very tired and hot. ⁶___ Later, when I felt better, I went for dinner at a restaurant. I had a dosa, which is a kind of pancake with curried potatoes and onions. Tomorrow, I'm going to visit Humayun's Tomb and the museum. I'm going to go to the markets and do some shopping too. ⁷___. Then I'll probably catch a flight to Varanasi. It's a very famous historical place. I'll let you know what it's like!

A It's going to be hotter tomorrow.

B I think I'll stay in Delhi for a few days.

C I didn't feel like exploring any more, so I went back to my hotel for a rest.

D He chatted for a bit and then showed me my room.

E That's why he met me at the airport.

F I took off my shoes and went in with the other tourists.

G I collected my luggage with no problems, left the airport and tried to find a taxi.

H It was a delicious meal of eggs, Indian breads and chutneys.

I I fell asleep in the middle of an article about street food.

## Listening

3 Read the Strategy. Then read sentences A–F in the task below and underline the key words.

4 🎧 2.29 Listen to five people talking about jobs. Match sentences A–F with speakers 1–5. There is one extra sentence.

A Get experience with your family. _____

B Have a fun job abroad. _____

C Get all the information you need in advance. _____

D Avoid problems at work. _____

E Learn to work for yourself. _____

F Learn different ways to perform. _____

## Use of English

5 Complete the text with the words below. There are two extra words.

about   after   as   before   but   for
from   that   the   to   what   who

### Being a tour guide

If you want to be a guide in a museum or an art gallery, you have to train before you can lead any tours. You do not have to be a historian, ¹_____ teaching and public speaking experience can help you to get a position. It's best to look ²_____ a voluntary position at first as this looks great on your CV. It can also help you get a paid museum job in ³_____ future. First, you should decide ⁴_____ kind of museum or gallery you want to work in. After ⁵_____ , you should contact the person in charge of volunteers. They may want to speak with you, so ⁶_____ you go for an interview, do some research. Find out ⁷_____ the kind of exhibits they have and how long they've had them. If it's an art gallery, ⁸_____ are the most famous and popular artists? The people at the museum want confident, friendly people to work ⁹_____ tour guides. Remember ¹⁰_____ show this side of yourself at the interview.

# Exam Skills Trainer

## Speaking

> **Strategy**
> A speaking task may ask you to role-play a conversation in which you have to make a choice between different options, e.g. which job to apply for, which holiday to go on, etc. During the conversation, make sure you use words like *however, even though, although* and *nevertheless*.

**6** Read the Strategy and the phrases below. Compare the pictures which show two summer jobs. Which would you prefer and why? Make sentences to show how you feel about each.

I'm sure I'll ...    even though ...
Although it's ... ,    I won't ...
The ... isn't very good.    Nevertheless, ...
I might find the job ...    However, ...

**7** Work in pairs. Do the task below. Use the phrases from exercise 6 to help you.

You aren't sure what job to get when you finish school or university. Discuss the three options you've read about on a careers website. Decide which one each of you will aim for. Say why it would suit you.
- teacher
- shop manager
- start your own business

**8** Summarise the decisions you made and your main reasons.

## Writing

> **Strategy**
> Using linking phrases makes your writing more coherent. It helps the reader to see logical connections between presented facts and opinions.

**9** Read the Strategy. Then complete the sentences with the linking phrases below.

as    because of    in order to    so    so that    that

1 Toby has a lot of experience, _____ finding a job isn't difficult for him.
2 I want to be a tour guide _____ I can work and travel at the same time.
3 There are so many unemployed people _____ finding work is very difficult.
4 Sally always gets a lot of job offers _____ she speaks seven languages.
5 Rob took a computer course _____ improve his computer skills.
6 Mike didn't get the job _____ his lack of experience.

**10** Read the task below and write the blog post.

You're looking for a summer job. Describe your job search on your blog, and ask for some advice from your readers:
- explain what kind of job you'd like to have and why.
- explain where and how you are looking for it.
- mention what difficulties you have finding a good job.

# 7
# Money

## 7A  Vocabulary

# Spending power
*I can talk about different shops and services.*

# Worth it?

Gold of Kinabalu orchid

white truffles

**1** white truffles – €_____ a kilo

**3** a pen – £_____ each

**2** a flower – £_____ each

Mont Blanc Lorenzo di Medici fountain pen

**1 SPEAKING** Look at the photos. In pairs, guess which of the items is the most expensive and which is the least expensive.

**2** Read aloud the numbers and currencies below. What other currencies do you know?

> Numbers and currencies
> $500 = five hundred dollars
> €3,500 = three thousand five hundred / three and a half thousand euros
> 250,000₹ = two hundred and fifty thousand rupees
> £1 million = a million pounds
> ¥3.5 billion = three point five / three and a half billion yen

**3** 🎧 **2.30** Listen to the descriptions of the items in exercise 1. Complete the prices using the numbers below. Which is the most surprising, in your opinion?

500   3,500   5,400   6,850   10,000   12,000

**4** 🎧 **2.31** **VOCABULARY** Work in pairs. Where would you buy the items in exercise 1? Match them with six of the shops and services below. Then listen and check.

**Shops and services** baker's  bank  butcher's  charity shop  chemist's
coffee shop  clothes shop  cosmetics store  deli (delicatessen)  DIY store
estate agent's  florist's  garden centre  greengrocer's  hairdresser's  jeweller's
launderette  newsagent's  optician's  post office  shoe shop  stationer's  takeaway

1 _____     3 _____     5 _____
2 _____     4 _____     6 _____

Yubari King melons

4 melons –
£_____ for two

Nike trainers

5 trainers –
$_____ a pair

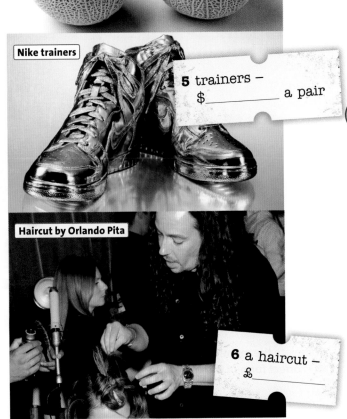

Haircut by Orlando Pita

6 a haircut –
£_____

**5** 🎧 **2.32** Listen and repeat all of the shops and services words from exercise 4. Copy the words into your notebook and mark where the stress falls on each word. Is it usually near the beginning or the end?

**6** 🎧 **2.33** Listen to six dialogues. Match them with six of the shops and services from exercise 4.

1 DIY store     3 _____     5 _____
2 _____     4 _____     6 _____

**7 VOCABULARY** Complete definitions 1–9 with the words and phrases below.

**Shopping**   bargain   coupons   discount   discount code price tag   receipt   refund   sale   special offer

1 'Buy one, get one free' is a common example of a
_____ .
2 If you think something is a _____ , you think it's a good price for what you are getting.
3 The _____ tells you how much something costs in a shop.
4 When a shop has a _____ , it sells some of its items at lower prices for a few days or weeks.
5 If a shop gives you a _____ , you pay less than the usual price.
6 Magazines sometimes have _____ that give you money off in a shop.
7 If you ask for a _____ in a shop, you ask for your money back.
8 A _____ is a small piece of paper that you get when you pay for something.
9 If you type in a _____ when you are shopping online, you can get something for less than the usual price.

**8** 🎧 **2.33** Listen again. Which word from exercise 7 do you hear in each dialogue? Add to your notes from exercise 6.

1 DIY store – coupon

> **RECYCLE!** **Present perfect with *ever***
> We use the present perfect with *ever* to ask about experiences.
> Have you ever bought a pair of really expensive trainers?
> Yes, I have. / No, I haven't.

**9** Read the Recycle! box. Then look at the questionnaire below and complete the questions with the present perfect form of the verbs in brackets and *ever*.

# Are you a crafty customer?

**SALE**

**1** _____ (you / ask) for a discount in a shop?

**2** _____ (you / use) coupons from magazines to get money off?

**3** _____ (you / compare) prices in two or three shops before buying something?

**4** _____ (you / wait) for something to be in the sale before buying it?

**5** _____ (you / see) something in a shop and then looked for it online to save money?

**10 SPEAKING** Do the questionnaire in pairs. Give your partner one mark for each 'yes' answer. What is his or her 'crafty customer' score out of five?

# Second conditional

*I can talk about imaginary situations and their consequences.*

**1 SPEAKING** Look at the photo of São Paulo. What does it tell you about the lives of people who live in this city?

**2 ⊙2.34** Read and listen to the dialogue. Who do you agree with more, the boy or the girl?

**Girl** What are you doing?

**Boy** I'm doing my geography project. Look at this photo. It's shocking that some people have so much and others have so little! The world would be much better if money didn't exist.

**Girl** What do you mean? If money didn't exist, how would you buy things?

**Boy** If you needed something, you would make it. If you couldn't make it, you would swap with somebody else.

**Girl** So if I wanted a new mobile phone, how would I get it?

**Boy** You don't need things like that! I'm talking about essentials: food, clothes, that kind of thing. At the moment, millions of people haven't even got those.

**Girl** If money didn't exist, life wouldn't be better for poor people.

**Boy** No? I think it would. If nobody had any money, everybody would be equal.

**3** Read the Learn this! box and complete rule a with *infinitive*, *past simple* and *would*. Use the examples to help you. Then find seven second conditional sentences in the dialogue in exercise 2.

---

**LEARN THIS! Second conditional**

**a** We use the second conditional to describe an imaginary situation or event and its result.

*If shops didn't exist, we would buy everything online.*

imaginary situation       result

We use the ¹_____ in the *if* clause and we use ²_____ + ³_____ in the main clause.

**b** We can put the main clause first.

*I'd buy you a present if I had enough money.*

**c** We use *could* to mean *would + be able to*. It is also the past simple of *can*.

*If I won the lottery, I could stop work.*
*If she could speak English, she'd get a job in the USA.*

---

➤ **Grammar Builder 7B** page 136

**4** Match 1–6 with a–f and make second conditional sentences using the correct form of the verbs in brackets.

1 If I _____ (need) money, _____
2 If tablet computers _____ (not cost) so much, _____
3 I _____ (be) upset _____
4 I _____ (can) buy clothes really cheaply _____
5 If I _____ (have) a credit card, _____
6 If I _____ (not have) a mobile phone, _____

a I _____ (ask) my dad to buy one for me.
b I _____ (can) shop online.
c if I _____ (shop) at the charity shop.
d I _____ (get) a holiday job.
e I _____ (use) my mum's laptop to send messages.
f if the coffee shop in my village _____ (close).

**5** Complete the money tips with the second conditional. Use the correct form of the verbs below.

can   get   make   save   sell   swap

## Money tips!

! Cosmetics are not cheap. You ¹_____ a fortune if you ²_____ your own. Olive oil, salt and lemon are three cheap and effective ingredients.

! Clothes shopping costs a lot of money. If you ³_____ clothes with your friends, all of you ⁴_____ something new to wear – for free!

! How many old books, DVDs and games have you got on your shelves? If you ⁵_____ them all online, you ⁶_____ use the money to buy new ones!

**6** Think about the questions below and make notes.

What would you do if …

1 there were no shops in your town?
2 you had a rich relative's credit card?
3 a shop assistant gave you too much change?
4 you saw somebody stealing from a shop?
5 you needed to earn money during the summer holiday?
6 you won €1 million?
7 you could have a free holiday anywhere in the world?
8 a friend needed money to buy some new clothes?

**7 SPEAKING** Work in pairs. Ask and answer the questions in exercise 6.

> What would you do if there were no shops in your town?

> I'd do all my shopping online. What about you?

**Listening**

# Honesty pays

*I can work out the kind of information I need to complete a listening task.*

**1 SPEAKING** Have you ever found any money that was not yours? What did you do with it?

**2** 🎧 **2.35** Listen to the story about Glen James. What did he do?

**Listening Strategy**

Before you listen, carefully read the summary and think about what you need to fill each gap. Think about the part of speech (noun, adjective, verb, etc.) and the kind of information (a time / date, number, age, place, an adjective that describes a feeling, etc.) that should go in each gap.

**3** Read the Listening Strategy and the summary below. What kind of information do you need for each answer?

Glen James lives in Boston, but for the past five years he ¹_____ . Last February, he found a bag in ²_____ . Inside the bag there was a lot of ³_____ . Instead of keeping it, he reported it ⁴_____ . They managed to find the owner of the bag, who was a ⁵_____ . Ethan Whittington heard the story on the news, and immediately decided to help Glen by setting up a ⁶_____ and asking people to donate money. He managed to raise ⁷_____ for Glen.

**4** 🎧 **2.35** Listen to the story again and complete the summary in exercise 3. Use between 1 and 3 words in each gap.

**5 SPEAKING** Work in pairs. Discuss your ideas. What would you do if you found a bag with $42,000 in it?

**6 VOCABULARY** Check the meaning of the verbs below. Find four pairs of verbs with opposite meanings.

**Verbs to do with money**   afford   be short of borrow   buy   charge   cost   get / give a refund lend   lose   owe   pay for   run out of   save save up   sell   spend   waste

**7** You are going to hear five speakers. Read the questions below and predict the kind of information you need to answer each one.

1 Where did the boy buy the present?
2 Who does the girl like to spend money on?
3 How did the boy pay for the baseball cap?
4 How much pocket money does the girl receive?
5 When did the girl return the item to the shop?

**8** 🎧 **2.36** Listen and answer the questions in exercise 7. Were your predictions correct?

**9** 🎧 **2.36** Listen again. Match speakers 1–5 with sentences A–F. There is one extra sentence.

This speaker:
A tried to borrow money from a family member. ___
B had an argument with a shop assistant. ___
C regrets buying something very expensive. ___
D returned something to a shop and got the money back. ___
E found some money in a shop. ___
F is saving money for an expensive item of clothing. ___

**10** Complete the questions with the correct form of the verbs from exercise 6. Do not use any verbs more than once.

1 Does anybody *owe* you any money?
2 Do you ever b_____ money from your family or friends?
3 Have you ever l_____ anyone any money?
4 Are you s_____ money for anything at the moment?
5 What's the most expensive thing you've ever b_____?
6 Has a shop assistant ever c_____ you too much for something in a shop?
7 How much do you s_____ on clothes when you go shopping?
8 About how much does a burger c_____ in a fast-food restaurant in your country?
9 Have you ever s_____ anything online?

**11 SPEAKING** Work in pairs. Ask and answer the questions in exercise 10. Where you can, give extra information with your answers.

Does anybody owe you any money?

Yes, my brother owes me €10. I lent it to him last week.

# Past perfect

*I can talk about events happening at different times in the past.*

## Buried treasure

In November 2013, James Howells started searching an enormous rubbish dump. He was looking for a computer hard drive which he had thrown away three months earlier. The hard drive contained 7,500 bitcoins (a virtual currency that people use online). He had bought the bitcoins for almost nothing in 2009, but by 2013 the value of a single bitcoin had risen to over $1,000. So, the value of Howells's collection had increased to $7.5 million.

In 2010, Howells, who works in IT, had taken his computer apart because he had spilled a drink on it. He had first kept the hard drive and had sold the other parts. When in 2013 he heard about the value of the virtual currency, it was too late. He had thrown the hard drive away! He had totally forgotten about the bitcoins. Howells never found the hard drive – and unfortunately, he hadn't saved any of his data.

**1** Read the text. Where is Howells's hard drive? How much is it worth? Did he find it?

**2** Look at the examples of the past perfect highlighted in the text in exercise 2. Find all the other examples. Complete rule a in the Learn this! box.

### LEARN THIS! Past perfect

**a** We form the past perfect with ¹_____ or ²_____ and the past participle.

**b** We use the past perfect when we are already talking about past events and we want to talk about an even earlier event.
*When I got to the classroom, the lesson had started.*

past | now | future
*The lesson started.* | *I got to the classroom.*

**c** We often use the past perfect with *after* or *when*.
*When I got to the bus station, the bus had already left.*
*After I'd called Maggie, I watched a film on TV.*

**3** Read rules b and c in the Learn this! box. Explain the difference in meaning between the sentences below.

1 When he threw away the computer, Howells forgot about the bitcoins.
2 When he threw away the computer, Howells had forgotten about the bitcoins.

➤➤ Grammar Builder 7D page 136

**4** Complete the sentences. Use the past perfect form of the verbs in brackets. Remember that *go* can have two past participles. (See Look out! box on page 64.)

1 After I _____ (leave) the newsagent's, I realised I _____ (forget) to buy a paper.
2 I didn't know that deli was so expensive. I _____ never _____ (buy) anything there before.
3 When I got to the shopping centre, most of the shops _____ already _____ . (close)
4 We didn't have any bread because I _____ (not go) to the baker's.
5 My sister wasn't there when I got home because she _____ (go) to the cinema.

**5** USE OF ENGLISH Rewrite each pair of sentences as one sentence, using *after*.

1 I bought a lottery ticket. Then I went home.
*After I'd bought a lottery ticket, I went home.*
2 I went to the cosmetics store. Then I went to the hairdresser's.
3 I paid for the flowers. Then I left the shop.
4 Jim did some shopping. Then he caught the bus home.
5 My dad left university. Then he became a teacher.
6 The chemist's closed down. Then a charity shop opened in the same building.

**6** Complete the text with the phrases below. Use the past perfect.

buy his ticket    not check the numbers    lose
lose his ticket    win the lottery    take the lottery company

When Martyn Tott learned that he ¹_____ , he was, of course, delighted. He ²_____ months earlier at his local newsagent's. He ³_____ at the time, but he knew he was the winner because he always chose the same six numbers. But there was a problem. He ⁴_____ ! Martyn Tott's computer records proved that he was the winner, but the lottery company refused to pay him without a ticket. Two years later, he was almost penniless. He ⁵_____ to court, but ⁶_____ the battle. He said he wished he had never played the lottery!

**7** Read the sentences below. Then think of explanations for the situation or event using the past perfect. What had happened?

1 A man was holding a lottery ticket and smiling.
2 The car drove onto the pavement and hit a lamp post.
3 A cleaner found a wallet under the seats in the cinema.
4 A security guard stopped a woman outside the department store.
5 The boy opened the envelope, read the letter and started to dance around.

**8** SPEAKING Take turns to ask and answer questions about the sentences in exercise 7.

Why was the man smiling?

He had won some money.

## 7E Word Skills

# Verb + infinitive or *-ing* form

*I can identify and use different verb patterns.*

**1 SPEAKING** Describe the picture. What do you think the woman is doing?

**2** Read the text. Then answer the questions.

1 What is 'showrooming'? Have you or someone you know ever showroomed?
2 Do you prefer to buy things in shops or online? Why?
3 Should you expect to pay more for goods in a shop than on a website? Why? / Why not?
4 What would you do if you had to pay to look around a shop?

## That'll be $5, please.

A health food shop in Adelaide, Australia, has decided to charge customers $5 for 'just looking'. The problem is that customers keep coming into the shop and leaving without buying anything. 'They pretend to be interested in a product and ask for advice,' says Kate Reeves, the shop owner, 'but they usually don't buy anything.'

This new phenomenon is called 'showrooming'. People visit a shop, examine a product, and then buy it online, where it is cheaper. Kate says she spends hours every day talking about products with customers. 'I can't stand working and not getting paid,' she says. 'I refuse to work for free!'

Everyone avoids paying more than they have to, but customers fail to realise that Kate's prices are mostly the same as in larger stores and on websites. They prefer to shop elsewhere as they expect to find the product at a lower price. 'If customers choose to buy something, I return the $5 fee,' says Kate.

Many shops face the same problem and some may end up introducing a similar charge. The danger is that it risks putting customers off. But Kate in Adelaide says it has made no difference to her business.

### LEARN THIS! Verb patterns

**a** Some verbs are followed by the infinitive of another verb.
Do you want <u>to go out</u>? She hopes <u>to be</u> a teacher.

**b** Some verbs are followed by the *-ing* form of another verb.
I fancy <u>going out</u>. He keeps on <u>interrupting</u>.

**c** Some verbs are followed by either the infinitive or the *-ing* form.
**like** to do / doing    **love** to do / doing
**start** to do / doing    **prefer** to do / doing

**3** Read the Learn this! box. Then find all the verbs in the text in exercise 2 that are followed by the infinitive or the *-ing* form of another verb. Make two lists in your notebook.

### Dictionary Skills Strategy

Entries for verbs in learner's dictionaries will show you patterns the verb is used in. They may show the pattern like this at the start of the entry: *suggest (doing), want (to do)* or give an example within the entry: *She suggested eating out.*

**4 DICTIONARY WORK** Read the Dictionary Strategy. Then study the dictionary entries below and answer the questions.

1 Which verb a) takes an infinitive, b) takes an *-ing* form, and c) can take either?
2 Which entries show the verb pattern a) at the start of the entry, and b) in an example?

**avoid** /əˈvɔɪd/ *verb* [T]  **1** avoid doing sth to prevent sth happening or to try not to do sth: *He always tried to avoid an argument if possible.* • *She has to avoid eating fatty food.* **2** to keep away from sb/sth *I leave home early to avoid the rush hour.* ▶ **avoidance** *noun* [U]

**hate¹** /heɪt/ *verb* [T]  **1** hate (sb/sth); hate (doing / to do sth) to have a very strong feeling of not liking sb/sth at all: *I hate grapefruit.* • *I hate it when it's raining like this. I hate to see the countryside spoilt.* • *He hates driving at night.*

**refuse¹** /rɪˈfjuːz/ *verb* [I, T] to say or show that you do not want to do, give or accept sth: *He refused to listen to what I was saying.* • *My application for a grant has been refused.*

**5** Look up these words in a dictionary and add them to the lists you made in exercise 3.

admit  agree  enjoy  mind  offer  promise

**6** Complete the sentences. Use the infinitive or the *-ing* form of the verbs in brackets.

1 Jason promised _____ (phone) me.
2 Tom admitted _____ (steal) a CD from the shop.
3 Joe enjoys _____ (shop) in town but refuses _____ (shop) online.
4 I decided _____ (order) groceries online as I don't like _____ (queue) in supermarkets.
5 Dad suggested _____ (eat out) this evening.
6 Mum offered _____ (give) me a lift to the shops.
7 You can expect _____ (pay) less online than in a shop.
8 Do you fancy _____ (go) to the cinema this evening?

**7** Complete the sentences with an infinitive or *-ing* form and true information about yourself.

1 I usually avoid …
2 I really can't stand …
3 I don't mind …
4 I spend a lot of time …
5 I sometimes pretend …
6 I really want …
7 I never agree …
8 I often decide …

**8 SPEAKING** Tell your partner your sentences. Are any of your answers the same?

## 7F Reading

### Aaron Levie

*I can understand an article about an unusual multi-millionaire.*

1 **SPEAKING** Look at the photo. What type of company do you think Aaron Levie runs? Why do you think 'Box' is a good name for this kind of company?

2 Read the first two paragraphs of the text and find the answers to the questions in exercise 1.

> **Reading Strategy**
>
> When you do a task with gapped sentences, study the sentence after each gap and look for any connections with the missing sentence. For example, if it begins with *but*, there is a contrast. Other words suggest other types of connection:
> - similarity: *too*
> - cause / result: *so*
> - a different option: *or*

3 Read the Reading Strategy. Then look at the underlined words in the sentences after the gaps in the text. What kind of connection do they imply: contrast, similarity, cause / result, or a different option?

4 Read the text. Match sentences A–G with gaps 1–5 in the text. Use your answers from exercise 3 to help you. There are two extra sentences.

A Back in 2005, cloud storage was quite a new idea.
B His success in business has brought him an enormous amount of money.
C He only goes to expensive restaurants if an important customer wants to eat there.
D For two and a half years, he spent nearly all his time at his office.
E Most people his age would lead an extravagant lifestyle if they had so much money.
F If you met him, you probably wouldn't realise that he is a multi-millionaire.
G Cloud storage is one of the fastest-growing areas of business.

5 **🎧 2.37** Listen and check your answers to exercise 4.

6 Are these sentences true or false? Write T or F.

1 Aaron Levie lives in a luxury apartment. ___
2 Levie doesn't mind working long hours because he is really enthusiastic about the work. ___
3 Levie was a student when he co-founded the company Box. ___
4 Mark Cuban was the first businessman to invest in Box. ___
5 Since he became rich and successful, Levie's lifestyle has not changed very much. ___

7 **VOCABULARY** Match the highlighted words in the text with the definitions below. Some definitions match with more than one word.

Business
1 money received by a business or person _____
2 money you receive every month for your work _____
3 a business person who takes risks _____
4 money that a business or person needs for a particular purpose _____
5 the money a business makes after paying its expenses _____
6 the person in charge of a large company _____
7 formal agreements to do business _____
8 people who support a business by lending it money _____

8 **SPEAKING** In pairs, ask and answer these questions. Give reasons for your answers and ask follow-up questions.

If you were a multi-millionaire ...
- would you eat in burger bars?
- would you live in a big house?
- would you work very long hours?
- would you go on expensive holidays?

> Would you eat in burger bars if you were a multi-millionaire?

> Yes, I would.

> Why?

> Because I really like burgers and I'm not keen on fancy restaurants!

🎧 2.37

**Aaron Levie** loves to eat tinned spaghetti, drives a six-year-old car, and has business meetings at a takeaway. He lives in an ordinary apartment, doesn't take holidays and, at the age
5 of 27, says his biggest luxury is his smartphone. ¹__ However, as co-founder and CEO of Box, a successful IT company, he is worth about $100 million. And he works very hard for his money: most days, he does not leave the office until after midnight. 'I work so many
10 hours because I love what I do. I'm incredibly excited about the business,' says Levie.

When Levie and his childhood friend Dylan Smith started their company in 2005, they had not even finished their university degrees. Box grew fast because
15 it offered a better way of storing data, and soon they had contracts with many of the biggest companies in the USA. Levie left university without finishing his course.

Like most new businesses, Box did not bring in much income at the start. Levie paid himself a salary of only
20 $500 a month, and lived off tinned spaghetti and instant noodles. ²__ Sometimes he even slept there too.

When Box began, Levie and Smith looked for funding.
³__ For that reason, nobody wanted to risk lending them money. They wrote letter after letter but could
25 not find any investors. Eventually, a well-known entrepreneur called Mark Cuban agreed to put money into Box. Once he had decided to do that, others followed and the business grew quickly.

That was eight years ago. Now, Box has grown a lot
30 and so have its profits, making Levie a multi-millionaire.
⁴__ But Levie says that it doesn't interest him. 'I'm certainly not into money. I don't live in the office – now I have an apartment six minutes' drive away – but there is no enormous house up in the hills.' ⁵__ Otherwise, he
35 has lunch meetings in burger bars. 'And I still really like tinned spaghetti. I'd be happy if I had it every day!'

CLOUD COMPUTING

# Photo comparison and presentation

*I can compare ideas for spending money on schools and justify my opinion.*

**1** Look at the photos. Where are the people? Match each photo with a place below.

In school   canteen   classroom   hall   library
playground   playing field   staff room   store room

➡ **Vocabulary Builder** In school: page 120

**2** Describe photo 1. What can you see? What is happening? Use the phrases below to help you.

the photo shows   in the foreground / background
on the left / right   in the top right corner
in the bottom left corner   judging by
it / they etc. must be …   she / they etc. can't be …

**3** **SPEAKING** Now compare photos 1 and 2. Describe a) the main similarities and b) the main differences. Use the phrases below to help you.

> **Similarities**
> The common theme in the photos is …
> You can see … in both photos.
> Both photos show …
> In both photos there are …
> **Differences**
> The first photo shows … , whereas the second photo shows …
> In the first photo … , but in the second photo …
> One obvious difference is (that) …
> Unlike the first photo, the second photo shows …
> In contrast to the first photo, the second photo …

**4** **SPEAKING** Does your school have a music or sports club? What other clubs are there? Are you a member of any?

> What should schools spend most money on: music, sport or school trips? Justify your opinions.

**5** Work in pairs. Discuss the question above and make notes.

**6** 🎧 **2.38** Listen to two candidates answering the question in an exam. Compare your ideas with theirs. Are any the same? Which are different?

> I agree with the girl that …

> I disagree with the boy that …

> **Speaking Strategy**
> When you are giving a short presentation, use set phrases to give opinions and justify them, and to structure your speech.

*Photointerest*

**1**

**2**

**7** 🎧 **2.38** **KEY PHRASES** Read the Speaking Strategy. Then listen again. Which phrases does the candidate use?

> **Structuring your speech**
> I'd like to start by saying / looking at …
> First of all, we need to decide / examine / look at / ask ourselves …
> I'll begin with …
> Now I'd like to move on to …
> This leads to my next point.
> Now let's look at / move on to (the question of) …
> **Ordering points or opinions**
> First, …   Second, …   Finally, …
> **Justifying your opinions**
> There are a number of reasons why I believe this. First, …
> I'll tell you why I think that.
> The reason I say that is …
> The main reason I feel this way is …
> **Summing up your opinion**
> To sum up, …   In conclusion, …   All in all, …
> Just to summarise the main points, …

**8** **SPEAKING** Work in pairs. Turn to page 142 and do the extra speaking task. Use the phrases in exercises 2, 3 and 7 to help you.

# An opinion essay

*I can write an essay suggesting how to spend €1 million.*

1 **SPEAKING** Read the task. In pairs, think of three possible things you could spend the money on.

> If you had €1 million to spend but couldn't spend any of it on yourself, what would you do with it? Write an essay and include three ideas. Give reasons for your choices and say what effect the money would have.

> I'd give money to a charity which helps ...

> I'd buy ... for ...

> I'd give money to ... so they could ...

2 **Read the essay. Does it mention any of your ideas from exercise 1? Which of the ideas in the essay do you think is best? Why?**

> If I had €1 million, it would be easy to find three good ways to use the money. It would be a great way to help people who deserve it.
>
> First of all, I would donate half of the money to the children's hospital in my town. They're raising money to build bedrooms for visiting families. They could probably start building immediately if I gave them half a million euros.
>
> Secondly, I would make a donation to my local primary school to buy sports equipment. As I see it, more sport at school would mean healthier children. Furthermore, the teachers would find it far easier to teach sports and PE if they had new equipment.
>
> Finally, I would buy a new bike for my brother. He borrows mine all the time, even though he's got one, because mine is better. If he had a new bike, he wouldn't do that!
>
> So to sum up, I would use the money to make life better for the families of children in hospital, to improve facilities at my school and to buy a gift for my brother.

3 **Answer the questions about the essay.**

1 How many paragraphs are there?
2 In which paragraph does the writer mention all three ways of spending the money?
3 In which paragraph does the writer explain who would get half the money, and why?
4 In which two paragraphs does the writer explain who would get the rest of the money, and why?
5 In which paragraph does the writer paraphrase the main point of the essay?

---

**Writing Strategy**

In your writing, avoid starting too many sentences which repeat the same words. Remember that you can:

- use a variety of expressions for introducing opinions (*It seems to me ...* , *In my opinion ...* , etc.) and for making additional points (*Moreover ...* , *Furthermore ...* , etc.).
- start conditional sentences with the *if* clause or the main clause.
- use concession clauses (*although ...* / *even though ...*) at the beginning or end of a sentence.

4 **Read the Writing Strategy. How well does the writer in exercise 2 follow this advice? Can you find ...**

1 an expression for introducing an opinion?
2 an expression for making an additional point?
3 a conditional sentence beginning with the *if* clause?
4 a conditional sentence beginning with the main clause?
5 a concession clause?

5 **Imagine you had €1 million to spend but could not spend any of it on yourself. Think of three ways to spend it. Make notes and complete the table below. Then compare ideas in pairs.**

| Choices (1–3) | Effect the money would have | Reason(s) for choice |
|---|---|---|
| 1 (50%) | | |
| 2 (25%) | | |
| 3 (25%) | | |

➡ **Vocabulary Builder** Money prepositions: page 120

6 **Write an essay using your plan from exercise 5. Include an introduction and a conclusion like the model in exercise 2.**

- Say what you would spend half the money on.
- Choose two more ways to spend the rest.
- Explain what effect the money would have.
- Give reasons for your choices.

---

**CHECK YOUR WORK**

 Have you ...

- checked the spelling and grammar?
- followed your plan carefully?
- used a variety of different ways to begin sentences?

# 8 Crime

## Unit map

## 8A Vocabulary

# Crimes and criminals

*I can describe different crimes.*

1 **SPEAKING** In pairs, describe photos 1–3 below. Do you recognise any of the film characters? What do they have in common?

2 **2.39** **VOCABULARY** Complete the table with the words below. (You need to use one of the words twice.) Then listen to the words and check your answers.

**Nouns** arsonist   burglar   burglary   mugging   mugger
murder   murderer   theft   thief
**Verbs** break   damage   kill   sell   steal

| Crimes and criminals | | |
| --- | --- | --- |
| **Crimes** | **Criminals** | **Verbs** |
| arson | 1 _____ | to set fire to (a building, etc.) |
| 2 _____ | 3 _____ | to burgle / 4 _____ into a house |
| drug-dealing | drug dealer | to 5 _____ / deal drugs |
| looting | looter | to loot / 6 _____ |
| 7 _____ | 8 _____ | to mug somebody |
| 9 _____ | 10 _____ | to murder / 11 _____ somebody |
| robbery | robber | to rob a person or place |
| shoplifting | shoplifter | to 12 _____ from a shop / shoplift |
| smuggling | smuggler | to smuggle |
| 13 _____ | 14 _____ (thieves) | to steal something |
| vandalism | vandal | to 15 _____ / vandalise |

**RECYCLE!** Comparatives and superlatives

Remember: we use comparatives for comparing two people or things, and we use superlatives for comparing a person or thing with all the other members of a group.

Molly is <u>taller</u> than Kieran.

Molly is <u>the tallest</u> person in the class.

**3 SPEAKING** Describe photos A–D above. Where are the people? What are they doing? Use words from exercise 2.

**4** 🎧**2.40** Listen to three news reports. Match them with three of the photos (A–D).

1 ___ 2 ___ 3 ___

**5 VOCABULARY** Work in pairs. Complete the verb + noun collocations.

appeal   identify   interview   launch
make   patrol   search   study

| Collocations: police work |  |  |  |
|---|---|---|---|
| 1 | _____ an investigation | 5 | _____ for witnesses |
| 2 | _____ a house | 6 | _____ CCTV footage |
| 3 | _____ a suspect | 7 | _____ a culprit |
| 4 | _____ an arrest | 8 | _____ an area |

**6** 🎧**2.40** Listen to the news reports again. Check your answers to exercise 5.

**7** Read the Recycle! box. Complete the questions below using the comparative or superlative form of the adjectives in brackets. Then make notes of your ideas.

1 What is *the most serious* (serious) crime, apart from murder?
2 Which type of theft is _____ (serious), shoplifting or robbery?
3 Which is _____ (bad), drug-dealing or drug-smuggling?
4 Which crime is _____ (difficult) to prevent?
5 Which crime is _____ (frightening) for the victim, mugging or burglary?

**8 SPEAKING** Work in pairs. Discuss your ideas from exercise 7. Give reasons for your opinions.

> I think arson is the most serious crime, apart from murder.
>
> Why?
>
> Because ...

## Grammar
# Reported speech (1)
*I can report what other people have said.*

**1 SPEAKING** Look at the photo. What do you think is going to happen? Why do you think that?

**2** Read the text. Why did most listeners think that the crime was a joke?

A radio reporter went onto the streets of London yesterday to do a report about crime and ended up learning more than he expected. He stopped a passer-by and said that he was doing a story on street crime in the area. The man said there was a lot of crime there. He said he had seen a mugging earlier that day. The reporter then said there weren't many police officers on the streets. The man said he didn't want more police around. Then he took the reporter's phone and ran off! The reporter, sounding upset, said that the man had stolen his phone. However, most listeners thought it was all a joke!

**3** 🎧 **2.41** Listen to the dialogue. Complete the words the reporter and the man actually say. Then find the parts of the text in exercise 2 where they are reported.

**Reporter** Hello. I ¹_____ (do) a report on street crime in the area.
**Man** There ²_____ (be) a lot of crime here. I ³_____ (see) a mugging earlier today.
**Reporter** But there ⁴_____ (not be) many police officers on the streets.
**Man** I ⁵_____ (not want) more police around.
**Reporter** Hey! He ⁶_____ (steal) my phone!

**4** Compare the dialogue in exercise 3 with the reported speech in the text in exercise 2. Complete rule a in the Learn this! box with the correct tenses.

**LEARN THIS!** Reported speech

**a** When you change direct speech to reported speech, the tense of the verbs usually changes.

| Direct speech | | Reported speech |
|---|---|---|
| present simple | → | ¹ |
| present continuous | → | ² |
| past simple | → | ³ |

**b** We can use *that* to introduce reported speech but we often omit it. *She said (that) she was feeling upset.*

**LOOK OUT!**

**a** Pronouns and possessive adjectives usually change in reported speech, depending on the speaker and context.
*'You're sitting at my table,' he said.*
*He said we were sitting at his table.*

**b** References to time and place can change as well.
*yesterday – the day before    tonight – that night*
*today – that day    a week ago – a week earlier*
*here – there    last Monday – the Monday before*
*this month – that month    now – at that moment*

**5** Read the Look out! box. Then look at the reported speech in exercise 2 again and find changes to pronouns, possessive adjectives and references to time and place.

➡ Grammar Builder 8B page 138

**6** Rewrite the quotations in reported speech. You may have to change pronouns and references to time or place.

1 'We searched a house yesterday,' said the police.
  *The police said they had searched a house the day before.*
2 'Two men are burgling the house next door!' she said.
3 'Teenagers often vandalise my shop,' he said.
4 'I found the money two days ago,' she said.
5 'We're launching an investigation into drug-dealing in the town centre,' said the police.
6 'The police arrested two suspects last Friday,' said the teacher.
7 'Crime is getting worse, in my opinion,' he said.
8 'Muggers often attack tourists,' she said.

**7 SPEAKING** Work in pairs. Imagine that a robbery has just taken place.

**Student A:** You saw the robbery and are talking to Student B about it over the phone.
**Student B:** Ask these questions and try to remember the answers.
1 What time did the robbery take place?
2 What kind of shop did they rob?
3 How did the robbers get away?
4 What were the robbers wearing?
5 How do you feel about the experience?

> What time did the robbery take place?

> It took place at 4 o'clock in the afternoon.

**8 SPEAKING** Work with another pair.

**Student B:** Report Student A's answers to the questions in exercise 7.
**Student A:** Listen and check Student B's memory!

> Anna said that the robbery had taken place at 4 o'clock in the afternoon.

# 8C

**Listening**
## A life of crime
*I can listen for paraphrase.*

Bonnie and Clyde

Butch Cassidy

Billy the Kid

**1** Look at the pictures of famous outlaws. What do you know about them? What nationality were they? When did they live? What crimes did they commit?

> **Listening Strategy**
> The information that you need to understand in the recorded text may be expressed differently in the task. Listen out for synonyms (e.g. *hate / can't stand*) and antonyms (e.g. *win / lose*), but also for information and ideas that are 'paraphrased' (worded differently).

**2** Read the Listening Strategy. Then read the sentences below and try to think of synonyms or ways of paraphrasing the underlined words and phrases.

a The police arrested the <u>woman they think committed the crime</u>. *suspect*
b The police arrested the <u>people who started the fire</u>.
c They <u>burgled</u> the house and stole some <u>expensive rings and necklaces</u>.
d They <u>searched for</u> the <u>culprits</u>.
e They <u>attacked the young man in the street</u> and stole his wallet and phone.

**3** 🎧 **3.02** Now listen to five sentences and match them with the paraphrased versions in exercise 2 (a–e).

1 ___  2 ___  3 ___  4 ___  5 ___

**4** 🎧 **3.03** Listen to a historian being interviewed about Bonnie and Clyde, the famous American outlaws. Answer the questions.

1 How many people did Bonnie and Clyde kill?
2 How old were they when they died?

**5** 🎧 **3.03** Listen again. Circle the correct answers. Sometimes both answers are correct.

1 Bonnie Parker
  a was clever.
  b got married before she left school.
2 Clyde Barrow's family
  a were not very well off.
  b worked on a farm which didn't belong to them.
3 The couple couldn't find a job when Clyde left prison because
  a Clyde had a criminal record.
  b unemployment was very high.
4 Bonnie and Clyde
  a frequently stole cars.
  b stayed in regular contact with their families.
5 Bonnie and Clyde
  a were constantly travelling around.
  b were fighting for ordinary people.

**6** How is the information in the correct options expressed in the listening?

Bonnie Parker was clever. – *'Bonnie was a bright student.'*

**7** **SPEAKING** Outlaws are 'on the side of ordinary people, and against authority'. Do you agree? Give reasons. Use the ideas below to help you.

**For** not hurt ordinary people   steal from the rich
romantic  young  free  always travelling
hide from the police   live by their own rules

**Against** violent  cruel and heartless  murdered people
greedy  people ignore the truth  false image  unrealistic

**8** **INTERNET RESEARCH** Find out and write about another famous outlaw. Include some or all of the information below.

- Where / When were they born?
- What crimes did they commit?
- How / When / Where did they die?

## 8D Grammar
# Reported speech (2)
*I can report what other people have said.*

**1** Read the text. Where did the burglar get stuck? How did he finally get free?

**2** Match the reported speech (1–5) in the text with the direct speech below.

  **a** You can stay where you are. ___
  **b** I won't help you because you tried to burgle my house. ___
  **c** I can't move. ___
  **d** I've been here for four hours. ___
  **e** I'll call the police. ___

**3** Complete the table in the Learn this! box below.

**LEARN THIS!** Reported speech

| Direct speech | | Reported speech |
|---|---|---|
| present simple | → | past simple |
| present continuous | → | past continuous |
| past simple | → | past perfect |
| present perfect | → | ¹ |
| can / can't | → | ² |
| will / won't | → | ³ |

➡ Grammar Builder 8D page 138

**4** Read the direct speech and write the reported speech. Remember to change the pronouns and time phrases if necessary.

  **1** 'I can't find my wallet,' Ben said.
    *Ben said that he couldn't find his wallet.*
  **2** 'I've never been jet-skiing,' said Cathy.
  **3** 'I'll watch the documentary with you tonight,' said Liam.
  **4** 'We can't go out because it's stormy,' said George.
  **5** 'The volcano has erupted twice this year,' said Harriet.
  **6** 'I'll probably study maths at college,' said Chris.
  **7** 'We can visit the aquarium today,' said Joe.
  **8** 'A new florist's has opened in town,' said Mandy.

**LOOK OUT!** *tell* and *say*

  **a** We always use a personal object with *tell*: *tell somebody something*.
    *He told me he was cold.* *He didn't tell Luke.*

  **b** With *say*, we do not need a personal object. If we say who we are speaking to, we use *to*: *say something (to someone)*.
    *John said he was hungry.* *You say that to everyone!*

# Bungling burglar!

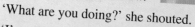

When Mary Holmes woke up at 5 a.m. one Sunday morning and went to the bathroom, she was shocked to discover a man half in and half out of the window.

'What are you doing?' she shouted.

'I'm stuck!' replied the man. 'I tried to climb in the window last night, but it's too narrow!'

¹The man told Miss Holmes that he had been there for four hours. ²He said he couldn't move. He asked Miss Holmes for help. ³Miss Holmes told the man that she wouldn't help him because he had tried to burgle her house. ⁴She said to the man that he could stay where he was and ⁵that she would call the police. Firefighters had to remove the window to rescue the man!

**5** Read the Look out! box. Find two examples of reported speech with *say* and two examples with *tell* in the story in exercise 2.

➡ Grammar Builder 8D page 132

**6** Complete the text with *say* and *tell*.

At the press conference, the police officer ¹_____ the journalists that the police had studied the CCTV footage. She ²_____ she could clearly see a man selling drugs. She ³_____ the police would launch an immediate investigation and she ⁴_____ the journalists that they were trying to identify him. She ⁵_____ they would arrest the suspect as soon as possible. Finally, she ⁶_____ the journalists she hoped more witnesses would come forward.

**7** Write five short sentences: one in the present perfect, one with *can*, one with *can't*, one with *will* and one with *won't*.

  *I've never been to Italy.*
  *Anna can speak three languages.*

**8** **SPEAKING** Say your sentences aloud to your partner. Your partner reports them to the class.

  I've never been to Italy.

  Adam said he'd never been to Italy.

## Adjective suffixes

*I can understand and use different adjective suffixes.*

# DI$APPEARING MONEY

One of the most mysterious unsolved bank robberies took place at the First National Bank of Chicago, USA. One Friday in 1977, an employee at the bank put $4 million in cash in a bank vault. When another employee came to make the weekly check on the vault, she discovered that only $3 million was there. A million dollars had simply disappeared. The robbery appeared in all the national newspapers. Because nobody had broken into the vault, the police suspected it was an 'inside job', and were at first hopeful that they would recover the money quickly. 'It's foolish to rob your own bank,' said one police officer. 'You are almost certain to get caught, unless you are very lucky.' Because most robbers are in a hurry, they are usually careless and leave clues, but the police could find nothing to identify the thief or thieves. The FBI were suspicious of one employee, but they didn't have enough reliable evidence to arrest him. Four years later, police discovered $2,300 of the money in a drugs raid, but have never found the thief or the rest of the money.

**1** Look at the title and the photo. What crime do you think the text is about?

**2** Read the text and check your ideas from exercise 1.

**3** Read the Learn this! box. Then find one example of each of the adjective suffixes in the text in exercise 2 and add them to the table.

**LEARN THIS!** Adjective suffixes

**a** Some suffixes have a particular meaning.

| Suffix | Add to ... | Meaning | Example |
|--------|-----------|---------|---------|
| -ful | nouns | full of or giving | helpful ¹ _____ |
| -less | nouns | without | tasteless ² _____ |
| -ish | nouns | like, similar to | greenish ³ _____ |
| -able | verbs | possible to | drinkable ⁴ _____ |

**b** Other suffixes have similar general meanings.

| Suffix | Add to ... | Meaning | Example |
|--------|-----------|---------|---------|
| -y | nouns | like, with the quality of | snowy ⁵ _____ |
| -ly | nouns | | friendly ⁶ _____ |
| -ous | nouns | | dangerous ⁷ _____ |
| -al | nouns | | economical ⁸ _____ |

**Dictionary Skills Strategy**

If you want to find out how to form an adjective from a noun or verb, look up the noun or verb in your dictionary. If the adjective does not appear in the same entry as the noun / verb, it will usually come as a separate entry after, e.g. *danger* followed by *dangerous*. But if the spelling changes, the adjective entry might be first, e.g. *beautiful* followed by *beauty*.

**4** **DICTIONARY WORK** Read the Dictionary Strategy. Then look up these words in a dictionary and find adjectives that are formed from them. (Sometimes there is more than one adjective.)

afford   coward   fury   pain   peace   self

**5** **USE OF ENGLISH** Complete the second sentence so that it has the same meaning as the first. Use adjectives from exercise 4.

1 The injection didn't hurt at all.
  The injection was *painless*.
2 The music created a calm and relaxing atmosphere.
  It was _____ music.
3 She doesn't think about others.
  She is _____ .
4 For some people, holidays abroad are too expensive.
  Holidays abroad aren't _____ for some people.
5 He didn't have enough courage to go to the dentist's.
  He was too _____ to go to the dentist's.
6 My dad was really angry that I stayed out late.
  My dad was _____ that I stayed out late.

**6** **SPEAKING** Work in pairs. Ask and answer the questions.

1 Who is the friendliest person you know?
2 What was your most painful experience?
3 Have you ever done anything dangerous?
4 What's the luckiest thing that's ever happened to you?
5 Who's the most helpful person in your family? Why?
6 Have you ever done anything careless?

# An Australian murder mystery
*I can understand a text about a mystery.*

**1 SPEAKING** Work in pairs. Do you know any stories about unexplained deaths? Think about TV dramas, films and books.

**2** Read the text on page 91. This mystery is sometimes called the Tamám Shud case. Why?

> **Reading Strategy**
>
> When you do a multiple-choice task, try to predict the answers just by looking at the beginning of each question, not the options. (It is not always possible, but sometimes you can.) Then look at the options. If one of them matches your prediction, it is probably the correct one. However, you still need to check carefully.

**3** Read the Reading Strategy. Then look at the sentence beginnings below. Can you complete them? Do not look at exercise 4 yet.

1 The suitcase did not help to identify the man because …
2 University professor John Cleland was the only person who …
3 The two clues contained in the book with the missing page were …
4 After they'd interviewed the nurse, the police wrongly thought that …
5 After many investigations, we now know …

**4** Circle the correct answers (a–d).

1 The suitcase did not help to identify the man because
  a nothing in it had a name.
  b nobody was sure that the suitcase belonged to him.
  c it only contained cigarettes, matches and a few other possessions.
  d they didn't find it until weeks after his death.
2 University professor John Cleland was the only person who
  a understood the meaning of *tamám shud*.
  b found the secret pocket in the dead man's trousers.
  c had read the poem.
  d looked for clues to the dead man's identity.
3 The two clues contained in the book with the missing page were
  a a soldier's telephone number and a secret message.
  b a message in Persian and a nurse's telephone number.
  c a secret message and a nurse's telephone number.
  d two telephone numbers and the name of a nurse.
4 After they'd interviewed the nurse, the police wrongly thought that
  a she had given Alfred Boxall a copy of the book.
  b the dead man was Alfred Boxall.
  c she could tell them what the secret message said.
  d the dead man had given her a copy of the book.
5 After many investigations, we now know
  a the identity of the dead man.
  b what the secret message in the book means.
  c how and why the man died.
  d where the piece of paper containing the words *tamám shud* came from.

**5 VOCABULARY** Find the words for these items in the first two paragraphs of the text.

**6 VOCABULARY** Complete the compound nouns (1–8) with the words below. Find them in the text. Which one is written as a single word?

car  code  gum  investigation
number  prints  records  ticket

**Compound nouns**

1 a murder _____
2 a train _____
3 chewing _____
4 finger _____
5 dental _____
6 an open-top _____
7 a telephone _____
8 a secret _____

**7** Work in pairs or groups. Work together to read this secret message and find out one more mysterious fact about the Somerton Man case.

> KEY: a = z, b = a, c = b … x = w, y = x, z = y
>
> Xifo uif ovstf tbx uif cpez, tif tbje tif eje opu lopx
>
> When the nurse saw the body, she said she …
>
> ijn, cvu tif tffnfe up sfdphojaf ijn boe mpplfe tdbsfe.

**8 SPEAKING** Discuss these questions in pairs. Give reasons.

1 Do you think people will ever solve the mystery of the Somerton Man? Why? / Why not?
2 What do you think happened? Did he kill himself or did a murderer kill him?
3 Do you think the information in exercise 7 is an important clue?
4 Does it matter who the man is or why he died? Why have people tried so hard to find out?

# Who was the Somerton Man?

🎧 3.04

It began at 6:30 a.m. on 1 December 1948 when some passers-by discovered the body of a man on Somerton Beach in Adelaide, Australia, just west of the city. The police arrived and launched a murder investigation. At the hospital, doctors examined the body but could not find out for sure how the man had died. In his pockets were a bus
5 ticket from the city, a train ticket, a comb, chewing gum, cigarettes and matches. There was no wallet or identification. Nobody knew who the man was.

The police continued their investigation. They could not identify the man using fingerprints or dental records. Then, two weeks after the discovery of the body, there was a breakthrough: they found a suitcase that the man had left at Adelaide station the
10 day before his death. Inside the case were some clothes, a knife, scissors and a brush.

However, these possessions did not reveal the man's identity. In fact, somebody had removed the labels from most of his clothes and another label from the suitcase itself.

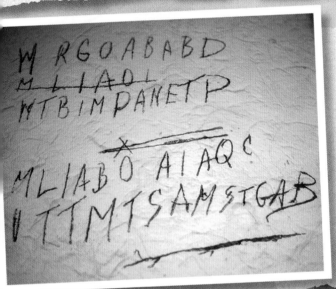

A new expert joined the investigation: John Cleland, a professor at the University of Adelaide. In April, he found a clue that everybody
15 else had missed: a small piece of paper in a secret pocket inside the dead man's trousers. On the paper were two words in Persian: *tamám shud*. The words are from a famous Persian poem, and they mean 'it is the end'. Somebody had torn the paper from an old copy of a book.

20 A few months later, a man gave police a copy of the book containing the poem. He said somebody had dropped it into his open-top car the day after the man on Somerton Beach died. The last page of the book – with the final two words – was missing. In the book, the police found two clues: a telephone number and a
25 message. The message was in a secret code. The second line was crossed out, and some letters were unclear.

The telephone number belonged to a nurse. She said she had given a copy of the book to a soldier called Alfred Boxall in 1945. Finally, the police had solved the mystery: obviously, the dead man was Alfred Boxall!

30 There was only one problem: Alfred Boxall was still alive. The police found him and interviewed him. What is more, he still had his copy of the book. The mystery of the body on Somerton Beach continued.

So what about the mysterious five-line message? Could
35 that contain the answer to this puzzle? Perhaps, but unfortunately we do not know what the message says. Nobody has ever solved the secret code.

# Photo description and comparison

*I can describe and compare photos of crimes.*

**1** Look at the photo of looting (A) and make deductions based on what you can see. Use *must* or *can't*. How do you know that:

1  the looters don't want people to recognise them?
2  it's a clothes store?
3  it's happening during the day?

*They can't want people to recognise them because …*

**2** ⏵**3.05** Listen to a student describing the photo. Does he make the same deductions as you made in exercise 1?

**3** Work in pairs. Choose one photo each (B or C) and describe it to your partner. Use the words below to help you.

**Nouns**  car window  balaclava  glass  handbag  phone  steering wheel  strap  subway

**Verbs**  grab  hold on  lean  pull  run away  smash

➡ **Vocabulary Builder** Describing people: page 121

**4** ⏵**3.06** Listen to a candidate comparing the photos from exercise 3. Do you agree with her final opinion? Why? / Why not?

**5** ⏵**3.06** Listen again. Complete the sentences with the words below.

both  difference  show  theme  unlike  whereas

1  The common _____ in the photos is crime.
2  You can see the criminal in _____ photos.
3  But _____ the first photo, the second photo does not show the victim.
4  Another obvious _____ is that the criminal in the first photo might not succeed.
5  Both photos _____ types of street crime.
6  The first photo shows a crime against a person, _____ the second photo shows the theft of some property.

**6** Look at the sentences in exercise 5 again. Which ones describe similarities? Which describe differences?

**7** ⏵**3.07** Read the examiner's question and listen to a candidate's answer. Do you agree?

In your opinion, is looting from a shop as bad as burgling a house? Why? / Why not?

**Speaking Strategy**
When you answer questions, try to use a variety of phrases for introducing your opinions, not just *I think* … . Use different phrases when you are less sure about your opinion.

**8** ⏵**3.07** **KEY PHRASES** Read the Speaking Strategy. Then listen again. Which phrases does the student use?

**Expressing an opinion**
I think / I don't think that …   It seems to me that …
I believe / don't believe that …   In my opinion, …
To be honest, …   As I see it, …   I imagine that …
**Giving a tentative opinion**
I'm not sure, really.   I agree to some extent.
I suppose it's true to say that …
**Making an additional point**
Moreover, …   Furthermore, …   What is more, …

**9** Work in pairs. Ask and answer the questions below. Use phrases from exercise 8.

In your opinion …
1  Is crime against a person always worse than property crime?
2  Is it OK to steal if you really need the money (for example, to buy medicine for your child)?

**10** **SPEAKING** Work in pairs. Turn to page 142 and do the extra speaking task. Use phrases from this lesson.

# 8H Writing

## An email
*I can write an email about a crime.*

**1** Do you prefer holidays in cities, on the coast, or in the country? Why?

**2** Read the task below and the email opposite. Does the writer cover all the points mentioned in the task?

> Imagine you went on a school trip to Dublin for three days last month. Write an email to your English friend Ed in which you:
> - describe the journey there.
> - describe the hotel you stayed at.
> - describe a crime that affected a classmate.
> - suggest an activity to do together in the summer.

> **Writing Strategy**
> Try to use a variety of phrases to move your narrative forwards. Choose ones which show that the next event happened immediately afterwards or some time later.

**3** **KEY PHRASES** Read the Writing Strategy. Then put the sequencing phrases below into the chart.

**Sequencing phrases**   a few moments later
after a while   a short while later   at that moment
before long   just then   shortly afterwards
soon   soon after   suddenly

| Immediately | Some time later |
|---|---|
|  |  |
|  |  |
|  |  |

**4** Find one more sequencing phrase for each group in the email in exercise 2.

**5** **USE OF ENGLISH** Rewrite each sentence using a different sequencing phrase. Include the word in brackets.

1 After a while, the rain stopped. (long)
2 Soon after, a black car arrived. (then)
3 Shortly afterwards, a second car appeared. (later)
4 Suddenly, a woman shouted for help. (moment)
5 A short while later, there were loud gunshots. (after)

**6** Complete the phrases with the correct preposition. They are all in the email in exercise 2.

1 go _____ a trip
2 travel _____ coach
3 _____ the end

> ➤➤ **Vocabulary Builder** Preposition + noun phrases: page 121

---

 **To:** ed@email.com

Hi Ed

How are you? Last week I went with my class on a three-day trip to Dublin. We travelled by coach to Liverpool and then took the ferry. I didn't enjoy the crossing because the sea was a bit rough.

We stayed in a hotel near the centre, so it was really easy to get to lots of places in the city. The rooms were great and had really good views. The restaurant was really small and crowded though, and the food wasn't very nice.

While we were having breakfast one morning, somebody broke into my classmate's room and stole his wallet. He reported the crime to the hotel manager at once. After a while, the police arrived and interviewed three of the hotel employees. In the end, they didn't make any arrests.

I'm looking forward to your visit in the summer. What time is your flight due to arrive?

Write soon!

Chris

**7** Read the task below. Make a plan for your email. Remember to cover each point in the task in a separate paragraph. Make notes under the paragraph headings.

> Imagine you have just returned home from a holiday in London with your family. Write an email to your English friend Sarah in which you:
> - describe the journey.
> - describe a tourist attraction you visited.
> - describe a crime you saw taking place.
> - ask for some information.

**Paragraph 1: journey**
transport: details (e.g. weather / time)
**Paragraph 2: tourist attraction**
what / where: adjectives
**Paragraph 3: crime**
what / where: what happened next
**Paragraph 4: request for information**
what / where: information needed

**8** Write your email. Use your notes from exercise 7.

> **CHECK YOUR WORK**
> Have you ...
> - written a logical and coherent email?
> - mentioned all four points and added extra detail?
> - used a sequencing phrase from exercise 3?
> - checked the spelling and grammar?

## Reading

**1** Read the Strategy. Then read the first paragraph of the text. Which topic (1–4) is the paragraph about?

1 One man's life of crime    3 The history of the mail train
2 Crimes through the 1960s    4 A plan for a crime

**2** Read the text and match statements A–G with paragraphs 1–6. There is one extra statement.

### The crime of the century

1 This is the story of one of Britain's most famous crimes: the Great Train Robbery. In 1963, an English criminal called Bruce Reynolds had an idea for a crime. He wanted to rob the night mail train from Glasgow to London because he knew the train carried thousands of pounds. He also knew he couldn't work alone, so he called fifteen other criminals and told them about the job. He called it 'the big one'.

2 The gang bought a farmhouse in the middle of the countryside to escape to after the crime. They also found a criminal train driver to help them drive the train after they stopped it, and they organised trucks to carry the money. Then, on the night of the robbery, they put up false signals on the track and waited.

3 The train appeared at around 3 a.m. and stopped at the false signals. The train driver, Jack Mills, was confused, so he got out and went to the signals. The thieves hit him on the head and then boarded the train. But now they had a problem – they needed to move the train to a bridge to unload the money, but their criminal train driver didn't understand the controls – he couldn't drive the train!

4 The thieves decided to drag the driver, Jack Mills, back onto the train to help them. Then they had a surprise. There was more than the thousands of pounds they thought would be on the train – there was over two and a half million! In those days that was a huge amount of money.

5 The men drove the money to their farmhouse and decided to wait there until the police ended their investigation. But this was a huge crime, and the police were looking everywhere. At last, the thieves became worried. They left the farmhouse with the money, and when the police found the house, they also found the men's fingerprints everywhere. The investigation continued, and the police started to arrest people. Many of the train robbers went to prison for thirty years for their crime.

6 In April 1965, one of the gang members, Ronnie Biggs, escaped from prison. He lived in Australia with his wife and children, and then he went to Brazil. During this time, the newspapers wrote many stories about him. In 2001, he returned to Britain because he was very ill. He went back to prison, but then left again in 2009 and died in an old people's home. Many people have made films and written books about the Great Train Robbery. It is one of Britain's most famous crime stories.

This paragraph tells you …
A how the thieves were discovered. _____
B how the men spent the money. _____
C how the thieves prepared for the robbery. _____
D the problem the robbers had on the night of the robbery. _____
E how their fame grew. _____
F what they found which was unexpected. _____
G why the thieves decided to work together. _____

## Listening

**3** Read the Strategy. Then read the questions and options in exercise 5 carefully. Who do you think will be talking in each extract? Match each extract with the best idea below.

a criminal    someone who works in a shop
a banker    an ordinary girl or woman    a teacher
a news presenter    a boy looking for a job

**4** 🎧 **3.08** Listen to the recording and check your answers to exercise 3.

**5** 🎧 **3.08** Listen to four texts and answer the questions. Circle the correct answer (A–D).

1 Where would you hear this announcement?
  A in a shopping centre
  B in a clothes shop
  C in a department store
  D in a camera shop
2 Who is the announcement for?
  A people who know something about a crime
  B police investigating a crime
  C the victims of a crime
  D visitors to an art gallery
3 What does Lucy do to save money?
  A She never goes out.
  B She works every weekend.
  C She doesn't buy many things.
  D She works every day.
4 What is Jake going to do?
  A apply for a job
  B make a phone call
  C work as a waiter
  D tell someone about a job

## Use of English

**6** Read the **Strategy**. Then read the text and complete gaps 1–8. Circle the correct answer A, B or C.

Shopping centres have become a ¹___ more than just places to shop and look for bargains. They are places of entertainment ²___ people meet and have fun. Some modern shopping centres are ³___ big they can take days to explore properly. For example, the Cehavir Shopping and Entertainment Centre in Istanbul covers 420,000 square metres and is considered to be the ⁴___ shopping centre in Europe. It has around 350 shops and 50 restaurants to choose from. And if you fancy ⁵___ your friends in the evening, there are 12 cinemas, a bowling alley and even a roller coaster ride.

Another huge shopping centre is the Mall of the Emirates in Dubai. As well as around 700 shops and restaurants, you can go to Magic Planet, which is a mini theme park, ⁶___ watch a film in one of the fourteen cinemas. And if that isn't enough, ⁷___ about visiting Ski-Dubai, the world-famous indoor ski slope? Some people want ⁸___ a more cultural experience. This is easy at the Mall of the Emirates. There is a Community Theatre and Arts Centre on the second floor of the building with a theatre, art galleries, a music school and a library.

| | | |
|---|---|---|
| **1** A much | B lot | C few |
| **2** A where | B who | C which |
| **3** A as | B such | C so |
| **4** A large | B larger | C largest |
| **5** A meet | B meeting | C to meet |
| **6** A while | B but | C or |
| **7** A how | B where | C much |
| **8** A to have | B have | C having |

## Speaking

**7** Read the **Strategy** and the phrases below. Decide which could be used for structuring your speech (St), ordering your points (O), justifying your opinions (J) and summing up (Su). Can you add any more phrases?

**1** There are a number of reasons why I believe this.
**2** I'll tell you why I think that.
**3** Secondly, …
**4** Now I'd like to move on to …
**5** In conclusion, …
**6** I'll begin with …

**8** Read the **Strategy**. Then do the exam task.

Look at the two photos showing modern school classrooms. Compare them, include the following:
- What makes a classroom a good place for learning?
- Which of the classrooms would you prefer to study in? Why?
- Is it more important for schools to spend money on new buildings or on new technology?

## Writing

**9** Read the **Strategy**. Then imagine that you discover your phone has been stolen. Write notes, including:
- three times when it might have happened.
- three ideas for what you did next.
- three adjectives to describe your feelings.
- *I think I lost it when I was …*

**10** Imagine you witnessed a robbery last week. Write an email to an English friend in which you:
- explain where you were.
- describe what you saw.
- say how it affected you.
- ask what similar experiences your friend has had.

# 9
# Science

## Unit map

**Vocabulary**
Materials
Describing technology
Collocations
Noun endings
Gadgets
Parts of gadgets

**Word Skills**
Verb + preposition

**Grammar**
The passive (present simple and past simple)

**Listening**
Intentions of the speaker

**Reading** Great inventions?

**Speaking** Making a complaint

**Writing** A formal letter

**Culture 9** Computer pioneers

**Vocabulary Builder** page 121

**Grammar Builder** page 140

**Grammar Reference** page 141

---

## 9A Vocabulary

### Gadgets
*I can describe gadgets and talk about their use.*

Dog water fountain

**1** SPEAKING Work in pairs. Look at the photos of gadgets (A–D). Do you think they are good or bad ideas? Which is your favourite and why?

**2** 3.09 VOCABULARY Check the meaning of the words below. Then listen and repeat. Which materials do you think are used to make the gadgets in exercise 1?

**Materials** aluminium cardboard ceramic concrete copper glass gold iron leather nylon paper plastic rubber steel stone wood

**3** Do the quiz in pairs. Then check your answers at the bottom of the page.

**1** During World War II (1939–45), scientists used dandelions (see photo) to make
**a** cardboard. **b** paper. **c** plastic. **d** rubber.

**2** The first bicycles had wheels made of
**a** wood with iron tyres. **b** iron with rubber tyres.
**c** iron with wooden tyres.

**3** Which one of these materials did the Ancient Romans not have?
**a** ceramic **b** concrete **c** glass **d** paper

**4** Are these sentences true or false?
**a** All types of wood float in water. **b** No type of stone floats in water.

**5** The earliest use of nylon was in
**a** women's clothing. **b** toothbrushes. **c** parachutes.
**d** guitar strings.

**6** Which of these metals is the hardest? Which is the heaviest?
**a** aluminium **b** copper **c** gold **d** iron **e** steel

1 d 2 a 3 d 4 a False b False 5 b 6 hardest: e heaviest: c

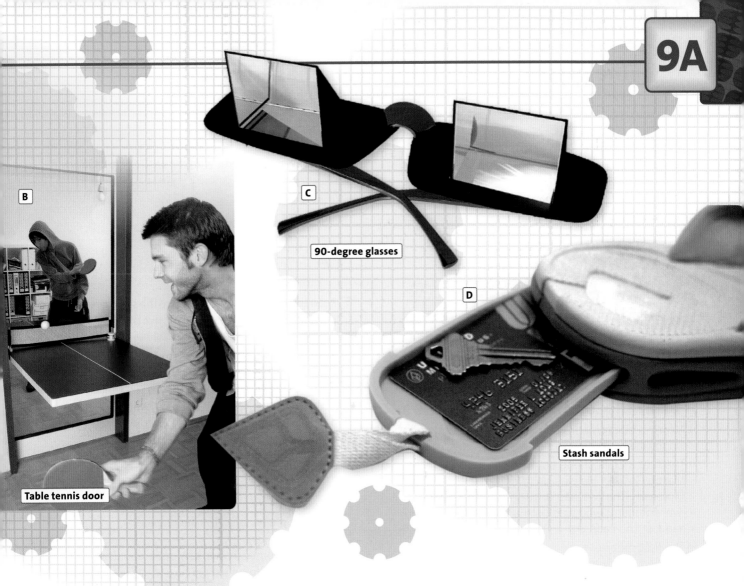

B

C

90-degree glasses

D

Stash sandals

Table tennis door

**4** SPEAKING Look around the classroom. What things are made of the materials in exercise 2? Think about furniture, the building, clothes and possessions.

> The windows are made of aluminium and glass. This book …

**5** VOCABULARY Look at the language for describing technology. Complete the phrases with the words below.

allows   base   handle   mains   mostly

| Describing technology
**Shape** straight curved rectangular spherical square triangular circular
**Power**
It's ¹_____ powered / battery powered / solar powered.
It's cordless / rechargeable.
**Construction**
It's made ²_____ of glass / steel, etc.
It's got wheels / a long ³_____ / a triangular ⁴_____ / a square lid, etc.
**Use**
You use it to …
It ⁵_____ you to …
It prevents you from (+ -ing) …

**6** 🎧 **3.10** Listen to the dialogues. Which phrases from exercise 5 do the people use?

**RECYCLE!** zero conditional
We use the zero conditional to talk about causes and effects which are always true.
If you heat aluminium, it melts.
A light comes on if there's no Wi-Fi signal.

**7** 🎧 **3.10** Read the Recycle! box. Then listen again. Complete the zero conditional sentences from the dialogues with the correct form of the verbs below.

come   get   go   post   press

1   If you _____ this button, the plug appears.
2   You don't need to put it away if friends _____ to visit.
3   If you choose 'share' mode, it automatically _____ your workout results on Facebook.
4   It _____ forward to the next track if you just touch here.
5   If you wave your hand once, it _____ louder.

**8** SPEAKING Work in pairs. Think of a gadget and describe it to your partner. Include phrases from exercise 5. Can your partner guess what you are describing?

> It's battery powered, I think. It's made of …

# The passive (present simple and past simple)

*I can use the present and past passive to talk about technology.*

**1 SPEAKING** Work in pairs. How many different things do people use mobile phones for? Think of as many as you can in two minutes.

**2** Read the text. What happened in 1973, 1986, 1992 and 1997?

## A brief history of mobile phones

›› Nearly a billion mobile phones **are sold** every year worldwide.

›› The first mobile phone call **was made** in 1973 **by** Martin Cooper. He was an inventor for the company Motorola. The call was answered by the boss of a rival company, who was not happy to hear that he had lost the race.

›› The first mobiles were powered by batteries that weighed nearly a kilo.

›› Voicemail was added to phones in 1986. Internet access was not added for another ten years.

›› The first text message was sent in December 1992. It was not typed on the phone itself but on a computer.

›› The camera phone was invented in 1997 by Philippe Kahn. Photos of his newborn daughter were shared via his phone with 2,000 friends and family.

›› In the UK, a mobile phone is stolen every three minutes.

›› What are mobile phones used for the most? It isn't texting or calling – it's checking the time!

**3** Study the first two sentences of the text in exercise 2. Then complete the Learn this! box.

**LEARN THIS!** The present and past passive

**a** The passive is formed with the correct form of the verb ¹_____ and the past participle.

**b** We use the ²_____ simple of *be* for the present passive and the ³_____ simple of *be* for the past passive.

**c** If we want to say who performed the action, we use ⁴_____ + their name.

**4** Find twelve examples of the passive in the text. Which examples are ...

**a** plural?　　**b** negative?　　**c** a question?

**LOOK OUT!**

When we use adverbs with the passive, we usually put them immediately before the past participle.

Phones <u>are sometimes used</u> as alarm clocks.

It <u>was probably invented</u> by accident.

➡ Grammar Builder 9B  page 134

**5** Read the Look out! box. Complete the sentences with the present simple or past simple passive of the verbs in brackets.

1 Mobile phones *are owned* (own) by about 4.3 billion people in the world today.

2 The best-selling phone ever was the Nokia 1100. More than 250 million _____ (sell).

3 In Japan, mobiles _____ (often / use) in the shower, so most of them are waterproof.

4 The average text message _____ (usually / answer) within 90 seconds.

5 In 2012, 340,000 iPhones _____ (buy) every day.

6 Today, the internet _____ (access) more often from a phone than from a computer.

7 More text messages _____ (send) every year in the Philippines than in any other country.

8 The world's toughest phone _____ (drop) 25 metres onto concrete and did not break.

**6** Complete the questions about the reading texts in Units 1–8 using the correct passive form of the verbs in brackets.

1 Why _____ Ashlyn Blocker _____ (watch) more carefully than all the other children at her school? [1F]

2 _____ Dan and Kate Suski _____ (rescue) by helicopter after their boat sank? [2F]

3 What skills _____ (improve) by playing online video games, according to a report? [3F]

4 Who _____ (nearly / kill) by a storm at a paragliding event? [4F]

5 Why _____ Jo Unsworth _____ (allow) to go to sleep at work? [5F]

6 Why _____ Terry Alderton _____ (laugh at) after sunbathing? [6F]

7 Where _____ meetings _____ (sometimes / hold), if Aaron Levie is choosing the venue? [7F]

8 Where _____ the words *tamám shud* _____ (find) in the Somerton Man case? [8F]

**7 SPEAKING** Work in pairs. Ask and answer the questions in exercise 6.

> Why was Ashlyn Blocker watched more carefully than all the other children at her school?

> Because ...

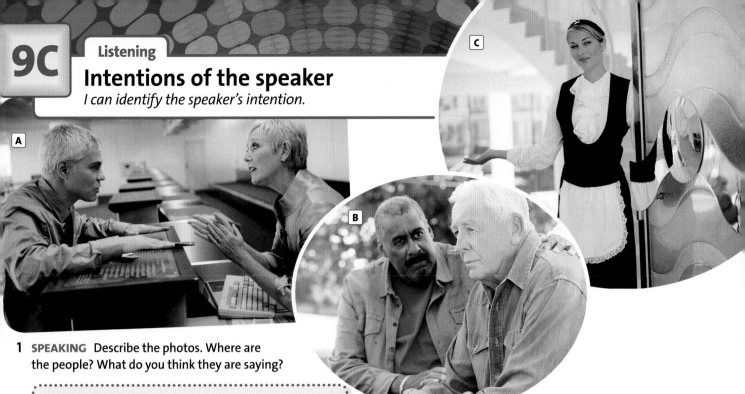

# 9C Listening
## Intentions of the speaker
*I can identify the speaker's intention.*

**1 SPEAKING** Describe the photos. Where are the people? What do you think they are saying?

> **Listening Strategy**
> You will sometimes have to identify the intentions of the speaker (e.g. to persuade, to warn, to inform, etc.). Listen for phrases such as *I think you should, be careful to, I'm going to tell you about* … that give you a clue to the speaker's intentions.

**2** Read the Listening Strategy. What is the intention of the speakers in sentences 1–6? Choose from the verbs below. Match three of the sentences (1–6) with the photos.

to apologise   to challenge   to comfort   to complain
to describe   to encourage   to enquire   to entertain
to inform   to persuade   to recommend   to tell a story
to thank   to warn   to welcome

1 'Be careful not to touch the cooker. It's hot.' ___
2 'This is ridiculous! Why is there such a long delay?' ___
3 'I'd go and see this film if I were you. It's brilliant.' ___
4 'Good morning. Let me show you to your table.' ___
5 'I'd like some information about opening times, please.' ___
6 'Don't worry, everything will be fine.' ___

**3** 🎧 **3.11** Listen and identify the intentions of the speakers. Circle the correct verbs.

1 a to persuade    b to thank       c to complain
2 a to describe    b to challenge   c to persuade
3 a to comfort     b to encourage   c to complain
4 a to warn        b to persuade    c to complain
5 a to comfort     b to challenge   c to warn
6 a to inform      b to welcome     c to recommend

**4** 🎧 **3.12** Read the questions below. Then listen and circle the correct answers.

1 The scientist's main aim is to
  a warn people about the dangers of overeating.
  b inform people about a scientific advance.
  c persuade people to try a new product.
2 The boy's main aim is to
  a compare his new motorbike with his previous one.
  b try to persuade someone to buy a second-hand motorbike.
  c complain that he can't afford a brand-new motorbike.

3 The doctor's main aim is to
  a encourage the patient to live a healthier lifestyle.
  b warn the patient of the dangers of eating too much.
  c recommend a course of treatment.
4 The speaker's main aim is to
  a describe a new invention.
  b advertise a new product he has invented.
  c persuade somebody to invest money in his invention.
5 The head teacher's main aim is to
  a persuade students to use the minibus.
  b inform people that the school will buy a minibus.
  c thank people for helping the school to raise money.

**5** 🎧 **3.12** Match the verbs in A with the words and phrases in B to make collocations. Then listen again and check.

**A** lose   get   prescribe   come up with   browse   run

**B** a good deal   an idea   on biofuel   drugs   the internet   weight

**6** Prepare a short speech (30–50 words) to do one of these things. Use the questions and phrases to help you.

1 persuade someone to come out with you
  *Where? When? Why will they enjoy it?*
  Why don't you … ?  I think you you'll enjoy …
  It'll be (great fun).  (George) is coming too.
2 thank the parents of your penfriend for their hospitality
  *How did they make you feel welcome? What did you particularly enjoy?*
  I had a (wonderful) time.  It was so kind of you to …
  I really enjoyed the …   I hope to see you again soon.
3 inform your cousin about your plans for your gap year
  *Where are you going and when? What kind of work are you going to do? How long will you stay?*
  I'm going to …  I'll be there for …
  I'm going to work (in a shop).
  When I come home, I'm going to …

**7 SPEAKING** Work in pairs. Deliver your speech to your partner.

**9D** Grammar

# The passive (present perfect and future)

*I can use different forms of the passive.*

**1** Look at the photo. What things do you think a wearable gadget can do?

**2** Read the text and check your ideas from exercise 1.

# The camera revolution

Over the past 20 years, ¹the way in which we take, keep and share photos has been transformed. Most people now use smartphones and digital cameras to take photos, and billions of photos have been uploaded to social networking sites. ²So have traditional celluloid film cameras been replaced by these gadgets? Not yet, but it won't be long.

But things are going to change again. Wearable gadgets have recently been developed that allow you to take a photo simply by blinking. You can also send messages and surf the internet. ³The technology hasn't been perfected, so ⁴these devices won't be sold in shops for a while.

⁵Will cameras and mobiles be replaced by wearable gadgets? They haven't been replaced yet, but it may happen sooner than we think. What's certain is that ⁶our lives will be changed by these devices in ways we haven't even thought of.

**3** Match the underlined passive forms in the text (1–6) with the tenses below (a–f). How many more examples can you find in the text?

a present perfect affirmative ___
b present perfect negative ___
c present perfect interrogative ___
d *will* future affirmative ___
e *will* future interrogative ___
f *will* future negative ___

➥ **Grammar Builder 9D** page 140

**4** What will life be like in cities 50 years from now? Complete the predictions with the verbs in brackets. Use the future passive.

1 Food _____ (grow) in huge vertical farms.
2 Everyone _____ (connect) to a super-fast fibre-optic network.
3 In shops we _____ (assist) by robots who will help us find what we are looking for.
4 Computers and mobiles _____ (wear), not carried.
5 People _____ (drive) around in robo-taxis which won't have drivers. Traffic lights _____ (not need).
6 Some people predict that we _____ constantly _____ (watch) by cameras!

**5** Complete the predictions with the affirmative future passive form of the verbs below.

build   control   drive   buy and sell   speak   connect

One hundred years from now:
1 the weather _____ by humans.
2 we _____ all _____ to computers so that we can think faster.
3 only two languages _____ in the world (English and Chinese).
4 cars _____ by robots.
5 all products _____ online.
6 hotels _____ on the moon.

**6** SPEAKING Work in pairs. Say if you agree or disagree with the statements in exercise 5. Use the phrases below to help you.

I don't agree that ...   I agree that ...
I'm not sure that ...   I wouldn't say that ...

**7** Complete the sentences with the verbs below. Use the present perfect passive.

sell   share   ~~take~~   upload   watch

In the past hour:
1 100 million photos *have been taken*.
2 208,000 mobile phones _____ .
3 1.7 million photos _____ to Instagram.
4 350 million photos _____ with friends on Facebook.
5 8.3 million hours of video _____ on YouTube.

**8** Write questions using the prompts below. Use the present perfect passive with *ever*.

1 photograph / at school?
   *Have you ever been photographed at school?*
2 punish / for something you didn't do?
3 involve / in an accident?
4 hurt / while doing sport?
5 criticise / by a good friend?
6 sting / by a bee?

**9** SPEAKING Work in pairs. Ask and answer the questions in exercise 8. Give extra information using the past simple.

Have you ever been photographed at school?

Yes, I have. We had a class photograph last year.

# Verb + preposition

*I can understand and use verb + preposition collocations.*

**1** Would you like to travel to another planet? Why? / Why not?

**2** Read the text. Do you think the Mars One project is a good idea? Give reasons for your answer.

The Mars One project is planning to send people to Mars to live there permanently. The idea of living on other planets clearly **appeals to** a lot of people, because over 200,000 individuals want to **take part in** the mission. But how will the settlers **adjust to** the conditions on Mars? Here are some of the problems they will face.

- The atmosphere **consists of** 95% carbon dioxide and almost no oxygen.
- The settlers will have to **cope with** very low temperatures (similar to Antarctica) and very high levels of ultra-violet radiation.
- Gravity is only 38% of that on Earth. We need to **learn more about** the effects that would have on their bodies.
- Mars Rovers have already **searched for** water on Mars but have found none that is in liquid form.

The plan is to send another Rover to Mars in 2018. Its job will be to prepare for the arrival of the first four settlers in 2025. It will construct 'houses' for the inhabitants, with a supply of fresh air, water and solar power. After that, four more settlers will arrive every two years. How long will the settlers stay? Nobody knows. The volunteer settlers will get a 'one-way ticket'. It may be possible to bring them back to Earth at some point in the future, but there is no guarantee!

**3** Look at the highlighted verb + preposition collocations in the text. Find six more (two with *for*, one with *about*, one with *of*, one with *to* and one with *with*).

> **Dictionary Skills Strategy**
>
> A dictionary will tell you if the verb is followed by a particular preposition.

**4** **DICTIONARY WORK** Read the Dictionary Strategy. Then look at the dictionary entry for *recover*. Which preposition is used with it?

> **recover** /rɪˈkʌvə(r)/ *verb* [I] **1** recover (from sth) to become well again after you have been ill: *It took him two months to recover from the operation.* **2** [I] recover (from sth) to get back to normal again after a bad experience, etc.

**5** Complete the sentences with the words below. Use a dictionary to check your answers if you need to.

about    apologised    asked    laugh    of    with

1  I _____ for my late arrival.
2  Dad complained _____ the noise from the neighbours.
3  I've often dreamed _____ flying to the moon.
4  We finished our meal and _____ for the bill.
5  Don't _____ at your little sister. It isn't kind.
6  Can you help me _____ my science homework?

**6** **SPEAKING** Do you think people will ever live on Mars? Why? / Why not? Use the phrases below to help you.

> I think / don't think …   I'm not sure, really.
> As I see it, …   To be honest, …
> For one thing, …   But then again, …
> It would(n't) be …   I would(n't) find it …

> **LOOK OUT!**
>
> Some verbs can be followed by more than one preposition, sometimes with a slight change in meaning, e.g. *shout at / shout to, agree with / agree to*.
>
> *My sister <u>shouted at</u> me because I lost her mobile.*
>
> *I saw Liz on the other side of the road and <u>shouted to</u> her.*

**7** Read the Look out! box. Circle the correct prepositions to complete the sentences.

1  **a** Have you ever heard **of / about** wearable gadgets?
   **b** Have you heard **of / about** John's new job?
2  **a** She has to care **for / about** her elderly mum.
   **b** I don't care **for / about** money.
3  **a** You look worried. What are you thinking **about / of**?
   **b** What do you think **about / of** my new dress?
4  **a** Throw the ball **at / to** me!
   **b** It was unkind to throw a ball **at / to** the dog.
5  **a** I write **to / about** my penfriend about once a month.
   **b** I wrote **to / about** my holiday on my blog.
6  **a** My teacher agreed **with / to** my request to leave early.
   **b** I don't agree **with / to** you.

**8** Complete the questions with the correct preposition.

1  What kinds of things do you worry _____ ?
2  When did you last argue _____ someone? Who? What _____ ?
3  Have you ever complained _____ anything in a restaurant or shop? What was the problem?
4  What kind of music do you listen _____ ?
5  When did you last take part _____ a race? How did you do?
6  If you were going to write a letter _____ someone famous, who would it be? Why?

**9** **SPEAKING** Ask and answer the questions in exercise 8. Give extra details if you can.

> What kinds of things do you worry about?

> I worry about school work and exams.

**Reading**

# Great inventions?

*I can understand a text about forgotten inventions.*

**1 SPEAKING** Look at the pictures. What do you think these inventions were for?

**2** Read the texts. Check your answers in exercise 1. Were any of your guesses correct?

**3** In pairs, decide which of the inventions is the most impressive and / or interesting, in your opinion. Give reasons.

**4** Number the pictures (A–D) in the order in which they were invented.

A ___  B _1_  C ___  D ___

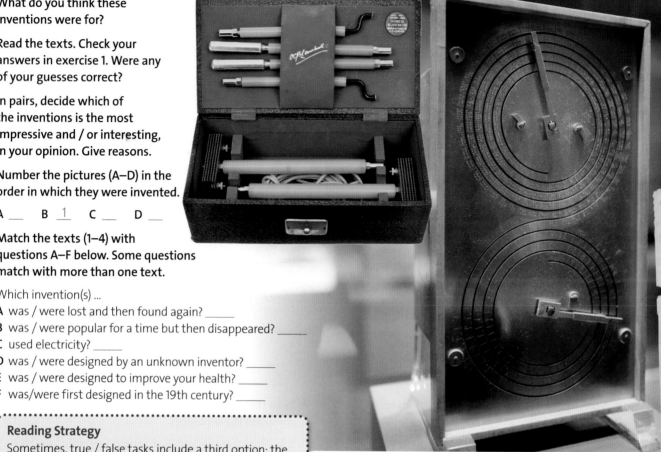

**5** Match the texts (1–4) with questions A–F below. Some questions match with more than one text.

Which invention(s) ...
A was / were lost and then found again? _____
B was / were popular for a time but then disappeared? _____
C used electricity? _____
D was / were designed by an unknown inventor? _____
E was / were designed to improve your health? _____
F was/were first designed in the 19th century? _____

> **Reading Strategy**
> Sometimes, true / false tasks include a third option: the text does not say. Choose the third option if the text does not contain enough information to clearly say if the sentence is true or false. Do not use your own knowledge (or guesswork) to fill any information gaps!

**6** Read the Reading Strategy. Explain why 'does not say' is the correct answer to this sentence.

The third of the three Telharmonium models was the heaviest. DNS

**7** Decide if the sentences below are true (*T*), false (*F*) or 'does not say' (*DNS*).

1 The Telharmonium was invented before the radio. _____
2 Thaddeus Cahill destroyed the final model of his invention before he died. _____
3 The Rejuvenator successfully cured deafness and baldness in hundreds of people. _____
4 The Rejuvenator was a commercial success even though it was not clear how it worked. _____
5 The Writing Ball was the first machine that used electricity for typing. _____
6 Other typing machines were cheaper to make because they were not made by hand. _____
7 The Antikythera Mechanism was at the bottom of the sea for nearly 2,000 years. _____
8 For about 70 years after it was found, the purpose of the mechanism was not known. _____

**8 VOCABULARY** Find nouns in the text related to these verbs and adjectives.

Noun endings

Text 1
a invent _____
b record _____

Text 2
c deaf _____
d bald _____

Text 3
e move _____
f arrange _____

Text 4
g discover _____
h reconstruct _____

**9 VOCABULARY** Look at your answers in exercise 8. How many different noun endings do they include? Can you think of other nouns with these endings?

**10 SPEAKING** In pairs, decide which three inventions and discoveries from history are the most important. Use the ideas below or think of your own. Give reasons.

aeroplanes  antibiotics  books  cars  computers
electricity  fire  printing  television  wheels

> If the wheel didn't exist, we couldn't travel by car or bus.

> If we didn't have aeroplanes, journeys would take much longer.

C

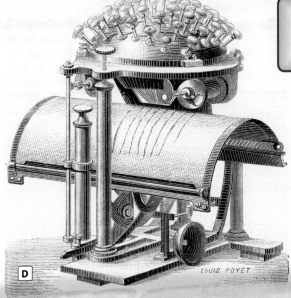

D

LOUIS POYET

# Inventions the world forgot

🎧 3.13

## 1 The Telharmonium

The Telharmonium was the world's first electronic musical instrument. It was designed by an American, Thaddeus Cahill, in 1897. Three models of the instrument were built; the first weighed about 7,000 kg, and the other two weighed nearly
5 200,000 kg! Music from the instrument was broadcast to people's homes using another new invention: the telephone. For the first time, people could stay at home and listen on their telephones to live music from another part of the country. (The radio had not been invented.) People loved these concerts, but there were
10 problems. Some telephone users who were not listening to the concert were interrupted by loud music half way through their conversation! By 1914, the world was no longer interested in the Telharmonium. After Cahill's death in 1934, his brother kept one of the three models, but in 1962 it was destroyed. No recordings
15 of the music were kept, so the Telharmonium and its unique sound have disappeared forever.

## 2 The Rejuvenator

In the early part of the 20th century, there was a lot of interest in the power of electricity to cure medical conditions. A device called the Rejuvenator was invented by
20 British scientist Otto Overbeck in 1925. It was used in the home to treat all kinds of medical problems, including deafness and baldness, and became very popular. It was advertised in newspapers and members of the public were invited to watch live demonstrations in theatres. The users placed electrodes on
25 any part of their body and a small electric current was passed through it. It was unclear exactly how the machine worked, but hundreds were sold all around the world and Overbeck became rich. In the 1950s, it was still possible to buy new parts for these machines, but today they are only seen in museums.

## 3 The Writing Ball

30 The Writing Ball was invented in 1865 by Rasmus Malling-Hansen from Denmark. It was a machine for typing onto paper. Malling-Hansen spent a long time working on the design. For example, he made sure all the keys were placed in the best positions for typing quickly. The machine even used electricity
35 to make the movement faster. There was one problem, however: you could not see the paper as you were typing. Nevertheless, the Writing Ball was sold all over Europe and was very successful. However, each model was made by hand. Soon, other machines became more popular because they were made in
40 factories and were cheaper. A new keyboard was developed with the keys arranged differently. This arrangement is now used on phones and computer keyboards all over the world, even though it was quicker to type using the Writing Ball. The once-popular Writing Ball was forgotten.

## 4 The Antikythera Mechanism

45 In 1901, a ship was discovered at the bottom of the sea near the Greek island of Antikythera. On the ship was an ancient machine. It had been made about 1,900 years earlier, in 2 BC. For many years after its discovery, nobody understood exactly what the machine was for. But in the 1970s, scientists used X-rays
50 to find out its secrets. Amazingly, they found that the machine was an ancient computer. It had been designed to predict the movements of the sun, the moon and the planets. It did this using more than thirty hand-made metal wheels of different sizes. A study of the mechanism in 2006 was led by Professor Michael
55 Edmunds from Cardiff University. He described the device as 'just extraordinary, the only thing of its kind' and 'more valuable than the *Mona Lisa*'. Reconstructions have been made and the device works perfectly.

## 9G Speaking
# Making a complaint
*I can complain about faulty goods in a shop.*

**1 Describe the photo. Answer the questions.**

1 What are the people saying, do you think?
2 Do you often take the things you have bought back to the shop? Why?
3 Tell us about a situation when you had to return a faulty item to a shop.

You are returning a gadget to a shop because something has gone wrong with it. Discuss these four issues during the conversation with the shop assistant:
• What the gadget is and when you bought it.
• What the problem is.
• What you want to happen next.
• What you will do if that isn't possible.

**2 🎧3.14 Read the task above. Then listen to a student doing the task. Circle the correct answers.**

1 The student is returning
  a a CD player.
  b a DVD player.
2 The student can't
  a charge the batteries.
  b turn on the player.
3 The student would like
  a an exchange.
  b a refund.
4 The sales assistant offers to
  a repair it.
  b exchange it.

**3 VOCABULARY Which of these gadgets do you own? Would you like to own any other? Why? / Why not?**

**Gadgets** digital camera   digital radio   DVD player
e-book reader   games console   headphones
mobile phone   MP3 player   smartphone   tablet

➤➤ **Vocabulary Builder** Gadgets: page 121

**Speaking Strategy**
When you are doing a speaking task, make sure you refer to all four points in the task. It is also important that you react and respond properly to what is said during the conversation.

**4 🎧3.14 Read the Speaking Strategy. Listen again and say if the student mentioned all the points in the task and responded well to the sales assistant's contributions.**

**5 VOCABULARY Look at the list of parts of gadgets below. Choose three gadgets from exercise 3. Which parts can you find on or with these gadgets?**

**Parts of gadgets** battery   case   charger   on/off button
power lead   remote control   screen   strap
USB port   volume control

**6 🎧3.15 Listen to another student. What parts of the gadget did she and the sales assistant mention?**

**7 KEY PHRASES Complete the phrases with the words below.**

broken   come   exchange   happy   manager   money
problem   repair   something   stopped   work   write

| Making a complaint |
| --- |
| There's a ¹_____ with … |
| There's ²_____ wrong with … |
| It doesn't ³_____ . |
| It has ⁴_____ working. |
| It's ⁵_____ . |
| The (dial) has ⁶_____ off. |
| Can I have my ⁷_____ back, please? |
| Can I ⁸_____ it, please? |
| Can you ⁹_____ it? |
| I'm not ¹⁰_____ about that. |
| Can I see the ¹¹_____ , please? |
| I'm going to ¹²_____ to (customer services). |

**8 🎧3.15 Listen again. Tick the phrases in exercise 7 that the student uses.**

**9 KEY PHRASES Match the sentence halves.**

Dealing with a complaint
1 What's wrong          a a refund?
2 When did you          b repair it.
3 Have you got          c a credit note.
4 Would you like        d the receipt?
5 We don't give         e refunds.
6 I can give you        f with it?
7 We can                g I can do.
8 There's nothing       h buy it?

**10 SPEAKING Work in pairs. Do the exam task in exercise 2. Take turns to be the shop assistant and the customer. Use words and phrases from this lesson to help you.**

# 9H Writing
# A formal letter
*I can write a formal letter.*

**1 SPEAKING** Work in pairs. Put these methods of transport in order from the most environmentally friendly to the least. Then compare ideas with another pair.

bicycle   bus   car (diesel or petrol)
electric car   motorbike   tram

**2** Read the task and the letter. Do you agree or disagree with the writer's opinions? Give reasons.

> Your local council has issued a new town planning policy and decided not to include any cycle lanes in the town centre. Write a letter of complaint about this decision.

Dear Sir or Madam,

**1** I am writing to express my disappointment at the council's recent decision not to include any cycle lanes in town. **Since** I do not have a car, I cycle everywhere, **so** this is a very important issue for me.

**2** My main reason for objecting to the decision is that cycles lanes improve the safety of cyclists. Without cycle lanes, more cyclists are injured in accidents, **as** it is far more difficult for drivers to see them.

**3** I realise that it is expensive to build cycle lanes. However, I believe it is a good use of public money. Pollution is a problem and we should be encouraging people to cycle **rather than** going by car because it is better for the environment.

**4** All in all, I believe this is a very bad decision. **Unless** the council reconsiders, there will be a negative effect on road safety and on the environment.

Yours faithfully,

*M Stafford*

Martin Stafford

> **Writing Strategy**
>
> Make sure you use a variety of different structures when writing formal letters. You can form complex sentences by joining two clauses together with a conjunction (*and, but, because, if, or*, etc.). Use different conjunctions depending on the meaning of the clauses they introduce.

**3** Read the Writing Strategy. Match the bold conjunctions in the letter with the meanings below.

1 because (×2) _____ , _____
2 instead of _____
3 except if / if it was not true that _____
4 for that reason _____

➼ **Vocabulary Builder** Conjunctions: page 121

**4** Match the paragraphs of the letter (1–4) with four of the headings below (A–F).

A Give the main argument for your opinion. ___
B Strongly re-state your overall opinion. ___
C Describe a personal experience. ___
D Explain the reason for writing. ___
E Make suggestions for the future. ___
F Mention one argument from the opposing view and say why you do not accept it. ___

**5 KEY PHRASES** Read the useful phrases for summing up. Then find one more in the letter in exercise 2. Which paragraph does it begin?

> Summing up
> On balance, I think …
> Overall, … in my opinion.
> In conclusion, …
> For these reasons, I strongly believe that …
>
> _____

**6** In pairs, read the task below. Plan your letter by following the instructions (1–3).

> Your local council has decided to stop giving under-18s cheap travel on buses. Write a letter of complaint about this decision, explaining why it is bad for teenagers and for the environment.

1 In pairs, brainstorm ideas for the pros and cons of offering young people cheap travel on buses.
2 Choose a main reason for complaining about the decision. Then choose one argument in favour of the council's decision and say why you do not accept it.
3 Make a paragraph plan for your letter. Use your answers in exercise 4 to help you.

**7** Write your letter following your plan from exercise 6. Use a phrase from exercise 5 to begin the final paragraph.

> **CHECK YOUR WORK**
>  Have you …
> • used conjunctions correctly?
> • checked the spelling and grammar?

# Exam Skills Trainer

## Reading

**Strategy**

Read each text quickly and decide what kind of text it is, e.g. an advert, a notice, a description, etc. This will help you answer questions about gist and intention.

**1** Read the Strategy. Then read the five short texts, ignoring the questions under them. Decide what kind of texts they are.

**2** Read the texts and answer the questions (1–5). Circle the correct answer (A–D).

### 1 TV opportunity!

*Great Inventions* is a new TV show and we are looking for young people to take part. Interested? We invite you to make a two-minute video that shows your idea for a new invention. Make sure you include:

- personal details: name, age, and address.
- the name of your invention, how you got the idea and how it works.

You can email us your video or send it to the address shown on our website. We'll choose the ones we think are most interesting. Your prize? The chance to appear on our TV show!

**1** What do the programme makers want?

A new inventors
B experienced film makers
C young TV presenters
D young actors

### 2 20th-century inventions

The most important modern invention has to be the mobile phone. It was only invented in the 1970s, but look at it now! Everyone has a phone. Originally, of course, phones were large and were only used to make phone calls. Now those phones are in museums! Modern mobile phones are mini-computers – you can do so much with them. You can buy very expensive phones, but you can also buy cheap models. That's why, in my view, it's the best 20th-century invention.

**2** What is the purpose of the text?

A to advertise mobile phones
B to invite people to a museum exhibition
C to give an opinion about an invention
D to advise people to avoid cheap phones

### 3 3D printers

3D printers are a new kind of machine that can make everyday objects. They're amazing because they can produce different things in different materials. A 3D printer can make anything from cups and plates to plastic toys and even chocolate cakes! So how do they work? First you design a 3D object on your computer, then you connect it to a 3D printer. Press 'print' and watch it work. The printer makes the object in very thin layers, like the pages of a book – one on top of the other until you have a complete object.

**3** What is the writer of the text doing?

A giving an idea about the future of printers
B describing an invention
C giving a short history of an object
D explaining different inventions

**4** Tim Berners-Lee is the British computer scientist who is given the credit for inventing the World Wide Web.

People had been developing the internet since the 1960s. However, Tim Berners-Lee put all the ideas together to create the World Wide Web. In 1990, he produced the first version and it was put online in 1991.

He could have made a lot of money from his invention, but he decided to offer it to the world as a gift.

**4** What would be the best title for this text?

A The inventor of the internet
B The advantages of the world wide web
C An expensive communication system
D The growth of the internet

### 5 What's my password?

These days we have so many computer passwords that it isn't surprising that we often forget them. That's why most people create passwords which are based on the people, places and things they know best. Using names and dates in different ways is popular. For example, combining part of your name with your date of birth. Using a childhood memory is also very common. You might use the name of the street you grew up in, or the name of your favourite teacher.

**5** According to this text, how do most people decide on their passwords?

A They only have one or two passwords for everything.
B They choose words which are very personal.
C They only use information about themselves.
D They use numbers rather than letters.

## Listening

**Strategy**

To decide if a statement is true or false, you should only use the information in the text. A *true / false* task is a test of comprehension, not your general knowledge.

**3** Read the Strategy. Which sentences in the exam task in exercise 4 do you think are true? Why do you think so? Discuss your ideas in pairs.

# Exam Skills Trainer

**4** 🎧 **3.16** Listen to the text. Are the sentences true or false? Write T or F.

1 Galileo invented the telescope.
2 Galileo immediately used the telescope to study space.
3 The United States sent the first person into space.
4 There was an astronaut in Vostok 1.
5 A woman explored space before men landed on the Moon.
6 Most spacecraft have successfully landed on Mars.
7 The speaker thinks it's useful to land on Mars.
8 The speaker is mainly describing the advantages of space exploration.

## Use of English

> **Strategy**
> Read the text quickly, ignoring the gaps, to get a general idea of what it is about. Then read it again more slowly and think about what type of words are missing, e.g. adjective, adverb, etc. When you have decided, look at the word given and consider how to change it. Think carefully about spelling, e.g *happy = happily* NOT ~~happyly~~.

**5** Read the Strategy. Then read the text in exercise 6 and work out what kind of words are missing from each gap.

**6** Complete the text with the correct form of the words in brackets.

### Food inventions

A lot of popular food was invented ¹_____ (ACCIDENT). For example, a chef called George Crum was working in a restaurant in Saratoga Springs in the US. One day, a ²_____ (CUSTOM) complained about his fried potatoes. He wanted them to be fried for a ³_____ (LONG) time than usual and to be cut into thinner slices. Maybe Crum was tired that day because he was very ⁴_____ (HAPPY) about this! He sliced the potatoes very ⁵_____ (THIN) and fried them for a very long time. ⁶_____ (STRANGE), the man loved them, and so, potato crisps were created! Another ⁷_____ (FAME) example is when a pharmacist named John Pemberton was working on some medicine for people who were tired or feeling ⁸_____ (NERVE). One of his assistants used carbonated water by mistake, not still water. The result was the fizzy drink: cola.

## Speaking

> **Strategy**
> Make sure you use appropriate language when doing a role-play exercise. You should learn suitable expressions that you can use for different situations, e.g. making a complaint, making a decision about what to buy.

**7** Read the Strategy. Then look at expressions 1–8. Which of these can you use to make a complaint? Can you think of any other expressions?

1 Can I have my money back, please?
2 It doesn't work.
3 It's perfect.
4 You're right about that.
5 There's something wrong with it.
6 I'm not happy about that.
7 That's a good idea.
8 Can I see the manager, please?

**8** Work in pairs. Do a role-play. You are complaining in a shop because an item you bought is faulty. Discuss these four issues during the conversation with the shop assistant and try to come to an agreement.

• What you bought.
• What the problem is.
• What you want to happen next.
• What you will do if that isn't possible.

**9** Summarise what you have agreed on. Say how you feel about the solution.

Now swap roles, and repeat the activity with a different complaint.

## Writing

> **Strategy**
> When you have finished writing, read through your work carefully and check for grammar mistakes.

**10** Read the Strategy. Then read the sentences below and find the errors.

1 I would like to sending you my latest invention.
2 I did not enter a competition before.
3 I always am working hard every day.
4 I going to send you a short video.
5 I write to you to find out more information.
6 I looking forward to hearing from you.

**11** Imagine you are entering a competition for a new invention or design. Write a formal letter to the organiser in which you:

• explain why you are writing.
• describe your invention.
• say what inspired you.
• explain why you think it would be useful.

# The British

**1 SPEAKING** Describe the photos. Do they match your idea of typical British people? Why? / Why not?

**2** Read the text. Are these sentences about the people who took part in the survey true or false? Write T or F.

a Most have a positive view of the British overall. ___
b More than half have a better opinion of the British now that they live in the country. ___

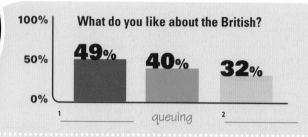

## HOW FOREIGNERS SEE THE BRITISH

🎧 3.17

*W*hat is a typical British person like? People who come to Britain from other countries probably have a few expectations: British people are polite, rather reserved, and enjoy drinking tea and standing in queues! But how accurate is this stereotype? In an online survey of 1,402 foreign nationals living in the UK, just over half said that the British matched their expectations.

The survey also asked which aspects of the British character the foreign nationals liked and disliked. British people's good manners were popular with 49% and 40% liked the ability to queue. Many agreed that the British are reserved and for 32% this was a good quality – but for 19% it was negative. Other negative aspects were the British sense of humour (31%) and British culture in general (28%). However, 77% said they liked British people in general and 61% said that their opinion of the British got better as a result of living in the UK.

A spokesman for the researchers said: 'People probably come to Britain with a stereotype of what to expect. It's good to see that, for the majority, the reality is better than the stereotype.'

**3** Complete the labels for the charts with the words below. Use information from the text to help you.

better   culture   good manners   reserve
reserve   sense of humour   the same or worse

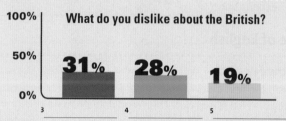

**What do you like about the British?**
49%   40%   32%
1 _____   queuing   2 _____

**What do you dislike about the British?**
31%   28%   19%
3 _____   4 _____   5 _____

**Is your opinion of the British better or worse now than before you lived here?**

39%   6 _____
61%   7 _____

**4** 🎧 3.18 Listen to five people from other countries talking about their view of the British. Which person do you think has the most negative view?

**5** 🎧 3.18 Listen again. Match the speakers (1–5) with sentences A–F below.

Which speaker(s) ...
A are not keen on the weather in the UK? ___ , ___
B makes a positive comment about the food? ___
C do not think British people are hard-working? ___ , ___
D have a negative opinion of young people's behaviour?
___ , ___
E are fans of British culture? ___ , ___
F are generally positive about the people in Britain?
___ , ___ , ___

**6 SPEAKING** Discuss the questions in pairs. Use the phrases below to help you.

People usually think we are ...
A lot of people see us as ...
It is / isn't right to say that we are ... because ...
However, it's probably true to say that ...

1 What do people from other countries think of your nationality? Is there a stereotype?
2 Do you think other people's view of your nationality is correct? Why? / Why not?

# Robinson Crusoe

**1 SPEAKING** Describe the photo. Where is the man? Why is he there? What is he doing? Do you know the name of the film and the actor?

**2 USE OF ENGLISH** Read the text and circle the correct answers.

| | | |
|---|---|---|
| **1 a** when | **b** before | **c** up to |
| **2 a** In | **b** On | **c** At |
| **3 a** which | **b** who | **c** it |
| **4 a** if | **b** why | **c** that |
| **5 a** stay | **b** to stay | **c** staying |
| **6 a** on | **b** over | **c** about |
| **7 a** so | **b** because | **c** however |

🎧 3.19

# The real Robinson Crusoe

Written by Daniel Defoe and published in 1719, *Robinson Crusoe* is one of the oldest and most famous adventure stories in English literature. In the story, Crusoe is marooned on a desert island and spends 27 years there **1**___ he is rescued. Defoe probably got the idea for his novel from the true story of the Scottish sailor, Alexander Selkirk. **2**___ the early 18th century, England was at war with Spain, and Selkirk joined the crew of an English ship, the *Cinque Ports*, **3**___ attacked Spanish colonies and ships in the South Pacific. In 1704, Selkirk's ship stopped at a remote island for fresh water and supplies. Selkirk was worried **4**___ the ship was in poor condition and, instead of returning to it, decided **5**___ on the island alone. He became very lonely and quickly regretted his decision, but he was right **6**___ the *Cinque Ports*: it sank. Selkirk survived by building a shelter and killing animals for food. Two ships visited the island the following year, but unfortunately they were Spanish, **7**___ Selkirk hid from sight. An English ship finally arrived at the island in February 1709 and Selkirk was able to return home.

**3** Read *The story so far*. Then work in pairs. What do you think happens next? Use the ideas below, or your own ideas.

1 They become friends.
2 The prisoner attacks Crusoe and runs away.
3 The prisoner becomes Crusoe's slave.
4 Crusoe learns to speak the prisoner's language.
5 The prisoner takes Crusoe to his home on another island.

**4** 🎧 3.20 Listen to the next part of the story and check your ideas.

**5** 🎧 3.20 Complete the questions with the words below. Use each word once. Then listen again and answer the questions.

how long    what    where    when    why

1 _____ did Crusoe call the man 'Man Friday'?
2 _____ did Crusoe teach Man Friday to do?
3 _____ did they go back to Crusoe's first house?
4 _____ did Crusoe and Man Friday live together?
5 _____ were they when Man Friday saw his country?

## The story so far ...

Robinson Crusoe is a sailor. On a voyage to Africa, his ship sinks in a storm. Crusoe manages to swim to an island but he is the only survivor. He manages to get ropes, wood, guns and tools from the ship. He builds shelters and a canoe, and hunts wild animals. Many years pass. One day he sees a footprint in the sand and then discovers that cannibals occasionally visit the island and eat their prisoners. On one of these visits, Crusoe kills two cannibals and helps one of the prisoners to escape ...

**6 SPEAKING** Work in pairs. Imagine that you are going to spend a year on a desert island. Decide which of the things below you will take with you and why. What else will you take? Use the phrases to help you.

blanket   first-aid kit   gun   knife   lighter
mobile phone   pencil and paper   sun cream
toothbrush   towel

Let's take ... so that we can ...
I (don't) think we need a ... because ...
A ... will be useful for ...
I think we should also take ...
Good idea. / I'm not sure about that.

# Screen exports

**1 SPEAKING** Look at the photos. Do you know these TV programmes? What types of programmes do you think they are? Choose from the words below.

chat show    documentary    drama
sitcom    talent show    science fiction

A *Downton Abbey*

B *Doctor Who*

POLICE PUBLIC CALL BOX

C *Strictly Come Dancing*

**2** Read the text. Check your answers to exercise 1.

**3** Are the sentences true or false? Write T or F.

1 Countries around the world spend more than £1 billion a year on British TV programmes. ___
2 The finished programmes which the UK exports are all dramas. ___
3 In India and Iran, you can watch British people taking part in a cookery programme. ___
4 *Doctor Who* is popular in Turkey but not in most other countries. ___
5 *Heartbeat* is popular in Finland but not in most other countries. ___

**4** 🎧 **3.22** Listen to the information about *Top Gear*. What is the most important reason for the show's popularity?

**5** 🎧 **3.22** Listen again. Circle the correct answers.

1 *Top Gear* is popular in **170 / 350** different countries.
2 Most countries show **their own / the British** version of the programme.
3 The programme first appeared in **1977 / 1987**.
4 It began a new format in 2002 with **three / two** main presenters.
5 About **14 / 40** per cent of the viewers are female.
6 The 2002 format introduced a new **presenter / racing driver** called The Stig.

**6 SPEAKING** Ask and answer the questions in pairs.

1 Do you ever watch any of the shows mentioned in the text in exercise 2? What do you think of them?
2 In general, do you prefer programmes from your own country or other countries? Why?

# BRITISH TV around the world

🎧 **3.21**

Selling British TV programmes to countries around the world is an important industry for the UK. It brings in around £1.3 billion a year. The top countries for British TV exports are 1) the USA, 2) Sweden, 3) Denmark, 4) Germany and 5) Norway.

There are two main types of TV export: finished programmes and formats. When countries buy a finished programme, it is ready to broadcast on their own channels. When they buy a format, they are just buying the idea for a programme. They then have to make the programme in their own language and with people and places from their own countries.

Many of the finished programmes are dramas. For example, the historical drama *Downton Abbey* is very popular in many countries. *Midsomer Murders*, a detective drama from

1997, is still a huge favourite around the world. Wildlife documentaries are also an important export.

Popular British formats include several talent shows: *The X Factor* and *Strictly Come Dancing* are two well-known examples. Cookery programmes are very popular too. For example, local versions of *Masterchef* are on TV in more than forty different countries, including India and Iran.

Different TV shows are popular in different countries. For example, the science fiction show *Doctor Who* is very popular in Turkey and many other countries. But when a TV company in Finland bought the programme, audiences there did not like it at all. They prefer an old police drama called *Heartbeat*, which was popular in the UK twenty years ago and only sells to a few countries.

# 4 Culture

## The English language

**1 SPEAKING** Work in pairs. Where are you most likely to see or hear English words in your country?

**2** Read the information about the history of English. Are the sentences true or false? Write T or F.

1 Britain's first inhabitants spoke Latin. ___
2 Old English arrived from Norway and Denmark. ___
3 The Vikings invaded parts of Britain between about 800 and 1000 AD. ___
4 After 1066, most powerful and important people in Britain spoke French. ___
5 Over half of all English words come from French and Latin. ___

**3** Read the information again and answer the questions.

1 Where did the Saxons come from?
2 What language did the Romans bring?
3 Where did the Celtic speakers go after the Saxons arrived?
4 What language did the Vikings speak?
5 After 1066, which language did most ordinary people speak?
6 Which very common English word came from Celtic?
7 What percentage of English words come from Old English and Norse?

**4** 🎧 3.23 Listen to an interview about English as a global language. Which one of these topics do they not mention?

1 The future of English
2 The number of English speakers
3 How English became a global language
4 The influence of technology
5 Foreign words in English
6 The effect of English on other languages

**5** 🎧 3.23 Listen again. What is the significance of these numbers and dates?

1 the 18th and 19th centuries
2 1945
3 55%
4 335 million
5 1.5 billion
6 half a million
7 one hundred years from now

**6 SPEAKING** Work in pairs. Ask and answer the questions.

1 What are the benefits of being able to speak English for people in your country?
2 Does your language have words borrowed from English and other languages? Give examples.

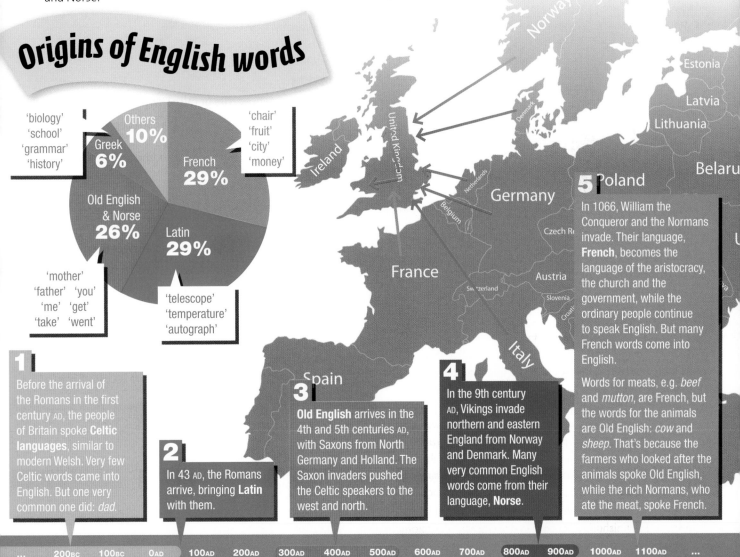

# Origins of English words

'biology'
'school'
'grammar'
'history'

Others **10%**

Greek **6%**

French **29%**

'chair'
'fruit'
'city'
'money'

Old English & Norse **26%**

Latin **29%**

'mother'
'father' 'you'
'me' 'get'
'take' 'went'

'telescope'
'temperature'
'autograph'

**1** Before the arrival of the Romans in the first century AD, the people of Britain spoke **Celtic languages**, similar to modern Welsh. Very few Celtic words came into English. But one very common one did: *dad*.

**2** In 43 AD, the Romans arrive, bringing **Latin** with them.

**3** **Old English** arrives in the 4th and 5th centuries AD, with Saxons from North Germany and Holland. The Saxon invaders pushed the Celtic speakers to the west and north.

**4** In the 9th century AD, Vikings invade northern and eastern England from Norway and Denmark. Many very common English words come from their language, **Norse**.

**5** Poland

In 1066, William the Conqueror and the Normans invade. Their language, **French**, becomes the language of the aristocracy, the church and the government, while the ordinary people continue to speak English. But many French words come into English.

Words for meats, e.g. *beef* and *mutton*, are French, but the words for the animals are Old English: *cow* and *sheep*. That's because the farmers who looked after the animals spoke Old English, while the rich Normans, who ate the meat, spoke French.

... 200BC 100BC 0AD 100AD 200AD 300AD 400AD 500AD 600AD 700AD 800AD 900AD 1000AD 1100AD ...

# 5 Culture
## British entrepreneurs

**1 SPEAKING** Look at the photo. Are there Body Shop stores in your country? What do they sell?

**2** Complete the text about British entrepreneur Anita Roddick. Write one appropriate word for each gap.

🎧 3.24

# Anita Roddick

Anita Perilli was born in 1942 in Littlehampton, a seaside town ¹_____ the south of England. Her parents were from Italy and ran a café. After leaving school, she trained ²_____ an English teacher, but before finding a job, she decided to travel round the world, working in a number of different countries. When she got back ³_____ Britain, her mother introduced her to a young Scottish man called Gordon Roddick. They fell in love immediately and ⁴_____ married. Together, they opened a restaurant and a small hotel in Anita's home town. They had two daughters and moved to Brighton, also on the south coast.

It was there in 1976 that Anita Roddick opened the first Body Shop store. Her husband was travelling in South America and she needed to earn money to support her young family. She wanted ⁵_____ sell cosmetics and skin-care products that were natural and not tested on animals. She also recycled the bottles ⁶_____ contained her products: customers could bring them back to the shop and refill them. 'Businesses have the power to do good,' she said. She opened a second shop six months ⁷_____ and by 1991, there were seven hundred Body Shop stores. By 2004, the Body Shop had over two thousand stores with 71 million customers in 51 countries.

Anita Roddick was passionate about social and environmental issues. She gave money ⁸_____ many charities, including Greenpeace and Amnesty International, and she campaigned for them too. She joined anti-globalisation protests and was very critical of big oil companies that did not invest in renewable energy.

Towards the end ⁹_____ her life, she sold Body Shop to the world's largest cosmetics company, L'Oréal. Many of her customers felt betrayed. But she gave away most ¹⁰_____ her money to charities. She died in 2007 at the age of 64.

**3** Read the text again. Answer the questions.

1 Where were Roddick's parents from?
2 What did she do immediately after leaving school?
3 What businesses did she and her husband run together?
4 Where was her husband when she opened the first Body Shop store?
5 What was different about the ingredients in Body Shop products?
6 Why did some of her customers feel betrayed?

**4** 🎧 3.25 Listen to a radio programme about Richard Branson, another British entrepreneur. Put the businesses in the order that Branson started them.

a airline ___
b mail-order record company ___
c mobile phone company ___
d recording studio ___
e space tourism company ___
f student magazine ___
g train company ___

**5** 🎧 3.25 Listen again. Are the sentences true or false? Write T or F.

1 Branson's head teacher made a correct prediction about Branson's future. ___
2 Branson was unable to attract famous bands to his record company. ___
3 He still owns his record company. ___
4 He has broken two world records. ___
5 Branson has set up a space tourism company. ___

**6 SPEAKING** Work in pairs. Ask and answer the questions.

1 What nationality are the entrepreneurs below? What are they famous for?

Roman Abramovich   Coco Chanel
Simon Cowell   Walt Disney   Henry Ford
Bill Gates   Steve Jobs

> Where is Bill Gates from and what is he famous for?

> He's American. He founded Microsoft.

2 Do you know of any entrepreneurs from your country? What are they famous for?

# 6 Culture

## Alcatraz

**1 SPEAKING** Look at the photo of the island of Alcatraz. Choose the correct answers.

1 Which country is it in?
   a the USA  b Britain  c Australia
2 What was it used for in the past?
   a a holiday resort  b a prison  c a private house
3 What is it today?
   a a government building  b a water sports centre
   c a tourist attraction

**2** Read the text and check your answers to exercise 1.

> 🎧 3.26
>
> Alcatraz is a small, rocky island in San Francisco Bay in the USA. It is 2.4 km from the shore and the sea around the island is very dangerous. The water is very cold and there are fast, strong currents. In the 19th century, the American government realised it was the ideal place to put dangerous prisoners, because it is very difficult to reach and even more difficult to escape from. So they built a prison on the island and from the 1930s to the 1960s it was the toughest prison in the USA. Over 1,500 prisoners stayed on the island, including America's most violent bank robbers and murderers. The most famous prisoner was the gangster Al Capone. But the prison was never full and it was very expensive to run, so the government finally decided to close it. Alcatraz became a museum and is now one of San Francisco's most popular tourist attractions, with more than one and a half million visitors a year.

**3 VOCABULARY** Find adjectives in the text in exercise 2 with the opposite meaning to the ones below.

**Opposites** cheap  easy  empty  hot  large  safe
slow  unpopular  weak

**4** Read the text again and answer the questions.

1 How far is Alcatraz from the coast?
2 Why is it dangerous to try to swim to or from the island?
3 For about how long was the island a prison?

4 Who was Alcatraz's most famous prisoner?
5 Why did the government decide to close it?
6 How many people visit Alcatraz every year?

**5 🎧 3.27** Listen to an interview. Are the sentences true or false? Write T or F.

1 Danny works at Alcatraz. ___
2 It was impossible to escape from Alcatraz but life was not too bad for the prisoners. ___
3 No prisoners ever tried to escape. ___

**6 🎧 3.27** Listen again and choose the correct answers.

1 The presenter is surprised that
   a black prisoners were separated from white prisoners.
   b the cell isn't very big.
   c there was so little furniture in the cells.
2 If the prisoners weren't well-behaved,
   a they had to stay in their cells during the day.
   b they had to work very hard.
   c they had to tidy all the cells.
3 The prisoners could
   a go outside for an hour a day.
   b play sports only on Saturdays and Sundays.
   c play instruments in their cell.
4 How many prisoners certainly died while trying to escape from Alcatraz?
   a 2  b 6  c 8
5 Danny thinks that the other five prisoners
   a successfully escaped.
   b were found by the FBI.
   c probably died while trying to escape.

**7** Make notes about a famous tourist attraction in your country. Use the questions below to help you.

• Where is it?
• When was it built?
• Why is it famous?
• What can you do / see there?

**8 SPEAKING** Tell the class about the tourist attraction.

# Wall Street

**1 SPEAKING** Look at the photo of people working at the New York Stock Exchange. What do you imagine their jobs are like? Use some of the adjectives below.

creative   challenging   repetitive   rewarding
stressful   tiring   varied   well-paid

🎧 3.28

Wall Street is a street ¹___ New York City's financial district. People also use Wall Street to mean the whole financial district. The Dutch gave the street ²___ name. They built a wall there to protect the area from the British in the 17th century.

Wall Street is one of the main financial centres in the world, ³___ with London, Hong Kong and Tokyo. The New York Stock Exchange opens every morning at 9:30 a.m. and closes at 4 p.m. The ⁴___ for opening and closing is a bell and they often invite a celebrity to ring it.

In the early part of the 20th century, Wall Street was the centre of the financial world. Millions of people wanted to invest money in the New York Stock Exchange because it was ⁵___ so well. Their money grew and grew and investors became rich. It seemed ⁶___ good to be true – and it was.

The Wall Street Crash began on 24 October 1929. The value of investments started to fall and soon everybody wanted to get their money back. Investors panicked and the situation got ⁷___ . The New York Stock Exchange lost 89% of its value very quickly and caused the worst global depression in history.

**2 USE OF ENGLISH** Read the text about the New York Stock Exchange. Circle the correct words to complete the text.

| | | | | | |
|---|---|---|---|---|---|
| 1 | **a** at | **b** in | **c** on |
| 2 | **a** its | **b** it's | **c** their |
| 3 | **a** also | **b** moreover | **c** together |
| 4 | **a** alarm | **b** signal | **c** symbol |
| 5 | **a** becoming | **b** being | **c** doing |
| 6 | **a** enough | **b** more | **c** too |
| 7 | **a** badly | **b** worse | **c** worst |

**3** Answer the questions about the text.

1 What two meanings are there for 'Wall Street'?
2 What are the opening hours of the New York Stock Exchange?
3 Was the Stock Exchange doing better before or after 1929?
4 What happened to the Stock Exchange on 24 October 1929?

**4** In pairs, study the infographic about the Great Depression. How many different pieces of information does it show?

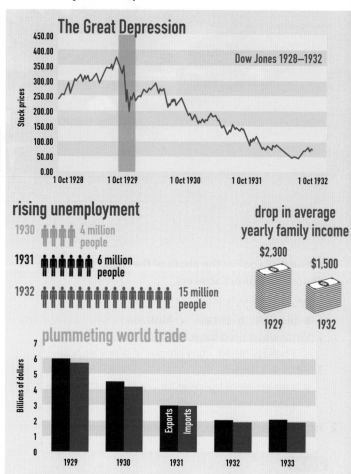

**5** 🎧 **3.29** Listen to the information about the Great Depression. Which two pieces of information from the infographic are not mentioned?

**6** 🎧 **3.29** Listen again. Make a note of a piece of information from the recording that is not in the infographic.

**7** Work in pairs. Decide how you could show the pieces of information you wrote down in exercise 6 on an infographic like the one in exercise 4. Then compare your ideas with other pairs.

**8 SPEAKING** Read the quotations about money. In pairs, decide if you agree or disagree. Give reasons.

'The love of **money** is the root of all evil.'

'The lack of **money** is the root of all evil.'

'Time is more valuable than **money**. You can get more **money** but you cannot get more time.'

'Too many people spend **money** they haven't earned, to buy things they don't want, to impress people they don't like.'

# Sherlock Holmes

SHERLOCK HOLMES

**1 SPEAKING** Look at the picture of Sherlock Holmes below. Describe his appearance using the words below to help you. What do you know about him? Can you describe his character?

coat   deerstalker hat   examine
magnifying glass   pipe

**2** Do the Sherlock Holmes quiz.

**1** When were the Sherlock Holmes stories written?
  **a** between 1847 and 1887
  **b** between 1887 and 1927
  **c** between 1927 and 1967

**2** Who wrote the stories?
  **a** Agatha Christie
  **b** Stephen King
  **c** Arthur Conan Doyle

**3** What is the name of Holmes's assistant?
  **a** Dr Watson   **b** Mr Watson   **c** Professor Watson

**4** What is Holmes's address in London?
  **a** 221b Bank Street
  **b** 221b Bond Street
  **c** 221b Baker Street

**5** Who is Holmes's worst enemy?
  **a** Professor Moriarty   **b** Mrs Baker   **c** Irene Adler

**6** What musical instrument does Holmes play?
  **a** trumpet   **b** guitar   **c** violin

**7** What was Watson's job before he met Holmes?
  **a** army officer   **b** teacher   **c** lawyer

**8** What is Holmes's most famous line?
  **a** I've got it, Watson!
  **b** Elementary, my dear Watson!
  **c** Simple, Watson!

**3** Read the fact file and check your answers to the quiz in exercise 2.

**4** 🎧 **3.31** Listen to an interview with a TV and film critic. Complete each sentence with one word.

**1** The character of Holmes has been played by at least _____ different actors.
**2** Holmes's personality is what makes the stories _____ .
**3** His coldness and lack of sympathy are evidence of a _____ side to his character.
**4** When Holmes is feeling depressed, he sometimes goes to _____ .
**5** In *Elementary*, the American TV drama, Watson is a _____ .
**6** In the original stories, Holmes isn't interested in women, but in *Elementary*, he has _____ .

**5 VOCABULARY** Below is a list of qualities that Sherlock Holmes possesses. Check the meanings and put them into two groups, positive and negative.

**Personality adjectives** arrogant  brave  cold  confident  curious  cynical  easily bored  imaginative  intelligent  logical  observant  proud  stubborn  unemotional  unsympathetic  vain

**6** 🎧 **3.31** Listen again. Write down the qualities in exercise 5 that the film critic mentions.

**7 SPEAKING** Work in pairs. Discuss the questions. Give reasons for your opinions.

**1** Have you read any Sherlock Holmes stories, or seen any on television or in the cinema? Did you enjoy them? What happens in the stories?
**2** Do you like reading crime stories or watching crime dramas on TV? Which ones are popular in your country?

**8 INTERNET RESEARCH** Find out about a famous fictional detective. Describe his / her appearance and personality. Say why you like or dislike his / her personality.

🎧 **3.30**

# SHERLOCK HOLMES: FACT FILE

* The author of the Sherlock Holmes stories was Arthur Conan Doyle (1859–1930). He was born in Scotland and studied medicine at Edinburgh University. He worked as a doctor but in his spare time he wrote detective stories.

* He wrote the first Sherlock Holmes story in 1887. His detective hero lives at 221b Baker Street in London.

* Holmes is tall and thin, with a long, sharp face. He usually wears a deerstalker hat, smokes a pipe or cigarettes, and carries a magnifying glass. He is extremely intelligent and is a brilliant violinist.

* Holmes's assistant is Dr Watson, an ex-army officer. Watson is less intelligent than Holmes. In one Sherlock Holmes film, when Watson asks Holmes how he solved a crime, Holmes's famous reply is 'Elementary, my dear Watson!'

* Holmes's greatest enemy is Professor Moriarty. At the end of one story, they both die. But Doyle's fans were so upset that he had to bring Holmes back to life in another story!

# Computer pioneers

Enigma machine

**1 SPEAKING** Look at the photos above and below and the title of the text. Guess the answers to these questions.

1 What is the large machine in the photo for?
2 What is the smaller machine for?
3 What period of history are the machines from?

**2** Read the text. Find out the answers to the questions in exercise 1.

# CODE-BREAKERS

The Bombe

🎧 3.32

During the 1930s, German military power was increasing. Its neighbours – in particular, Poland and France – were becoming more and more worried about the danger of an invasion. In Poland, a team of brilliant young mathematicians worked hard to break Germany's military codes. It was difficult because the Germans used a complex machine called Enigma to send and receive their codes. But by 1938, the Polish team could understand 75% of Germany's secret messages. This was mainly thanks to an invention by Marian Rejewski called the *bomba*. However, that year, the Germans changed their Enigma machines and made the codes far more difficult to break. As World War II began, the Polish team shared their ideas about Enigma with British and French code-breakers.

**3** Put the events in the order they happened, according to the text.

a Marian Rejewski worked as an accountant. ___
b Alan Turing invented the Bombe computer. ___
c World War II began. ___
d Marian Rejewski invented a machine for breaking codes. ___
e Marian Rejewski spoke publicly about his code-breaking work. ___
f A group of code-breakers started work at Bletchley Park. ___
g World War II ended. ___

**4** In pairs, discuss the following question. Give reasons for your answer.

Which happened first, do you think: the first computer was built or the first computer program was written?

**5** 🎧 3.33 Listen to the information about Ada Lovelace. What is the answer to the question in exercise 4?

**6** 🎧 3.33 Listen again. Are the sentences true or false? Write T or F.

1 Ada Lovelace grew up with a famous writer. ___
2 As a child, Lovelace showed no particular ability at maths. ___
3 Charles Babbage designed complex machines but didn't finish building them. ___
4 Lovelace realised that Babbage's invention could do complex calculations by following a program. ___
5 Lovelace described the idea behind computer programs but she did not actually write one. ___
6 Ada is now the name of a type of computer. ___

**7 INTERNET RESEARCH** Find out five more facts about Bletchley Park and the people who worked there during World War II. Then share your information with the class.

A team of code-breakers – men and women – worked at a secret location in the south of England: Bletchley Park. They included Alan Turing, a mathematician with an interest in computing. At Bletchley Park, he designed an early form of computer which they called the Bombe. (It was based on Rejewski's design.) They used it to help break complex codes. Compared to today's computers, the Bombe was huge and not very powerful. But at the time, it was some of the most advanced technology in the world. It made the work of the code-breakers much faster.

Marian Rejewski worked as a code-breaker in Britain during the war. In 1946, he returned to Poland and worked as an accountant. He kept his code-breaking work secret from everybody until 1967! But today, his work is celebrated each year at Bletchley Park.

# V Vocabulary Builder

## Introduction

### IA Sports and hobbies

**1** Match the icons with eight of the sports and hobbies below.

basketball   board games   bowling   chess   cycling
dancing   drama   drawing   football   gymnastics
ice hockey   ice skating   listening to music   skateboarding
swimming   video games   volleyball   watching films

**2** Which sports and hobbies from exercise 1 can you do ...

**a** on your own?   **b** at home?   **c** in a team?

### IC Clothes

**3** Look at the pictures and complete the descriptions. Use the words below.

boots   cardigan   coat   dress   gloves   hat   hoodie
jacket   jeans   leggings   scarf   shirt   shoes   shorts
skirt   socks   sweater   sweatshirt   T-shirt   tie   top
tracksuit   trainers   trousers

**A** Mia is wearing ...        **B** Luke is wearing ...

**C** Georgia is wearing ...      **D** Ben is wearing ...

**4** Write which clothes from exercise 3 you are wearing now.

## Unit 1

### 1G *get*

> **LEARN THIS!** Basic meanings of *get*
>
> The verb *get* has several basic meanings.
>
> **a** to receive – *What did you get for your birthday?*
>
> **b** to buy or collect – *He went out to get a newspaper.*
>
> **c** to catch or take (transport) – *Which train did she get?*
>
> **d** to arrive – *We got home at midnight.*
>
> **e** to become – *I'm getting hungry.*

**1** Complete the sentences with the correct form of *get*. In your notebook, match the sentences to the correct basic meaning (a–e) in the **Learn this!** box.

1 It was dark when we _____ to the hotel. ___
2 It was too far to walk so we decided to _____ a taxi. ___
3 We live on the equator, so it _____ dark at the same time every evening. ___
4 On the way to the hospital yesterday, we _____ some flowers for my aunt. ___
5 My brother is really excited because he _____ a new phone for his birthday. ___

**2** Write one more example for each basic meaning (a–e) of *get*.

### 1H Phrasal verbs and register

> **LEARN THIS!**
>
> **a** Most phrasal verbs are neutral in register, neither formal nor informal.
>
> *I woke up at seven, got out of bed and turned on the radio.*
>
> **b** Some phrasal verbs have more formal equivalents.
>
> *They put off the match until next Saturday.*
>
> *They postponed the match until next Saturday.*

**3** Rewrite the sentences using the phrasal verbs below. Use the correct tense and form.

carry on   come back   get away   give back   look up to
make up   put up with   run after   talk about

1 My sister often invents funny stories.
2 The robbers escaped in a stolen car.
3 The dog chased the cat.
4 I respect my older sister.
5 Please continue reading.
6 I won't tolerate your rudeness any longer!
7 Please return the money when you can.
8 My teacher wants to discuss my exam results with my parents.
9 My grandad went to live in Australia but returned to Britain twenty years later.

# V Vocabulary Builder

## Unit 2

### 2G Sports clothing and equipment

1 Match the items (1–12) in the photos with the words below. Check the meaning of all the words.

ball  bat  boots  gloves  goal  goggles  helmet
hoop  mask  net  puck  racket  rope  running shoes
safety harness  shirt  shorts  skates  socks
stick  surfboard  swimming trunks (men) /
swimming costume (women)  vest  wetsuit

2 Put the words in exercise 1 into two groups: *clothing* and *equipment*.

*Clothing: gloves, … Equipment: rope, …*

3 Match at least three of the words in exercise 1 with each of the sports below.

basketball  climbing  football  surfing

*basketball: shorts, …*

### 2H Outdoor activities

4 Which of the activities below usually take place a) in water, b) in the air, c) in the street and d) in the mountains?

bungee jumping  camping  canoeing  cycling
hang-gliding  hiking  karting  paddleboarding
riding  rollerblading  snorkelling  walking  windsurfing

5 Decide which activities in exercise 4 you would like to do. Which would you not like to do? Why?

*I wouldn't like to do bungee jumping. I think it's scary.*

## Unit 3

### 3G Expressing likes and dislikes

1 Complete the sentences using the prepositions below. One sentence does not need a preposition.

about  for  for  in  of  on  about

1 My sister isn't **keen** _____ video games.
2 When I was young, I wasn't **interested** _____ sport.
3 Lucy isn't a big **fan** _____ horror films.
4 My parents **can't stand** _____ loud music.
5 I like comedy but I can't get **excited** _____ sitcoms.
6 Hailey doesn't **go** _____ combat games, but she likes driving games.
7 My cousin is **mad** _____ vampire films.
8 My best friend is always **up** _____ a trip to the cinema.

2 Use the bold phrases in exercise 1 (including the correct prepositions) to write your own opinions about the things below.

going bowling  watching horror films
going out for dinner  playing board games  cooking

### 3H Social activities

> **LEARN THIS!**
> a go to the park / the cinema / the shopping centre / a café / a restaurant / a friend's house
> b go for a walk / a run / a bike ride
> c go out for lunch / dinner / a coffee / the day / the evening
> d go dancing / skating / skateboarding / rollerblading
> e watch TV / a DVD / a film
> f play video games / volleyball / tennis

3 Study the Learn this! box. Then use the underlined verbs to complete the phrases below. Use each verb once.

1 _____ a meal
2 _____ swimming
3 _____ the beach
4 _____ a talent show
5 _____ board games
6 _____ a jog

4 SPEAKING Work in pairs. Find out what your partner does at weekends. Ask and answer about the activities in the Learn this! box and exercise 3.

Do you ever go to the cinema at weekends?

Yes, I do. / No, I don't. / Not very often.

# Vocabulary Builder

## Unit 4

### 4G In the street

**1** Are all of the things below in the picture?

billboard   bus stop   fire hydrant   parking meter
pedestrian crossing   phone box   postbox   road sign
roadworks   rubbish bin   shop sign   shop window
street lamp   telegraph pole   traffic lights

**2** **SPEAKING** In pairs, ask and answer about the picture in exercise 1. Use *next to*, *behind*, *in front of* and *between* in your answers.

> Where's the fire hydrant?

> It's next to the rubbish bin. / It's in front of the billboard.

### 4H Climate change

**3** Complete the collocations with the verbs.

emit   rely on   ~~use up~~

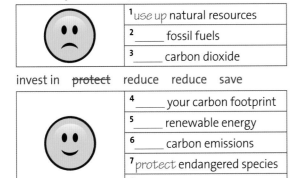

| | |
|---|---|
| 1 | *use up* natural resources |
| 2 | _____ fossil fuels |
| 3 | _____ carbon dioxide |

invest in   ~~protect~~   reduce   reduce   save

| | |
|---|---|
| 4 | _____ your carbon footprint |
| 5 | _____ renewable energy |
| 6 | _____ carbon emissions |
| 7 | *protect* endangered species |
| 8 | _____ energy |

**4** Complete the sentences with the correct form of collocations from exercise 3.

1 The government should _____ such as wind and solar power.
2 You can _____ by insulating your house, turning off lights and using public transport.
3 At the moment, we _____ such as coal, shale gas and oil to give us energy.
4 Factories _____ and other greenhouse gases into the atmosphere.
5 How can we _____ such as orang-utans, gorillas and tigers?
6 If we don't _____ , the amount of $CO_2$ in the atmosphere will go up.

## Unit 5

### 5G Personal qualities

**1** Match the adjectives with the descriptions of the people.

~~confident~~   enthusiastic   friendly   good at communicating
honest   physically fit   sensitive

1 She feels sure that she can do the job well.  *confident*
2 He smiles and talks to everyone at work. _____
3 She's good at explaining things to people. _____
4 He always tells the truth. _____
5 She's always excited and interested in new ideas. _____
6 He is active and strong. _____
7 She understands other people's feelings. _____

~~flexible~~   hard-working   organised   outgoing   patient
punctual   reliable

8 He doesn't mind if things change at work.  *flexible*
9 She plans her work very well. _____
10 He always arrives at work on time. _____
11 She likes being with other people. _____
12 He works very hard. _____
13 You can trust her to do her job well. _____
14 He doesn't mind waiting. _____

**2** How many adjectives do you know with the opposite meanings of those in exercise 1? You can use the prefixes *un-*, *dis-*, *in-* and *im-* with some of them.

*patient – impatient, hard-working – …*

**3** **SPEAKING** Which adjectives in exercise 1 a) describe you and b) do not describe you?

> I'm very … and I'm sometimes …

> I'm not very …

### 5H Formal language

**4** Replace the underlined words in the sentences with the more formal words below.

available   discuss   manager   many   obtain   opportunity
possess   require   sit   succeed   telephone   wish

1 Please <u>call</u> me if you <u>need</u> more information.
2 I can <u>get</u> a reference from my current <u>boss</u>.
3 I <u>have got</u> the personal qualities that are necessary to <u>do well</u> in business.
4 I <u>do</u> my exams in June and will be <u>free</u> to start work immediately afterwards.
5 There are <u>lots of</u> reasons why I <u>would like</u> to become a teacher.
6 I would be grateful for the <u>chance</u> to <u>chat about</u> my application in person.

# Vocabulary Builder

## Unit 6

### 6G City tourism

**1** Put the words below in the correct groups, A, B or C.

boat trip   ~~bus fare~~   day trip   excursion
fish and chip shop   food van   ~~open-top bus tour~~
restaurant   route   sandwich bar   ~~street café~~   tea room
timetable   travel pass   travel zone   walking tour

**A** Places to eat: *street café*, …
**B** Organised sightseeing: *open-top bus tour*, …
**C** Getting around: *bus fare*, …

**2** Complete the sentences with words from exercise 1.

1 The _____ is valid for one day on all buses and underground trains.
2 Can I have a _____ with bus and tram times, please?
3 You can get takeaway burgers at the _____ in the main square. But they close and drive away at about 11 p.m.
4 You get the best views of the city if you take the _____ . It leaves every 30 minutes from the bus station.
5 You must have the correct _____ when you get on. The driver won't give you change.
6 This ticket is only valid in two of the nine _____ in London.
7 If you want traditional British food, try the _____ on Queen Street.
8 Make sure you're wearing comfortable shoes if you're planning to go on a _____ of the city.
9 I recommend taking a _____ on the river.

### 6H Holiday activities

**3** Complete the phrases with the verbs below.

eat   buy   go   go   hire   lie   play   visit

| Holiday activities |
| --- |
| 1 _____ a museum / a castle / a cathedral / a theme park / a water park |
| 2 _____ shopping / swimming / cycling / surfing / kayaking / abseiling / mountain biking |
| 3 _____ for a walk / for a bike ride / on an excursion / on a boat trip / up a tower |
| 4 _____ a bike / a kayak / a car / a boat |
| 5 _____ table tennis / beach volleyball / cards / board games |
| 6 _____ on the beach |
| 7 _____ out |
| 8 _____ souvenirs |

**4** **SPEAKING** Work in pairs. Ask and answer about the activities in exercise 3. Find three you both like and three neither of you like.

> Do you like visiting museums?

> No, I don't. Do you?

## Unit 7

### 7G In school

**1** Match pictures 1–5 with five of the places below.

canteen   classroom   corridor   gym   hall   library
head teacher's office   language lab   playground
playing field   reception   science lab   staff room
stairs   store room   toilets

**2** Choose six of the places in exercise 1 and say where they are in your school. Use the examples below to help you.

*The staff room is on the first floor, next to the language lab.*
*The gym is at the end of the corridor on the ground floor.*
*There's a store room near the stairs opposite reception.*

### 7H Money: prepositions

**3** Complete the sentences with the prepositions below. You need to use some prepositions more than once.

for   from   in   off   on   to

1 How much did you spend _____ those trainers?
2 I'm saving up _____ some new clothes.
3 You shouldn't lend money _____ friends. It can cause arguments!
4 Don't worry – my mum is paying _____ everything.
5 I don't want to borrow money because I don't like being _____ debt.
6 Use this coupon to get £1 _____ your next sandwich.
7 How much do they charge _____ a haircut?
8 I borrowed some money _____ my brother.
9 Don't waste money _____ a new phone – your old one is fine.
10 The company owes thousands of pounds _____ the bank.
11 They'll replace the battery in your phone _____ £35.

**4** **SPEAKING** In pairs, talk about:

- what you spend your money on.
- something you would like to save up for.
- the best person to borrow money from.

# V Vocabulary Builder

## Unit 8

### 8G Describing people

**1** Put the words below in the correct group: A or B.

a beard    curly / straight / wavy hair    earrings
eyebrows    a moustache    a necklace    plaits
a ponytail    sunglasses    a scarf

**A** hair    **B** accessories

**2** Describe the people in the photos. Use as many words from exercise 1 as you can.

### 8H Preposition + noun phrases

> **LEARN THIS!**
> Some nouns are used in phrases with a fixed preposition.
> *travel by car, plane*, etc.    *go on holiday    be in a hurry*

**3** Read the Learn this! box. Then complete the phrases. Use the prepositions below.

at    by    for    in    on    on    on    on

1 go _____ an excursion
2 do something _____ mistake
3 be _____ the phone
4 go _____ a walk
5 _____ the morning
6 _____ night
7 _____ Friday afternoon
8 go _____ foot

**4** Complete the sentences with a preposition + noun phrase from the Learn this! box or exercise 3.

1 Jess is _____ . She's talking to her cousin in Canada.
2 We went _____ to Greece last year. We stayed in a villa by the sea.
3 I go _____ every morning with the dogs. We usually walk around the park.
4 My cat goes out _____ and sleeps all day.
5 Sorry, I can't stop to talk to you now. I'm _____ !
6 While we were in London, we went _____ to Oxford.
7 I took my sister's phone _____ – they look the same.

## Unit 9

### 9G Gadgets

**1** Match six of the gadgets below with pictures A–C. Check the meaning of all the words.

Blu-ray player    camcorder    digital camera    digital radio
digital photo frame    DVD player    e-book reader
games console    hard disk recorder    headphones
laptop    mobile    MP3 player    satnav    smart TV
(solar-powered) battery charger    tablet    wireless speakers

**2** Read the sentences below. Which gadget is each person talking about?

1 'It connects to the internet so I can watch films and TV programmes online.'
2 'I can record my favourite TV programmes and watch them later. It can store about 100 programmes.'
3 'Dad has one – Mum gave it to him for Christmas. But he never uses it. He prefers to use maps.'
4 'I use them with my smartphone. They're quite small so I can take them anywhere and the sound quality is really good.'
5 'I can store hundreds of books on it. Much easier than carrying them around with me!'

> **LEARN THIS! Conjunctions**
> When we join two clauses together, we use a conjunction. Common conjunctions in English include *and, but, because, if, even if, so, or* and *although*.

### 9H Conjunctions

**3** Choose the correct conjunction (a–c) to complete the sentences. Use a dictionary to help you if necessary.

If there were no cars, lorries, vans etc. in the world, ...
1 You couldn't travel long distances ___ you went by public transport.
  **a** rather than    **b** so    **c** unless
2 You would probably shop locally ___ going to a big supermarket.
  **a** rather than    **b** although    **c** but
3 The motorways would be empty ___ you could cycle on them safely.
  **a** as    **b** because    **c** so
4 We would eat more food from our local area ___ it would be difficult to transport it from other places.
  **a** so    **b** since    **c** although

# Grammar Builder

## IB Contrast: present simple and continuous

**1** Complete the sentences with the present simple affirmative form of the verbs below. ➡ I.1, I.2

go   have   live   miss   play   study   visit   watch

1 My aunt _____ in Scotland.
2 Carl _____ his grandparents every weekend.
3 Audrey _____ TV in her bedroom every evening.
4 My mum's a scientist: she _____ climate change.
5 Brooklyn _____ the piano really well.
6 My cousin _____ to school in Switzerland.
7 Now that she's at secondary school, she _____ her old teachers from primary school.
8 Grace _____ double maths every Tuesday.

**2** Make the sentences negative. ➡ I.1

1 Sophie has a guitar lesson every Saturday.
   *Sophie doesn't have a guitar lesson every Saturday.*
2 My cat likes cheese.
3 Jack and Ellie live near the city centre.
4 Maya goes bowling every weekend.
5 My next-door neighbours work in London.
6 Amelia wears sports clothes at home.

**3** Look at the picture and correct the sentences. Use the verbs in brackets. ➡ I.3, I.4

1 The woman in a dress is cooking. (eat)
   *She isn't cooking. She's eating.*
2 The old man is reading. (sleep)
3 The two girls are skateboarding. (read)
4 The dog is drinking water. (play)
5 The man with the hat is washing. (cook)
6 The two boys are playing volleyball. (chat)

**4** Circle the correct tense. ➡ I.5, I.6, I.7

1 Cats **sleep** / **are sleeping** for about sixteen hours a day.
2 Mason **walks** / **is walking** to school every day.
3 Jack and Emily **don't belong** / **aren't belonging** to our sports club.
4 Don't forget your scarf – **it snows** / **it's snowing**.
5 **I meet** / **I'm meeting** Paul for a coffee this afternoon.
6 Why **do you wear** / **are you wearing** shorts? It's cold today!
7 He's laughing, but he **doesn't understand** / **isn't understanding** the joke.
8 Let's continue with the game. **I have** / **I'm having** fun!

**5** Complete the dialogue. Use the correct present simple or present continuous form of the verbs in brackets. ➡ I.5, I.6, I.7

**Ryan**  Hi, Ava. What **1**_____ (you / do)?
**Ava**   I **2**_____ (look) for a present for Laura.
         I **3**_____ (go) to her party tomorrow night.
**Ryan**  Me too. But I **4**_____ usually _____ (not buy) her a birthday present.
**Ava**   I **5**_____ (want) to get her something.
         **6**_____ (she / like) DVDs?
**Ryan**  She **7**_____ (prefer) books, I think. She **8**_____ (read) the *Twilight* novels at the moment. Maybe she would like a new one.
**Ava**   Great idea. Thanks!

## ID Articles

**6** Complete the sentences with *a / an*, *the* or no article. ➡ I.8, I.9, I.10, I.11

1 There's ___ zoo and ___ wildlife park near my home, but ___ wildlife park isn't open in the winter.
2 Don't use ___ DVD player, it's broken.
3 Can you pass me my sunglasses, please? They're on ___ table.
4 I've got ___ computer and ___ laptop, but I have to share ___ laptop with my brother.
5 My sister is at ___ home. She's playing ___ guitar.
6 My dad is ___ teacher and my mum is ___ doctor.
7 There's ___ CD player in my room so I can lie in ___ bed and listen to ___ music.
8 Do you want to go to ___ cinema this evening, or watch ___ TV at ___ home?

**7** Complete the sentences with *the* or no article. Remember: we do not use *the* with generalisations. ➡ I.12

1 Children need ___ milk for healthy teeth and bones.
2 I love the UK, but I don't like ___ weather here.
3 On holiday, I prefer to stay in ___ nice hotels.
4 I'm not a sports fan, but ___ table tennis is fun.
5 It's freezing, but the children are enjoying ___ snow.
6 At school, students learn how to use ___ computers.
7 I'm not interested in ___ science fiction films.
8 These dancers are great but I don't really like ___ music.

# Grammar Reference

## Present simple

**I.1**

| Affirmative | Negative | Questions |
|---|---|---|
| I work | I don't work | Do I work?<br>Yes, I do. / No, I don't. |
| you work | you don't work | Do you work?<br>Yes, you do. / No, you don't. |
| he / she / it works | he / she / it doesn't work | Does he / she / it work?<br>Yes, he does. / No, it doesn't. |
| we / you / they work | we / you / they don't work | Do we / you / they work?<br>Yes, we do. / No, you don't. |

**I.2 Spelling: 3rd person singular (*he / she / it*)**
We add -*s* to the end of most verbs.
+ -*s*:   start → starts    play → plays

We add -*es* if the verb ends in -*ch*, -*ss*, -*sh* or -*o*.
+ -*es*:   teach → teaches    miss → misses
          do → does          go → goes

If the verb ends in a consonant + -*y*, we change -*y* to -*i* and add -*es*.
-*y* → -*ies*:   study → studies    carry → carries

The 3rd person singular form of *have* is *has*.

## Present continuous

**I.3** We form the present continuous with the present simple form of *be* and an -*ing* form:

| Affirmative | Negative | Questions |
|---|---|---|
| I'm playing | I'm not playing | Am I playing?<br>Yes, I am. / No, I'm not. |
| you're playing | you aren't playing | Are you playing?<br>Yes, you are. / No, you aren't. |
| he's / she's / it's playing | he / she / it isn't playing | Is he / she / it playing?<br>Yes, he is. / No, she isn't. |
| we're / you're / they're playing | we / you / they aren't playing | Are we / you / they playing?<br>Yes, we are. / No, you aren't. |

**I.4** To form the -*ing* form, we add -*ing* to the end of most verbs.
+ -*ing*:   work → working    study → studying

With most verbs ending in -*e*, we drop the -*e* and add -*ing*.
-*e* → -*ing*:   dance → dancing    write → writing

But if the verb ends in -*ee*, we simply add -*ing*.
+ -*ing*:   agree → agreeing    see → seeing

And if the verb ends in -*ie*, we change the -*ie* to -*y* and add -*ing*.
-*ie* → -*ying*:   die → dying    lie → lying

If the verb ends in a short accented vowel + a consonant, we double the consonant and add -*ing*.
-*p* → -*pping*:   drop → dropping
-*n* → -*nning*:   plan → planning
-*t* → -*tting*:   chat → chatting

## Contrast: present simple and present continuous

**I.5** We use the present simple:
- for something that always happens or happens regularly (e.g. every week, often, sometimes).
  *Tamer cycles to school every day.*
- for facts.
  *Cows eat grass.*

**I.6** We use the present continuous for:
- something happening at this exact moment or around this time.
  *Dan is wearing a T-shirt.* (at this moment)
  *Dan is working hard this term.* (around this time)
- for future arrangements.
  *We're playing volleyball tomorrow.*

**I.7** We don't use the present continuous with certain verbs. Their meaning is usually connected with a state rather than an action. They include:
- *hate, like, love, need, prefer, want, wish*
- *believe, know, mean, realise, recognise, remember, suppose, understand*
- *belong, contain, depend, matter, owe, possess*

I don't understand the task. ✓
NOT I'm not understanding the task. ✗

## Articles

**I.8** We use *a* when we talk about something for the first time. We use *the* if we mention it again.
I've got *a* cat and *a* dog. *The* cat is black and white.

**I.9** We use *the* when it is clear what we are talking about, perhaps because there is only one of them.
Let's go to *the* park. (There's only one park near here.)
Pass me *the* cup. (I'm pointing to it.)
Look at *the* moon!

**I.10** We use *a* to say what someone's job is.
My uncle is *a* taxi driver.

**I.11** Some set expressions include *the*:
listen to *the* radio    go to *the* cinema    play *the* guitar
Some set expressions don't have an article:
watch TV    listen to music    go to bed    go to school
be at home / at work / in hospital / at university

**I.12** We don't use an article when we are making a generalisation.
I don't like spicy food. ✓
NOT I don't like the spicy food. ✗

# 1 Grammar Builder

## 1B Past simple (affirmative)

**1** Write the past simple form of verbs 1–20. Verbs 1–10 are regular and verbs 11–20 are irregular. ➡ 1.2, 1.3

1 look _____
2 study _____
3 stop _____
4 die _____
5 move _____
6 compare _____
7 agree _____
8 enjoy _____
9 realise _____
10 drop _____
11 feel _____
12 leave _____
13 spend _____
14 have _____
15 give _____
16 win _____
17 begin _____
18 go _____
19 get _____
20 say _____

**2** Write the correct past simple affirmative form of the verb *be*. ➡ 1.4, 1.5

1 I _____ very relieved about my exam results.
2 The sports centre _____ shut last weekend.
3 You _____ cross with me for being late.
4 There _____ five winners in last week's lottery.
5 Nobody _____ at home this morning.
6 My grandfather _____ a student at Harvard University.
7 We _____ on holiday in China last August.
8 Adam's party _____ amazing.

**3** Complete the sentences with the past simple affirmative form of the verbs in brackets. All the verbs are regular. ➡ 1.1, 1.2. 1.5

1 The train to Birmingham _____ (stop) at Oxford.
2 My friends _____ (work) very hard for their exams.
3 We _____ (try) some interesting dishes at the Lebanese restaurant.
4 Last night, I _____ (plan) my summer holiday.
5 You _____ (seem) very upset yesterday.
6 I _____ (chat) with my cousin for hours last night.
7 My uncle _____ (marry) his next-door neighbour.
8 Theo _____ (move) house three times last year.

**4** Complete the email. Use the past simple affirmative form of the verbs in brackets. ➡ 1.1, 1.2, 1.3, 1.4, 1.5

Dear Abby

How are you? I **1**_____ (see) Ryan yesterday and we **2**_____ (chat) for hours about Zak's party. We both **3**_____ (have) a great time. We really **4**_____ (enjoy) the music and the food **5**_____ (be) good too. Ryan **6**_____ (leave) just before midnight, but I **7**_____ (stay) until 2 a.m.! I **8**_____ (feel) so tired the next day! I hope Ryan's parents **9**_____ (be) OK about the mess. They **10**_____ (go) out for the evening.

See you soon!

Ella

## 1D Past simple (negative and interrogative)

**5** Complete the sentences with the past simple negative form of the verbs below. ➡ 1.5, 1.6, 1.7

be   can   enjoy   feel   leave   spend   study   win

1 I _____ the film. It was terrible!
2 Ben _____ talk until he was three.
3 We _____ the match. The score was 2–1 to the other team.
4 The weather _____ very good yesterday.
5 I _____ very well yesterday. I had a headache.
6 Joe failed the exam because he _____ for it.
7 We were late because we _____ early enough.
8 Fred _____ all his pocket money. He saved some.

**6** Complete the dialogue with the correct past simple form of the verbs *be* and *can*. ➡ 1.7

Sam    You **1**_____ (not be) at the party last night. Where **2**_____ (you / be)?
Leah    I **3**_____ (not can) go. My cousins **4**_____ (be) here, so I had to stay in.
Sam    **5**_____ (it / be) fun?
Leah    Yes, it **6**_____ (be) good. We watched a film. It **7**_____ (be) a really funny comedy. **8**_____ (there / be) a lot of people at the party?
Sam    No, not many. It **9**_____ (not be) much fun. And the music **10**_____ (be) too loud! I **11**_____ (not can) hear what people were saying. The film sounds better!

## 1D Question words

**7** Complete the questions with the words below. ➡ 1.8

How   How often   What   When   Where   Who

1 _____ do you live?
2 _____ did you do on Saturday evening?
3 _____ did you get up this morning?
4 _____ did you travel to school this morning?
5 _____ do you go to the cinema?
6 _____ do you sit next to in English lessons?

**8** SPEAKING Work in pairs. Ask and answer the questions in exercise 7.

**9** Read the answers and complete the questions. ➡ 1.8

1 What *are you thinking about*?
   I'm thinking about my next holiday.
2 Who _____?
   She danced with Tom.
3 Who _____?
   I'm looking for Zoe.
4 Where _____?
   They walked to the beach.
5 What _____?
   He's worried about his exams.

# Grammar Reference

## Past simple (affirmative)

**1.1** The affirmative form of the past simple is the same for all persons, singular and plural (*I, you, he, we*, etc.).

*I watched a football match last night.*
*She watched TV.  They watched a DVD.*

### 1.2 Spelling: past simple (affirmative) form of regular verbs

We form the past simple (affirmative) form of regular verbs by adding -*ed*.

+ -*ed*:    work → worked    play → played

If the verb ends in -*e*, we add -*d*.

+ -*d*:    dance → danced    die → died

If the verb ends in a consonant + -*y*, we change -*y* to -*i* and add -*ed*.

-*y* → -*ied*:    study → studied    cry → cried

If the verb ends in a short accented vowel + a consonant, we double the consonant and add -*ed*.

-*p* → -*pped*:    drop → dropped
-*n* → -*nned*:    plan → planned
-*t* → -*tted*:    chat → chatted

**1.3** Some verbs have irregular past simple (affirmative) forms. There are no spelling rules for these forms; you need to learn them by heart. See the list in the Workbook.

### 1.4 Past simple affirmative of *be*

The verb *be* has two past simple affirmative forms: *was* and *were*.

| | | |
|---|---|---|
| I | was | |
| you | were | |
| he / she / it | was | sad |
| we | | |
| you | were | |
| they | | |

**1.5** We use the past simple:
- for a completed action or event at a definite point in the past.
  *We played volleyball last Saturday.*
- for actions or events that happened one after another.
  *Joanna got up, had a shower, got dressed and left the house.*

## Past simple (negative and interrogative)

**1.6** In negative sentences and questions, we use *did / didn't* + the infinitive without *to* (NOT the past simple form) for regular and irregular verbs. The forms are the same for all persons, singular and plural (*I, you, he, we*, etc.).

| Negative | Questions |
|---|---|
| I didn't watch | Did I watch? |
| he / she / it didn't watch | Did he / she / it watch? |
| we / you / they didn't watch | Did we / you / they watch? |

| Short form and full form | Short answers |
|---|---|
| didn't = did not | Yes, I did. / No, I didn't. |

**1.7** We don't use *did* or *didn't* for the past simple negative and question forms of *be* or *can*.

| Negative | Questions and short answers |
|---|---|
| I / He / She / It wasn't happy. | Was I / he / she / it happy? Yes, I was. / No, she wasn't. |
| We / You / They weren't happy. | Were we / you / they happy? Yes, we were. / No, they weren't. |

The forms of *could* are the same for all persons (*I, he, we, they*, etc.)

| Negative | Questions and short answers |
|---|---|
| I / He / She / It / We / You / They couldn't see. | Could I / he / she / it / we / you / they see? Yes, I / he / we could. / No, she / you / they couldn't. |

## Question words

**1.8** Examples of question words:
*where   who   what   which   why   when   how   what time   how often   how much / many   how long / wide / tall*
When a *Wh-* question includes a preposition, the preposition usually goes at the end.
*Where are you from?*
*Who did you talk to?*
*What are you waiting for?*

## 2B Past continuous

**1 Complete the sentences. Use the past continuous form of the verbs in brackets.** ➡ 2.1, 2.2, 2.3, 2.4

1. At eight o'clock yesterday evening, Josh _____ (text) his girlfriend.
2. 'Why _____ they _____ (laugh) at me?'
3. You _____ (not pay) attention while I _____ (speak), were you?
4. Dave _____ (walk) down the street, _____ (eat) a sandwich.
5. Emma _____ (watch) TV and Lisa _____ (read) a magazine.
6. At midnight, Wendy _____ still _____ (do) her homework.

**2 Complete the text with the past continuous form of the verbs below.** ➡ 2.1, 2.2, 2.3

get   make   put   shine   sing   talk

It was a beautiful morning. The sun **1**_____ and the birds **2**_____. We **3**_____ ready to go to the beach. Dad **4**_____ our bags in the car and Mum and Tom **5**_____ sandwiches in the kitchen. I **6**_____ to my friend on the phone.

**3 Complete the dialogue with the past continuous form of the verbs in brackets.** ➡ 2.1, 2.2, 2.3

| | |
|---|---|
| **Policeman** | What **1**_____ (you / do) at 9 o'clock yesterday evening? |
| **Woman** | I **2**_____ (watch) TV in the living room. |
| **Policeman** | What **3**_____ (you / watch)? |
| **Woman** | Er … I can't remember. I **4**_____ (not pay) attention. I was sleepy. |
| **Policeman** | What **5**_____ (your husband / do) at that time? |
| **Woman** | He **6**_____ (make) chicken pie in the kitchen. |
| **Policeman** | How do you know? |
| **Woman** | Because our dog **7**_____ (go crazy). He loves the smell of chicken! |

**4 What were you doing last Saturday at these times? Write sentences.** ➡ 2.1, 2.2, 2.3

| | |
|---|---|
| 1  7 a.m. | 4  6 p.m. |
| 2  10 a.m. | 5  9 p.m. |
| 3  1 p.m. | 6  11.30 p.m. |

At 7 a.m., I was having a shower.

1. _____
2. _____
3. _____
4. _____
5. _____
6. _____

## 2D Contrast: past simple and past continuous

**5 Complete the sentences with the past simple or past continuous form of the verbs in brackets.** ➡ 2.5, 2.6

1. When Molly _____ (drop) her phone on the floor, it _____ (break).
2. When my parents _____ (get) home, they _____ (find) a mouse in the kitchen.
3. Martin _____ (not hear) the phone because he _____ (have) a shower.
4. At 8 p.m. last night, I _____ (sit) at my desk but I _____ (not work).
5. When I _____ (see) Ben and Tia, they _____ (sit) on a bench, _____ (laugh) and _____ (chat).
6. It was a warm afternoon, but the sun _____ (not shine).
7. While we _____ (take) my grandmother to hospital, our car _____ (break down).
8. I _____ (lose) my watch while we _____ (play) volleyball in the park.

**6 Complete the second sentence so that it means the same as the first.** ➡ 2.5, 2.6

1. While we were having dinner, my dad arrived home.
   We _____ when my dad _____ .
2. I was trying to sleep when the phone rang.
   The _____ while I _____ .
3. She was climbing up some rocks when she fell.
   As she _____ , she _____ .
4. While you were shopping, I tidied your room.
   You _____ when _____ .
5. The boat hit some rocks as it was sailing towards the shore.
   The boat was _____ when it _____ .

**7 Complete the text with the past simple or past continuous form of the verbs in brackets.** ➡ 2.5, 2.6, 2.7

It was past midnight when Helen **1**_____ (arrive) home. She **2**_____ (close) the door quietly because her parents **3**_____ (sleep) upstairs. As she **4**_____ (take off) her coat, she **5**_____ (see) a letter on the floor with her name on it. She **6**_____ (open) the letter and **7**_____ (read) it. Then she **8**_____ (put) it in her pocket, **9**_____ (pick up) her coat and **10**_____ (go) out again. It **11**_____ (be) a cold night but it **12**_____ (not rain). A few people **13**_____ (walk) towards the High Street, so Helen **14**_____ (cross) the road and **15**_____ (follow) them. She **16**_____ (not know) where they **17**_____ (go) – but she **18**_____ (not want) to be alone.

# Grammar Reference

## Past continuous

**2.1** We form the past continuous with *was* or *were* + the *-ing* form of the verb.

| Affirmative | Negative | Questions |
| --- | --- | --- |
| I was playing | I wasn't playing | Was I playing? |
| you were playing | you weren't playing | Were you playing? |
| he/she/it was playing | he/she/it wasn't playing | Was he/she/it playing? |
| we/you/they were playing | we/you/they weren't playing | Were we/you/they playing? |

**2.2** To form the *-ing* form, we add *-ing* to the end of most verbs.
+ *-ing*:   work → working   study → studying

With most verbs ending in *-e*, we drop the *-e* and add *-ing*.
*-e* → *-ing*:   dance → dancing   write → writing

But if the verb ends in *-ee*, we simply add *-ing*.
+ *-ing*:   agree → agreeing   see → seeing

And if the verb ends in *-ie*, we change the *-ie* to *-y* and add *-ing*.
*-ie* → *-ying*:   die → dying   lie → lying

If the verb ends in a short accented vowel + a consonant, we double the consonant and add *-ing*.
*-p* → *-pping*:   drop → dropping
*-n* → *-nning*:   plan → planning
*-t* → *-tting*:   chat → chatting

**2.3** We often use the past continuous to set the scene.
*The sun was shining brightly. Some tourists were standing in the square. A man was selling ice creams.*

We use the past continuous to talk about an action that was in progress at a particular time.
*At seven o'clock this morning, I was eating my breakfast.*

**2.4** When we use the past continuous with two or more actions, we do not need to repeat the subject (*I*, *we*, etc.) or *was/were* if the subject is the same.
*We were sitting at a table, chatting and drinking coffee.*

## Contrast: past simple and past continuous

**2.5** We use the past simple for a sequence of events in the past. The events happened one after another.
*She walked into the room and sat down. Then she opened her bag and took out a letter.*

We use the past continuous to describe a scene in the past. The events were in progress at the same time.
*She was sitting in the room, reading a letter. A man was looking out of the window.*

**2.6** We use the past simple and the past continuous together for a single event that interrupted a longer event in the past. We use the past continuous for the longer event and the past simple for the interruption.
*As she was reading the letter, the phone rang.*
       *(longer event)          (interruption)*

We can use *as* or *while* with the past continuous. We usually put a comma between the longer action and the interruption.
*While we were having lunch, my uncle arrived.*
*As we were having lunch, my uncle arrived.*

If we don't use *as* or *while* with the past continuous, we use *when* with the past simple. In these sentences, we usually do not include a comma.
*We were having lunch when my uncle arrived.*

**2.7** We do not use the past continuous – or any continuous tense – with certain verbs. The meaning of these verbs is usually connected with a state rather than an action. They include:
- *hate, like, love, need, prefer, want, wish*
- *believe, know, mean, realise, recognise, remember, suppose, understand*
- *belong, contain, depend, matter, owe, possess*

*They weren't dancing because they didn't like the music.* ✓
NOT ~~They weren't dancing because they weren't liking the music.~~ ✗

Some verbs are not used in continuous tenses when they have a particular meaning, e.g. the verb *have* when it means 'to own or possess'.
*He had dark hair and was wearing a white T-shirt.* ✓
NOT ~~He was having dark hair and a white T-shirt.~~ ✗

# Grammar Builder

## 3B Quantity

**1 Complete the dialogue with *some* or *any*.** ➡ 3.1, 3.2

**Aiden** There aren't ¹_____ good programmes on TV. Have you got ²_____ DVDs?

**Emily** Yes. There are ³_____ DVDs on the shelf behind the TV.

**Aiden** Let's see … You've got ⁴_____ great films here! What do you fancy watching?

**Emily** How about *Grown Ups 2*? My sister says there are ⁵_____ funny scenes in that.

**Aiden** Really? I heard it wasn't very good. But there are ⁶_____ good actors in it: Adam Sandler, Chris Rock …

**Emily** Let's try it. Would you like ⁷_____ popcorn?

**Aiden** Yes, please!

**Emily** Oh, actually, we haven't got ⁸_____ popcorn. Sorry! But there are ⁹_____ crisps.

**Aiden** Great. Can I have ¹⁰_____ water too?

**Emily** Yes, of course.

**2 Complete the recipe with *a little* or *a few*.** ➡ 3.1, 3.3

Take your ready-made pizza base and add ¹_____ cheese. Slice ²_____ mushrooms and ³_____ ham and sprinkle on top. Cut ⁴_____ small tomatoes in half and put them between the mushrooms. Finally, add ⁵_____ more cheese and ⁶_____ olives and cook the pizza in a hot oven. Ten minutes later, enjoy your pizza with ⁷_____ salad on the side. Why not invite ⁸_____ friends to join you?

**3 Replace *a lot of* with *much* or *many*.** ➡ 3.1, 3.4

1 Do you get a lot of tourists here in the summer?
2 I don't spend a lot of time in my bedroom.
3 There aren't a lot of people in our village.
4 Have you got a lot of information about university courses?
5 They never do a lot of homework.
6 Did a lot of people go to see your school show?

**4 Complete the email with the words and phrases below. Use each word or phrase once only.** ➡ 3.1, 3.2, 3.3, 3.4, 3.5

a few   a little   any   How many   How much   many   much

Hi Hailey

How are you? I hope you enjoyed your trip to London.
¹_____ money did you spend? Did you do ²_____ sightseeing? I'm inviting ³_____ friends round for a film night next week. There won't be ⁴_____ people – just four or five. Can you come? ⁵_____ DVDs can you bring? We can spend ⁶_____ time choosing the ones we want to watch. Don't bring ⁷_____ food or drink, though. My mum is making dinner for us!

See you soon!

Isabella

## 3D *must, mustn't* and *needn't / don't have to*

**5 Circle the correct answers.** ➡ 3.2, 3.3

1 You **must / mustn't** finish your breakfast or you'll be hungry later.
2 I **must / mustn't** leave before 8.30 or I'll be late for school.
3 You **must / mustn't** eat that bread. It's a week old!
4 In football, you **must / mustn't** touch the ball with your hand.
5 You **must / mustn't** visit Paris some time. It's a wonderful city.
6 You **must / mustn't** go near the edge of the cliff. It's very dangerous.

**6 Complete the sentences with *must, mustn't* or *needn't*.** ➡ 3.2, 3.3, 3.4

1 You _____ take off your shoes if they are clean.
2 Students _____ turn off their mobiles during lessons or the teacher will take them away.
3 You _____ go to the check-in desk if you have checked in online.
4 In most Arab countries, you _____ eat with your left hand. You should use your right hand.
5 When you're driving, you _____ stop if someone steps onto the pedestrian crossing.
6 We _____ waste any more time.

**7 Complete the sentences with *must* or *have to* and the verbs below.** ➡ 3.5

drive   eat   get up   phone   stop   take   take   wear

1 At school, we _____ a white shirt and a blue sweater.
2 We _____ at the new Chinese restaurant in town. I've heard it's really good.
3 In Britain, we _____ on the left.
4 Sue really _____ eating so many sweets – it's bad for her teeth!
5 You _____ your grandparents more often. You know how much they enjoy talking to you.
6 We _____ exams at the end of our final year at school.
7 You _____ your mobile with you so that I can call you.
8 Jason _____ early because he's got a doctor's appointment at eight in the morning.

# Grammar Reference

## Quantity

### 3.1 Countable and uncountable nouns

Countable nouns can be singular or plural.

*a car – three cars   an island – lots of islands*
*a woman – two women*

Uncountable nouns only have a singular form. We cannot use *a* or *an* with uncountable nouns.

*food   pollution   money*

Some nouns can be countable or uncountable depending on the meaning. Compare:

*We haven't got much <u>time</u> for dinner.* (uncountable)
*I told him the answer three <u>times</u>.* (countable)
*Nothing can travel faster than <u>light</u>.* (uncountable)
*He turned on the <u>lights</u> in the kitchen.* (countable)

### 3.2 *some* and *any*

We usually use *some* in affirmative sentences and *any* in negative sentences and questions. We use them with plural nouns and uncountable nouns.

*There are some traffic lights at the end of the road.*
*There's some pasta on the table.*
*The dog doesn't want any biscuits.*
*They haven't got any money.*
*Are there any cinemas in your town?*
*Do you need any help?*

We usually use *some* when we offer or ask for something, even if it is a question.

*Would you like some tea?   Can I borrow some money?*

### 3.3 *a little, a few*

We use *a little* with uncountable nouns. We use *a few* with plural nouns. They mean 'a small quantity of'.

*Julia ate a little rice.   Mike ate a few chips.*

### 3.4 *much, many, a lot of*

We use *much* with uncountable nouns. We use *many* with plural nouns. We use *a lot of* with uncountable or plural nouns. *Much*, *many* and *a lot of* all mean 'a large quantity of'.

*French people don't drink much tea.*
*Are there many pedestrian crossings in the town centre?*
*Bill Gates has got a lot of money.*
*There are a lot of tall buildings in Tokyo.*

We often use *much* and *many* in negative sentences and questions. We do not often use them in affirmative sentences, except in very formal writing.

*Charlotte's got a lot of friends.* ✓
NOT ~~Charlotte's got many friends.~~ ✗

### 3.5 *How much ... ?* and *How many ... ?*

We use *How much ... ?* and *How many ... ?* to ask about quantity. We use *How much ... ?* with uncountable nouns and *How many ... ?* with plural nouns.

*How much food did you eat?   How many films did you watch?*

## *must* and *mustn't*

### 3.6 The form of *must* or *mustn't* is the same for all persons (*I, you, he*, etc.).

| Affirmative |
| --- |
| I must go home. |
| You must tell the truth. |

| Negative |
| --- |
| You mustn't tell anybody. |
| They mustn't be late. |
| (full form = *must not*) |

| Questions* |
| --- |
| Must you leave so early? |

| Short answers |
| --- |
| Yes, I must. |
| No, I don't have to / needn't. |

\* We do not often make questions with *must*. It is more common to use *Do you have to ... ?*

### 3.7 We use *must* + infinitive without *to* to say that something is necessary, and it is very important to do it.

*I've got a maths test tomorrow. I must revise for it this evening.*

We use *mustn't* + infinitive without *to* to say that something is prohibited, and it is very important not to do it.

*We mustn't be late for school.*
*You mustn't use a mobile phone in the cinema.*

We often use *must* or *mustn't* to express rules and laws.

*In the UK, you must be 17 to drive a car.*
*You mustn't smoke on aeroplanes.*

## *needn't* and *don't have to*

### 3.8 We use *needn't* or *don't have to* + infinitive without *to* to say that something is not necessary but isn't against the rules.

*You don't have to bring a towel. There are towels at the swimming pool.* (But you can bring one if you want.)
*You needn't take sandwiches as lunch is provided.* (But you can bring them if you want.)

## *must* and *have to*

### 3.9 *Must* and *have to* have very similar meanings. However, *must* often expresses the feelings and wishes of the speaker.

*You must read this book. It's brilliant!*
*I'm really tired. I must go home.*

*Have to* often expresses an 'external obligation'.

*You have to show your passport when leaving the country.*

*Mustn't* and *don't have to* do NOT have the same meaning: *don't have to* means that something is not necessary.

*We don't have to wear a school uniform.*

*Mustn't* means 'it's prohibited'.

*We mustn't wear jeans to school.*

# 4 Grammar Builder

## 4B Comparison

**1** Write the comparative form of the adjectives and quantifiers. ➡ 4.1

1 small _____
2 large _____
3 early _____
4 powerful _____
5 much _____
6 bright _____
7 few _____
8 many _____
9 far _____
10 wet _____
11 pretty _____
12 frightening _____

**2** Complete the email with the comparative form of the adjectives and quantifiers in brackets. ➡ 4.1

Dear Aunt Polly,

I hope you're well. Jake seems **1**_____ (happy) at his new school. It's **2**_____ (small) and **3**_____ (friendly) than his old school. His grades are **4**_____ (good) than last year. He gets **5**_____ (a little) homework but the lessons at school are **6**_____ (difficult), he says. The only bad thing about his new school is that it's **7**_____ (far) from our house. At the moment he cycles there, but he's planning to go by bus when the weather gets **8**_____ (cold) and **9**_____ (wet).

I'm working hard for my exams but I'm not enjoying it. It's always **10**_____ (bad) at the weekend because I want to go out!

Write soon.

Eva

**3** Write sentences comparing a and b. Include the correct form of the words in brackets. ➡ 4.1, 4.2

1 a Iceland  b Egypt  (far / cold)
  *Iceland is far colder than Egypt.*
2 a the Earth  b the sun  (much / small)
3 a gold  b silver  (heavy)
4 a rock-climbing  b hiking  (dangerous)
5 a cycling  b skiing  (much / easy)
6 a the USA  b the UK  (far / big)
7 a Porsches  b Skodas  (expensive)
8 a ice storms  b thunderstorms  (far / rare)
9 a a broken ankle  b a sprained ankle  (bad)

**4** Write sentences based on the information. Use (not) as ... as and the adjective in brackets. ➡ 4.3

1 Tom and Karen both weigh 72 kg.  (heavy)
  *Tom is as heavy as Karen.*
2 The pen costs £12.95 and the book costs £8.50.  (expensive)
3 Darren is 154 cm tall and Lucy is 165 cm tall.  (tall)
4 London is 150 km away and Leeds is 180 km away.  (far)
5 The skiing holiday costs £500 and the beach holiday costs the same.  (cheap)
6 About a hundred students choose to study Spanish each year and only fifty choose French.  (popular)

## 4D (Part 1) Superlative adjectives

**5** Write the superlative form of the adjectives. ➡ 4.4

1 big _____
2 scary _____
3 bad _____
4 far _____
5 good _____
6 intelligent _____

**6** Complete the sentences with superlative adjectives. Add *in* or *of* before the final noun. ➡ 4.4, 4.5

1 Joe is _____ (intelligent) boy _____ the school.
2 Friday is _____ (good) day _____ the week.
3 This is _____ (bad) restaurant _____ London.
4 Lake Superior is _____ (big) _____ the five Great Lakes.
5 21 December is _____ (short) day _____ the year.
6 Ben Nevis is _____ (high) mountain _____ Britain.

**7** Write the questions. Use the superlative form of the adjective, and add *in* or *of* where necessary. ➡ 4.4, 4.5

1 Who / intelligent / person / the class / ?
  *Who's the most intelligent person in the class?*
2 What / good / day / the week / ?
3 What / bad / day / the week / ?
4 What / beautiful / city / your country / ?
5 Who / good-looking / actor on TV / ?

**8** SPEAKING Work in pairs. Ask and answer the questions in exercise 7. Give your opinions.

## 4D (Part 2) too and enough

**9** Write sentences with words from the table below. Use *too* and the infinitive. ➡ 4.6, 4.8

*James is too young to take his driving test.*

| James | cold | reach that shelf. |
|---|---|---|
| You | ~~young~~ | swim in the sea. |
| This pizza | cloudy | lift. |
| The sky's | short | eat. |
| It's | heavy | ~~take his driving test.~~ |
| This suitcase | hot | see the stars. |

**10** Rewrite the sentences in exercise 9 with the adjectives below and *enough*. ➡ 4.7, 4.8

clear  cool  light  ~~old~~  tall  warm

*James isn't old enough to take his driving test.*

## 4H Zero conditional

**11** Complete the sentences with the correct form of the verbs in brackets. ➡ 4.9

1 If we _____ (use) public transport instead of cars, we _____ (reduce) our carbon footprint.
2 If we _____ (cut down) rainforests, we _____ (destroy) many animals' natural habitat.
3 We _____ (can) combat climate change if we _____ (conserve) energy.
4 You _____ (save) electricity if you _____ (not leave) the lights on.
5 If you _____ (burn) a fossil fuel, it _____ (give off) carbon dioxide.

# Grammar Reference

## Comparative adjectives

### 4.1 Forming the comparative

We add -er to all one-syllable adjectives.

+ -er:  long → longer   straight → straighter

If a one-syllable adjective ends in -e, we add -r.

+ -r:  wide → wider   large → larger

If a one-syllable adjective ends in a short vowel + a single consonant, we double the consonant and add -er.

-t → -tter:  hot → hotter   wet → wetter

-n → -nner:  thin → thinner

If a two-syllable adjective ends in consonant + -y, we drop the -y and add -ier.

-y → -ier:  friendly → friendlier   sunny → sunnier

A few other two-syllable adjectives have comparative forms ending in -er:

quiet → quieter   narrow → narrower   gentle → gentler

simple → simpler

For most two-syllable adjectives and all adjectives with three or more syllables, we use the word more to form the comparative.

boring → more boring   difficult → more difficult

A small number of adjectives have irregular comparative forms. They are:

good → better   bad → worse   far → further

Some quantifiers have irregular forms.

few → fewer   much / many → more   a little → less

### than

**4.2** We use than to compare two things or people.

Horror films are usually scarier than thrillers.

We usually use the object pronoun (me, you, he, him, us, them) after than, not a subject pronoun.

You're taller than me.

We can make a comparison stronger by using far or much before the comparative form.

Dolphins are far more intelligent than sharks.

Hungarian is much harder to learn than English.

### (not) as ... as

**4.3** We use (not) as ... as to compare two things or people. Not as ... as means 'less ... than'.

Jack is twelve. Liam is fourteen. Jack isn't as old as Liam.

As ... as means 'equally ...'.

My brother and I both weigh 62 kg. I'm as heavy as my brother.

We usually use the object pronoun (me, you, he, him, us, them) after (not) as ... as, not a subject pronoun.

We aren't as rich as them.

She's as excited as me.

## Superlative adjectives

### 4.4 Spelling

We put the in front of short (one-syllable and some two-syllable) adjectives and add -est.

+ -est        long → the longest

If the short adjective ends in -e, we add -st.

+ -st        wide → the widest

If the short adjective ends in a short vowel + a single consonant, we double the consonant and add -est.

-t → -ttest     hot → the hottest

If the adjective ends in -y, we drop the -y and add -iest.

-y → -iest      friendly → the friendliest

If the adjective is long (two syllables or more), we use the word most.

gripping → the most gripping

A small number of adjectives have irregular superlative forms. They are:

good → the best   bad → the worst   far → the furthest

**4.5** We can use of after superlative adjectives.

the longest day of the year

We use in, not of, with nouns for groups or places.

the tallest man in the world     the longest river in China

### too and enough

**4.6** Too comes before an adjective. Enough comes after an adjective.

This jacket is too small for him.

This jacket isn't big enough for him.

**4.7** Enough comes before a noun.

He can't buy it. He hasn't got enough money.

**4.8** We often use an infinitive with to after too + adjective or adjective + enough.

He's too young / old enough to join the army.

### Zero conditional

**4.9** We use the zero conditional to talk about a result which follows a particular action. We use the present to describe the action and the present simple to describe the result.

If I eat too much, I feel ill.

The if clause can come before or after the main clause. If it comes after, we don't use a comma.

If I drink a lot of coffee, I can't sleep.

I can't sleep if I drink a lot of coffee.

# 5 Grammar Builder

## 5B will and going to

**1** Complete the sentences with the correct affirmative or negative form of will. ➡ 5.1

1 Don't worry. My dad _____ pay for our tickets.
2 '_____ Tamer be at the party?' 'No, he _____ .'
3 Suzie's the best student in the class. She _____ pass all her exams easily.
4 '_____ your friends be at the beach?' 'Yes, they _____ .'
5 Max is good at keeping secrets. He _____ tell anyone.
6 August is always very dry, so it _____ rain then.
7 '_____ you be in Year 5 next year?' 'No, I _____ .'
8 Kyle wants to have a motorbike, but his parents _____ allow it.

**2** Write offers or promises in reply to sentences 1–6. Use the verbs and object pronouns below. ➡ 5.1, 5.2

**Verbs** ask ~~carry~~ eat invite tell video
**Pronouns** her him ~~it~~ them you us

1 This bag is too heavy for me.
  I'll carry it.
2 I don't really like these crisps.
3 I really want Emma to come to my party.
4 Let's send a video message to Grandma.
5 I want to know what happens at the end of the film.
6 Maybe we can borrow my dad's laptop.

**3** Write decisions with will in reply to sentences 1–6. Use your own ideas. ➡ 5.1, 5.2

1 Somebody's knocking at the door.
  I'll answer it.
2 Would you like the blue T-shirt or the red one?
3 There's chicken or fish for lunch.
4 It looks freezing outside.
5 The next bus into town is in an hour.
6 What would you like to drink?

**4** Look at the pictures and write predictions with going to and the prompts. ➡ 5.3, 5.4

1 they / catch / the bus

2 the boat / sink

3 the rope / break

4 she / get / a shock

**5** Complete the dialogue with the correct form of will or going to. ➡ 5.3, 5.4, 5.5, 5.6

| | |
|---|---|
| Tara | Hi, Matt. Where are you going? |
| Matt | Into town. I **1**_____ buy some new trainers. |
| Tara | I **2**_____ go with you. I can help you choose. |
| Matt | Thanks! Look, here's our bus. |
| Tara | It's going very fast. It **3**_____ stop! |
| Matt | That's strange. Maybe it's full. |
| Tara | I know. I **4**_____ phone my sister, Lucy. She usually drives into town on Saturdays. She **5**_____ probably give us a lift. And her car is OK now, after the accident. |
| Matt | Accident? Actually, I think I **6**_____ go by bike. |

## 5D First conditional

**6** Complete the sentences with the verbs below. Use the present simple. ➡ 5.7, 5.8

become drop have not hurry up
not understand want

1 If you _____ , you'll be late for school.
2 If I _____ time, I'll phone you later.
3 She'll earn a lot of money if she _____ a solicitor.
4 If you _____ your phone into water, it'll stop working.
5 I'll help you if you _____ the exercise.
6 She'll have to work very hard if she _____ to go to university.

**7** Complete the sentences with the will form of the verbs in brackets. ➡ 5.7, 5.8

1 If you text me, I _____ (reply) immediately.
2 We _____ (not go) skiing this winter if there isn't enough snow.
3 If you come home late, your parents _____ (worry).
4 You _____ (have) a great time if you come to the party.
5 If we leave before 10 o'clock, we _____ (not be) late.
6 I _____ (lend) you my phone if you can't find yours.

**8** Match 1–6 with a–f below and write six first conditional sentences. For each sentence, write the if clause first, then second. ➡ 5.7, 5.8

1 ~~you / study hard~~ ___
2 the weather / be bad ___
3 you / not listen to the instructions ___
4 she / not invite Joe to her party ___
5 we / not leave now ___
6 the match / be / on TV ___

a you / not know what to do
b we / miss the train
c ~~you / pass all your exams~~
d I / watch it
e he / be upset
f we / not have a barbecue

1 If you study hard, you'll pass all your exams.
  You'll pass all your exams if you study hard.

# 5 Grammar Reference

## will and *going to*

**5.1** We form sentences with *will* like this:
*will* + infinitive without *to*
I will go.
The form of *will* is the same for all persons (*I, you, he, she,* etc.). In the affirmative, we usually use the short form *'ll* with subject pronouns (*I, you, he, she,* etc.). However, we never use the short form in an affirmative short answer. In the negative, we usually use the short form *won't*. We use *won't* in negative short answers too.

| Affirmative | Negative |
|---|---|
| I'll see you later.<br>She'll be angry.<br>(full form = will) | I won't tell anybody.<br>They won't listen.<br>(full form = will not) |
| **Questions** | **Short answers** |
| Will you be at home?<br>Will it work?<br>When will we know? | Yes, I will.<br>No, I won't. |

**5.2** We use *will*:
- to make factual statements about the future.
  There will be a solar eclipse in 2026.
- to make predictions, especially when they are based on what we know or when they are just a guess. We often use *I think / don't think* ... to make these predictions.
  I think you'll do well in your exams.
  I don't think England will win the next World Cup.
- to make offers.
  I'll carry your bags.
  I'll lend you my phone.
- to make promises.
  I'll always love you.
  I won't forget.
- to make instant decisions (decisions that we make while we are speaking).
  Look! There's Tommy. I'll go and say hello.

**5.3** We form sentences with *going to* like this:
present simple of *be* + *going to* + infinitive without *to*
I'm going to take my driving test next year.
Djokovic isn't going to win this match.
Are you going to be at home this weekend?
Yes, I am. / No, I'm not.

**5.4** We use *going to*:
- to make predictions, especially when they are based on what we can see or hear.
  Look at that man! He's going to jump in the river!
  Listen to the thunder. There's going to be a storm.
- to talk about our plans and intentions.
  I'm going to invite her to my party.

**5.5**

|  | will | going to |
|---|---|---|
| **Predictions** | based on our own knowledge and opinions:<br>*Messi will score. He always scores in important games.* | based on the situation and what we can see or hear:<br>*Messi's got the ball. He's going to score!* |
| **Decisions** | instant decisions that we make while speaking:<br>*Show me the menu. Hmm. I'll have chicken.* | intentions – things that we have already decided:<br>*I'm going to have chicken tonight. I bought it this morning.* |

**5.6** We can make predictions and plans with *will* or *going to* more certain or uncertain by adding *definitely* or *probably*. Pay attention to the position of the adverb.
I'll definitely / probably be at home this weekend.
I definitely / probably won't finish my homework.
I'm definitely / probably (not) going to invite friends round.

## First conditional

**5.7** We use the first conditional to predict the result of a future action. We use the present simple to describe the action and *will* + infinitive without *to* to describe the result.
If the weather's fine tomorrow, we'll play tennis.
   (action)        (result)
If you go to bed early, you won't be tired tomorrow.
   (action)        (result)

**5.8** The *if* clause can come before or after the main clause. If it comes after, we do not use a comma.
If you work hard, you'll do well at school.
You'll do well at school if you work hard.

# 6

# Grammar Builder

## 6B Present perfect

**1** Write the words in the correct order to make sentences. ➡ 6.1

1 exams / finished / hasn't / my / sister / her
2 you / new / game / played / computer / have / this / ?
3 dog / its / my / leg / has / broken
4 parents / New York / been / have / to / my
5 you / my / have / trainers / seen / ?
6 cousin / has / my / applied / job / new / for / a

**2** Write the past participles of these regular and irregular verbs. ➡ 6.2

1 visit  *visited*
2 ask _____
3 take _____
4 meet _____
5 use _____
6 see _____

7 do _____
8 reach _____
9 stop _____
10 put _____
11 be _____
12 spend _____

**3** Complete the sentences with the present perfect form of the verbs in brackets. ➡ 6.1, 6.2, 6.3

1 Oh no! You _____ (drop) my laptop!
2 My friends _____ (buy) lots of new clothes in the sale.
3 We _____ (be) on holiday for a week but we _____ (not spend) much money.
4 This train _____ (stop) at every town and village!
5 I _____ (have) a shower and I'm ready to go out.
6 _____ (you / met) my best friend from school?
7 How long _____ (he / have) that motorbike?
8 My grandparents _____ (live) in London since 2010.

**4** Circle *for* or *since*. ➡ 6.3

1 We've been in this queue **for / since** two hours!
2 I've known my best friend **for / since** we were at primary school.
3 Have you had that phone **for / since** a long time?
4 You've needed a new car **for / since** years.
5 I've had a headache **for / since** this morning.

**5** Complete the sentences with *been* or *gone*. ➡ 6.4

1 I'm sorry, Adam isn't here. He's _____ to the shops.
2 My parents have _____ on holiday. They'll be back next week.
3 My hair is wet because I've _____ to the swimming pool.
4 Bess was here earlier, but now she's _____ .
5 I've _____ to Paris but I don't remember it very well.

## 6D Contrast: past simple and present perfect

**6** Some of the sentences are incorrect. Rewrite them correctly. ➡ 6.5

1 I've read six books last year. ✗
   *I read six books last year.*
2 Jo washed her hair last night.
3 I had this watch since March.
4 Have you ever been to Spain?
5 'Tidy your room, please.' 'I already tidied it.'
6 We've eaten at that restaurant last Tuesday.
7 Peter has gone to the shops on Friday morning.
8 I've been kayaking twice in the last year.
9 'Did you do your homework yet?' 'No, not yet.'

**7** Complete the sentences. Use the past simple form of the verb in one sentence, and the present perfect in the other. ➡ 6.5, 6.6

1 have
   a I _____ this laptop since my birthday.
   b We _____ dinner in the garden last night.
2 not buy
   a I _____ a new jacket in the sale last weekend.
   b I _____ any new clothes for months.
3 leave
   a I _____ home at seven and arrived at school at eight.
   b I _____ your dinner in the fridge. You can heat it up later.
4 not text
   a I _____ you last night because I don't have your number.
   b Jim _____ his girlfriend since Monday. She's a bit upset about it.
5 go
   a I _____ to Turkey three times. The last time was in 2011.
   b Liam _____ to Morocco last summer.

**8** Complete the dialogues with the verbs. Use the past simple or the present perfect. ➡ 6.5, 6.6

go  go  never go  not have  stay  visit

Max  **1**_____ you _____ to Portugal?
Lucy  Yes, I **2**_____ there last summer.
Max  **3**_____ you _____ Porto?
Lucy  No, we **4**_____ time. We **5**_____ in Lisbon.
Max  I'd like to see Lisbon. I **6**_____ there.

be  be  not go  see  see

Tom  I **7**_____ the new *Iron Man* film last Saturday.
   **8**_____ you _____ it?
Sarah  No, I haven't. I **9**_____ to the cinema for ages.
   **10**_____ it good?
Tom  Yes, it **11**_____ great. You should see it.

# Grammar Reference

## Present perfect

**6.1** We form the present perfect with the present tense of the auxiliary verb *have* and the past participle.

| Affirmative | | Full forms |
|---|---|---|
| I've / you've / we've / they've | finished | 've = have |
| he's / she's / it's | | 's = has |
| **Negative** | | |
| I / you / we / they haven't | finished | haven't = have not |
| he / she / it hasn't | | hasn't = has not |
| **Questions** | | **Short answers** |
| Have I / you / we / they | finished? | Yes, I have. / No, you haven't. |
| Has he / she / it | | Yes, he has. / No, she hasn't. |

**6.2** The past participle of regular verbs is the same as the past simple. It ends in *-ed*. (See 1.2 on page 125 for past simple spelling rules.)

> play → played   dance → danced
> study → studied   drop → dropped

With irregular verbs, sometimes the past participle is the same as the past simple, but sometimes it is different:

| Infinitive | Past simple | Past participle |
|---|---|---|
| buy | bought | bought |
| put | put | put |
| see | saw | seen |
| take | took | taken |

There is a list of irregular verbs in the Workbook.

**6.3** We use the present perfect:
- to give news, when we do not say exactly when the event happened.
  *Guess what! I've passed my exam!*
- to talk about events during a period of time (for example, a holiday) that is still continuing.
  *I'm in Paris. I've visited a museum but I haven't seen the Eiffel Tower.*
- to ask how long a situation has existed.
  *How long have you been in Spain?*
- with *for* or *since* to say how long a situation has existed. We use *for* with a period of time or *since* to say when it started.
  *We've been in Spain for a week / since Tuesday.*

**6.4** We use both *been* and *gone* as the past participle of the verb *go*. We use *been* when somebody has returned.
*John has been shopping.* (He went shopping but he's here now.)
We use *gone* when somebody has not returned.
*John has gone shopping.* (He is still at the shops.)

## Past simple and present perfect contrast

**6.5** We use both the past simple and the present perfect to talk about completed actions in the past.
*I finished 'The Hobbit' last night. I really enjoyed it.*
*I've finished 'The Hobbit'. You can read it now.*

- We use the past simple to talk about a specific occasion in the past, at a definite time.
  *I went to the cinema last Saturday night. I saw the new Spiderman film.*
- We use the present perfect to talk about an experience at any time in the past. The exact time of the experience isn't stated.
  *I've been to Italy three times.*
  *'Have you ever eaten Chinese food?' 'Yes, I have.'*
- We can use finished-time expressions with the past simple, but not with the present perfect.
  *I visited my cousin yesterday / last Tuesday / on 1 May / in January*, etc.
  (NOT ~~I've visited my cousin yesterday~~, etc.)

See point **6.3** for a list of the uses of the present perfect.

**6.6** We often use the present perfect to ask and answer about an experience, and then the past simple to give specific information about it.

*'Have you ever broken a bone?' 'Yes, I broke my leg when I was 12.'*

# Grammar Builder

## 7B Second conditional

**1** Match the two halves of the conditional sentences. Which sentences are true for you? ➡ 7.1, 7.2, 7.3

1 If I won the lottery, ___
2 I'd feel bad ___
3 If I found a spider in my bed, ___
4 I would download a film illegally ___
5 If I went on holiday with my friends, ___

a I'd be terrified.
b if I couldn't afford to buy it.
c I'd buy a new house for my parents.
d we'd go camping.
e if my best friend was cross with me.

**2** Complete the second conditional sentences with the correct form of the verbs in brackets. ➡ 7.1, 7.2, 7.3

1 I _____ (do) more homework if I _____ (spend) less time online.
2 If children _____ (not watch) TV so much, they _____ (be) healthier.
3 If a big rock _____ (hit) the Earth, it _____ (cause) a huge explosion.
4 Global warming _____ (slow) down if people _____ (change) their lifestyles.
5 If you _____ (apply) for a job at the hotel, I'm sure you _____ (get) it.
6 If you _____ (visit) Rome, you _____ (can) see the Trevi Fountain.
7 If I _____ (want) to become a millionaire, I _____ (start) my own business.

**3** Rewrite these sentences using the second conditional. ➡ 7.1, 7.2, 7.3

1 My job is repetitive. That's why I don't enjoy it.
   *If my job wasn't repetitive, I'd enjoy it.*
   *OR I'd enjoy my job if it wasn't repetitive.*
2 She doesn't like swimming. That's why she doesn't go to the pool.
3 He doesn't earn a lot of money. That's why he doesn't rent an apartment on his own.
4 The Louvre Museum is crowded. That's why I don't like it.
5 We won't go on holiday this year. We can't afford it.
6 I don't understand my homework. That's why I can't finish it quickly.

**4** Complete the second conditional questions with the correct form of the verbs in brackets. ➡ 7.1, 7.2, 7.3

1 What _____ (you / do) if you _____ (be) outside in a thunderstorm?
2 If you _____ (can) meet one film star, who _____ (you / choose)?
3 _____ (you / behave) well on holiday if your parents _____ (not be) there?
4 How _____ (you / feel) if you _____ (win) the lottery?

5 If you _____ (can) visit any country, where _____ (you / go)?
6 If you _____ (have to) spend a month alone on a desert island, what _____ (you / take) with you?

**5** SPEAKING In pairs, ask and answer the questions in exercise 4. ➡ 7.1, 7.2, 7.3

## 7D Past perfect

**6** Complete the sentences with the past perfect form of the verbs in brackets. ➡ 7.4, 7.5

1 I didn't have any chocolate because my sister _____ (eat) it.
2 I couldn't buy the magazine because I _____ (forget) to bring my wallet with me.
3 I didn't recognise my cousin. He _____ (grow) a beard.
4 We couldn't get home because we _____ (miss) the last bus.
5 After I _____ (write) the answer, I realised I _____ (make) a mistake.
6 I didn't watch the programme because I _____ (see) it before.

**7** Complete the sentences. Use the past simple or past perfect form of the verbs in brackets. ➡ 7.4, 7.5

1 I _____ (can't) remember where I _____ (leave) my keys.
2 Last Saturday, I _____ (eat) at a Japanese restaurant. I _____ (never eat) Japanese food before that.
3 I _____ (find) a £10 note that I _____ (lose) last year.
4 Last weekend I _____ (meet) a girl who _____ (be born) in the same hospital as me.
5 I _____ (not play) volleyball because I _____ (hurt) my hand.
6 The pavement _____ (be) wet because it _____ (rain).

**8** Rewrite each pair of sentences as one sentence using the past simple and the past perfect. Start with the word given. ➡ 7.4, 7.5

1 I had dinner. I watched TV.
   After *I'd had dinner, I watched TV.*
2 We bought a newspaper. We had a coffee.
   After _____
3 We played tennis. We went home.
   After _____
4 I went to sleep. My cousin phoned.
   When _____
5 Messi scored two goals. We arrived at the match.
   When _____
6 The children did the housework. Their mother got home.
   When _____

# Grammar Reference

## Second conditional

**7.1** We use the second conditional to describe an imaginary situation or event and its result.

*If I lived near the sea, I would go to the beach a lot.*
(imaginary situation)          (result)

We use the past simple in the *if* clause and we use *would +* infinitive without *to* in the main clause. The short forms of *would* are *'d* and *wouldn't*.
*If she had a car, she'd learn to drive.*
*If she learned to drive, she wouldn't use her bike.*

**7.2** We can put the main clause first and the *if* clause second.
*I'd buy you a present if I had enough money.*
When the main clause is first, we usually do not put a comma between the clauses.

**7.3** In the main clause, we can use *could* to mean *would + can*. *Could* is also the past simple of *can*, so we can use it in the *if* clause too.
*If I won the lottery, I could stop work.*
*If I could remember his number, I'd call him.*

## Past perfect

**7.4** We form the past perfect like this:

| Affirmative |
| --- |
| I'd / you'd / he'd / she'd / it'd gone |
| **Full form** |
| 'd = had |
| **Negative** |
| I / you / he / she / it / we / you / they hadn't gone |
| **Full form** |
| hadn't = had not |
| **Questions** |
| Had I / you / he / she / it / we / you / they gone? |
| **Short answers** |
| Yes, I had. / No, she hadn't. |

The past participle of regular verbs is the same as the past simple.
   *finished   danced   studied   chatted*
Sometimes irregular verbs have the same past participle as the past simple form, sometimes they are different.
   *go – went – been / gone*
   *buy – bought – bought*
   *see – saw – seen*
For a list of irregular verbs, see the Workbook.

**7.5** We use the past perfect to talk about an event in the past which happened before another event in the past.

| past | | future |
| --- | --- | --- |
| they ran out of milk   I arrived at the shop | Now | |

*When I arrived at the shop, they had run out of milk.*

## 8B Reported speech (1)

**1 Complete the reported speech. ➡ 8.1**

1 'I'm wearing my sister's jacket,' she said.
   She said she _____ her sister's jacket.
2 'I didn't arrive on time,' he told me.
   He told me he _____ on time.
3 'The DIY store isn't open at the weekend,' he said.
   He said the DIY store _____ open at the weekend.
4 'It's snowing heavily,' my dad said.
   My dad said that it _____ heavily.
5 'I'm not enjoying the film,' Zak said.
   Zak said he _____ the film.
6 'My grandma makes really good pizzas,' said Gino.
   Gino said that his grandma _____ really good pizzas.
7 'I don't like horror films,' said Joel.
   Joel said he _____ horror films.
8 'I went to Paris at New Year,' my cousin told me.
   My cousin told me he _____ to Paris at New Year.
9 'I know all the answers,' my friend said.
   My friend said she _____ all the answers.
10 'We didn't take many photos,' my parents said.
   My parents said they _____ many photos.

**2 Complete the sentences with the correct pronouns and possessive adjectives. ➡ 8.2**

1 'I'm cleaning your brother's room,' my dad told me.
   My dad told me he was cleaning my brother's room.
2 'I love your sunglasses,' my uncle said to me.
   My uncle said that _____ loved _____ sunglasses.
3 'You need our help,' Anna told him.
   Anna told him that _____ needed _____ help.
4 'Your sister has left her bike in our garage,' my friend's mum said to me.
   My friend's mum told me that _____ sister had left _____ bike in _____ garage.
5 'You're hurting my finger,' Dan said to his brother.
   Dan told _____ brother that _____ was hurting _____ finger.

**3 Rewrite what Emma said using reported speech. ➡ 8.1, 8.2**

1 'I'm on the High Street.'
   *She said she was on the High Street.*
2 'It's raining quite hard here.'
3 'I need to buy a present for my sister.'
4 'It's her birthday soon.'
5 'I'm looking for a silver bracelet.'
6 'I saw a nice one yesterday in the jeweller's.'
7 'Unfortunately, it isn't there any more.'
8 'I think somebody bought it.'

## 8D Reported speech (2)

**4 Complete the reported speech. Use the past perfect, *could / couldn't* and *would / wouldn't*. ➡ 8.3**

1 'Burglars have broken into our house twice,' said Di.
   Di said that burglars _____ into their house twice.
2 'I'll carry the bags for you,' said Ryan.
   Ryan said that he _____ the bags for me.
3 'I've lost my glasses,' said my grandma.
   My grandma said that she _____ her glasses.
4 'We can get some bread at the corner shop,' said Dad.
   Dad said that we _____ some bread at the corner shop.
5 'I've never been to Spain,' Kelly said.
   Kelly said that she _____ never _____ to Spain.
6 'You can't go out tonight,' said Mum.
   Mum said I _____ go out that night.
7 'You haven't locked the door,' said George.
   George said that I _____ the door.
8 'Barcelona will win the Champions League again,' said Harry.
   Harry said that Barcelona _____ the Champions League again.

**5 Change the direct speech to reported speech. Remember to change the pronouns and references to time where necessary. ➡ 8.2, 8.3**

1 'I'll see you tomorrow,' said Sally.
   *Sally said that she would see me the next day.*
2 'We haven't been to London since last January,' said Emma.
3 'Tom can't speak French,' said Wendy.
4 'I'll get a holiday job next summer,' said Kylie.
5 'We can play tennis tomorrow,' said Jake.
6 'Kate has decided to study medicine,' said her brother.
7 'I won't tell anyone what Josh has done,' said Andy.

## 8D Reported speech (2) *tell* and *say*

**6 Complete the reported speech with *said* or *told*. ➡ 8.4**

1 Kate _____ me that she wasn't feeling well.
2 Sally _____ she wouldn't be late.
3 Jordan _____ that he didn't like Vanessa.
4 Amy _____ James that she'd text him later that day.
5 Charlie _____ he wanted to go home.
6 Beth _____ us she was going to the café.

# Grammar Reference

## 8B Reported speech (1)

**8.1** We use reported speech to report what somebody else said. We can use *that* to introduce reported speech, but we often omit it. The tense of the verb usually changes.

| Direct speech | Reported speech |
|---|---|
| **Present simple** | **Past simple** |
| 'I don't like dogs,' Ben said. | Ben said (that) he didn't like dogs. |
| 'My dad is at work,' Becky said. | Becky said (that) her dad was at work. |
| **Present continuous** | **Past continuous** |
| 'He's wearing a blue top,' Michelle said. | Michelle said (that) he was wearing a blue top. |
| **Past simple** | **Past perfect** |
| 'We moved to London in 2010,' Phil said. | Phil said (that) they had moved to London in 2010. |

**8.2** Pronouns and possessive adjectives usually change in reported speech, depending on the speaker and context.
'You're eating my chips,' he told us.
He told us we were eating his chips.
References to time and place can change as well.

| Direct speech | Reported speech |
|---|---|
| *yesterday* | *the day before* |
| 'I sold my bike yesterday,' he told me. | He told me (that) he'd sold his bike the day before. |
| *today* | *that day* |
| 'I'm revising today,' she said. | She said (that) she was revising that day. |
| *here* | *there* |
| 'My grandparents live here too,' she told him. | She told him (that) her grandparents lived there too. |

## 8D Reported speech (2)

**8.3** See **8.1** and **8.2** above for general information about changes of tense and pronouns in reported speech.

| Direct speech | Reported speech |
|---|---|
| **Present perfect** | **Past perfect** |
| 'I've finished,' he said. | He said (that) he had finished. |
| *can / can't* | *could / couldn't* |
| 'He can't swim,' she said. | She said (that) he couldn't swim. |
| *will / won't* | *would / wouldn't* |
| 'I'll phone later,' he said. | He said (that) he would phone later. |

**8.4** *say* and *tell*
If we want to mention who is spoken to, we usually use *tell*.
'Tom, I'm hungry,' said Mel. → Mel told Tom she was hungry.

We don't use *to* with *tell*.
~~Mel told to Tom she was hungry.~~ ✗

After *say*, we don't usually mention the person who is spoken to.
'Tom, I'm hungry,' said Mel. → Mel said she was hungry.

If we do mention the person who is spoken to, we use *to*.
Mel said to Tom that she was hungry. ✓
NOT ~~Mel said Tom that she was hungry.~~ ✗

# Grammar Builder

## 9B The passive (present simple and past simple)

**1** Write the past participle of these verbs.

1 break _____
2 take _____
3 make _____
4 send _____
5 spend _____
6 fly _____
7 try _____
8 show _____
9 grow _____
10 know _____

**2** Complete the sentences with the correct form of the verb *be*. ➠ 9.1

1 I _____ mugged last summer in New York.
2 The museum _____ renovated two years ago.
3 Good food _____ served every night in our restaurant.
4 Nowadays, most food _____ made in factories.
5 The video clip _____ viewed over a million times that day.
6 Most newspapers _____ published online these days.
7 The first TV programmes _____ broadcast about 90 years ago.
8 Every year, we _____ invited to my aunt's house for New Year, but we never go!

**3** Complete the description using the present simple passive form of the verbs in brackets. ➠ 9.1

Our pizzas ¹_____ (make) freshly every evening from a recipe which ²_____ (know) by only a few people. Only the finest ingredients ³_____ (use). The tomatoes ⁴_____ (grow) in the south of Italy and the cheese ⁵_____ (produce) using only the finest buffalo milk. The pizzas ⁶_____ (prepare) by our skilled pizza chefs. Then they ⁷_____ (cook) in our traditional pizza ovens. They ⁸_____ (serve) with fresh salad.

**4** Complete the broadcasting facts. Use the past simple passive form of the verbs in brackets. ➠ 9.1, 9.2

1920 The first radio broadcast ¹_____ (transmit) by KDKA in the USA.
1925 The first soap opera, *The Smith Family*, ²_____ (broadcast) on the radio.
1928 A television image ³_____ (send) from England to the USA for the first time.
1928 The first television set ⁴_____ (sell).
1936 The first BBC TV programmes ⁵_____ (make) in the UK.
1940 Colour TV sets ⁶_____ (demonstrate) by CBS in New York.
1947 Baseball games ⁷_____ (televise) for the first time.
1954 More money ⁸_____ (earn) by TV broadcasters than by radio broadcasters.
1964 Colour TV sets ⁹_____ (buy) by families across the USA.

1983 The final episode of the comedy series *M*A*S*H* ¹⁰_____ (watch) by more than 125 million viewers.
1990 The first episode of *The Simpsons* ¹¹_____ (show) on Fox.

## 9D The passive (present perfect and future)

**5** Complete the sentences. Use the correct affirmative, negative, or interrogative form of the present perfect passive. ➠ 9.4

1 My watch *has been stolen* (steal).
2 These socks _____ (not wash).
3 _____ your ticket _____ (check)?
4 A new road _____ (build) between Kingsbridge and Abbotsville.
5 The latest *Avengers* film _____ (not show) in our local cinema yet.
6 _____ your parcel _____ (deliver) yet?
7 They're going to cancel the concert because not enough tickets _____ (sell).
8 How many people _____ (invite) to Emily's party?
9 My homework _____ (not mark) by the teacher.

**6** Complete the advertisement. Use the future passive form (*will*) of the verbs in brackets. ➠ 9.5

### SuperCloud ☁

**FREE cloud storage for your computer data!**

It's so easy! Simply select the files you want to store and they ¹_____ (upload) to SuperCloud. They ²_____ (scan) for viruses and then ³_____ (store) on our servers.

Your files and photos ⁴_____ (back up) automatically, so they ⁵_____ (not lose).

Remember, you ⁶_____ (not charge) for the SuperCloud service. It's FREE!

Click here to sign up. Once you sign up, an email ⁷_____ (send) to you with full instructions.

What are you waiting for?!

**7** Rewrite the sentences. Use the present perfect or future passive. Use *by* where necessary.
➠ 9.2, 9.3, 9.4, 9.5

1 Robots will build the cars in the new factory.
*The cars will be built by robots in the new factory.*
2 The police have arrested three men.
3 We probably won't need desktop computers ten years from now.
4 Youths have vandalised the bus stop.
5 Digital cameras have replaced celluloid film cameras.
6 The police will study the CCTV footage.
7 They haven't invented computers that can think like humans.

# Grammar Reference

## The passive (present simple and past simple)

**9.1** We form the passive with the correct tense of the verb *be* and the past participle.

*These cars are made in China.* (present)
*This computer was made in Japan.* (past)

The passive can be affirmative, negative or interrogative.

| Present simple | Past simple |
| --- | --- |
| **Affirmative** | |
| They are powered by electricity. | It was powered by steam. |
| **Negative** | |
| Cricket isn't played in many countries. | Basketball wasn't played in the 18th century. |
| **Questions and short answers** | |
| Are they grown in Europe? Yes, they are. / No, they aren't. | Was it built by the Romans? Yes, it was. / No, it wasn't. |

**9.2** We use the passive when either we do not know who or what performed the action, or we do not want to focus on who or what performed the action.

*My laptop was stolen last weekend.*

If we want to say who performed the action, we use *by*.

*My house was designed by a famous architect.*

**9.3** When we use adverbs with the passive, we usually put them immediately before the past participle.

*Phones are often used as video cameras.*
*It was probably discovered by the Ancient Greeks.*

## The passive (present perfect and future)

**9.4** We form the present perfect passive like this:
present perfect of the verb *be* + past participle of the main verb

| Affirmative |
| --- |
| The room has been tidied. |
| **Negative** |
| The room hasn't been tidied. |
| **Questions and short answers** |
| Has the room been tidied? Yes, it has. / No, it hasn't. |

**9.5** We form the future passive like this:
*will / won't* + *be* + past participle of the main verb

| Affirmative |
| --- |
| Teachers will be replaced by robots. |
| **Negative** |
| Teachers won't be replaced by robots. |
| **Questions and short answers** |
| Will teachers be replaced by robots? Yes, they will. / No, they won't. |

## S Extra Speaking Tasks

## Unit 4

**SPEAKING** Work in pairs. Take turns to compare and contrast photos A and B.

1 Describe each photo in general.
2 Describe any differences and similarities between the photos.
3 Speculate on how people in the situations may be feeling.

## Unit 5

**SPEAKING** Work in pairs. Take turns to do the task below. Spend about a minute preparing your answer. Use phrases from exercise 4 in lesson 3G and exercises 4 and 5 in lesson 5G to help you.

After leaving school, you have decided to take a gap year and work in Britain. Discuss the three jobs shown in the pictures with a member of staff at the job agency. Decide which job you will apply for and why.

## Unit 7

**SPEAKING** Work in pairs. Take turns to do the tasks below.

**Student A:** Describe photo A in detail first, then briefly compare it with photo B.
**Student B:** Describe photo B in detail first, then briefly compare it with photo A.

- Discuss this statement together:
  'It is more important for schools to spend money on teaching materials than extra-curricular activities'.
  Do you agree? Why? / Why not?

## Unit 8

**SPEAKING** Work in pairs. Take turns to compare and contrast photos A and B. Then answer the questions.

1 How do you think the person is feeling? Why?
2 What are the pros and cons of punishing criminals in this way, in your opinion?

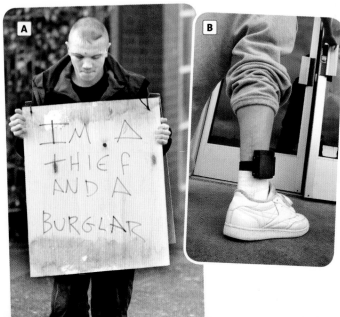

# OXFORD
## UNIVERSITY PRESS

Great Clarendon Street, Oxford, OX2 6DP,
United Kingdom

Oxford University Press is a department of the
University of Oxford. It furthers the University's
objective of excellence in research, scholarship,
and education by publishing worldwide. Oxford
is a registered trade mark of Oxford University
Press in the UK and in certain other countries

ISBN: 978 0 19 451056 1

Printed in China

This book is printed on paper from certified
and well-managed sources.

ACKNOWLEDGEMENTS

*Back cover photograph:* Oxford University Press
building/David Fisher

*The authors and publisher are grateful to those who have
given permission to reproduce the following extracts and
adaptations of copyright material:* p.68 Adapted
extract from "Teenage trips: that first parent-free
holiday" by Hilary Bradt, Kevin Rushby and Terry
Alderton, The Guardian, 12 June 2010. Copyright
Guardian News & Media Ltd 2010. Reproduced by
permission. p.58 Adapted extract from "Best job in
the world? Meet the duvet tester who spends her
working day getting ready for bed" by Emily Allen,
Daily Mail Online, 31 December 2012. Reproduced
by permission of Solo Syndication. p.109 Extract
from Oxford Bookworms Library Stage 2: Robinson
Crusoe by Daniel Defoe, retold by Diane Mowat.
© Oxford University Press 2008. Reproduced by
permission. 123RF pp.51 (family on beach/Graham
Oliver), 58 (watching tablet/Andriy Popov),
142 (boy with cello/Cathy Yeulet); Alamy Images
pp.19 (Walking in Lake District/Trevor Ronson
Photographic), 27 (Hikers looking at map/Alaska
Stock), 110 (Downton Abbey 2010/AF Archive),
142 (water polo players/Cultura Creative); Alamy
Stock Photo pp.8 (angry man/Alamy), 10 (lottery
tickets/Fire Pig Images), 11 (girl comforting friend/
Catchlight Visual Services), 14 (warning sign/
D Johnson), 14 (takeaway coffee/Chih-Chung
Johnny Chang), 14 (mind your head sign/
imageBROKER), 15 (swimming sign/Bill Bachman),
19 (rock climber/Africa Media Online), 35 (data
security symbol/imageBROKER), 36 (tablet game/
veryan dale), 37 (racing game/pumkinpie),
40 (foggy park/Steve Vidler), 40 (cars in blizzard/
Avico Ltd), 41 (car in ice storm/Shotshop GmbH),
43 (flooding/Jeremy Pardoe), 43 (earthquake
destruction/Tommy E Trenchard), 44 (tsunami
aftermath/DOD/S.Dupuis), 46 (paragliders/Arterra
Picture Library), 48 (Glastonbury festival/Roger
Cracknell 01/classic), 53 (female sports coach/
Blend Images), 55 (man making keys/Jeff Morgan

08), 55 (groundsman/Gerrit de Heus), 57 (teen with
new iPad/Peter Barbe), 60 (picking strawberries/
Andrew Fox), 60 (washing up/keith morris),
65 (cabin crew/David R. Frazier Photolibrary, Inc),
68 (silhouette of crowd/Kirsty Pargeter), 68 (coast
walker/Steve Taylor ARPS), 71 (kayaker/Jane
Hallin), 74 (white truffles/Maurizio MIlanesio),
74 (Gold of Kinabalu orchid/Renato Granieri),
75 (pair of Yubari King melons/Fotosearch), 76 (Sao
Paulo landscape/Mike Goldwater), 79 (woman
scanning barcode/Cultura Creative), 85 (van
vandalising car/john norman), 87 (Bonnie and
Clyde/GL Archive), 88 (open window/Radharc
Images), 89 (bank vault/Radius Images), 97 (ping
pong invention/WENN Ltd), 97 (stash sandals
invention/WENN Ltd), 99 (angry man at airport/
Eyecandy Images), 100 (testing Google Glasses/dpa
picture alliance), 102 (the Antikythera mechanism/
Hercules Milas), 102 (Overbeck Rejuvenator/Marc
Tielemans), 103 (typewriter/Mary Evans Picture
Library), 104 (customer complaint/allesalltag),
108 (afternoon tea/Bailey-Cooper Photography 2),
110 (Dr Who toy/Pete Jenkins), 110 (Strictly Come
Dancing/Carolyn Jenkins), 110 (Top Gear Live
show/WENN Ltd), 112 (The Body Shop logo/PSL
Images), 112 (Richard Branson/jim forrest),
116 (Enigma machine/NTERFOTO), 116 (Ada
Lovelace/AgencyPictorial Press Ltd), 118 (tennis
player/Juergen Hasenkopf), 118 (ice hockey/dpa
picture alliance), 142 (snowball fight/Micheko
Productions, Inh. Michele Vitucci), 142 (electric
ankle monitor/Art Directors & TRIP); Caters News
Agency pp.58 (Jo Unsworth), 96 (dog/Caters News
Agency – Hayley Pugh); Corbis p.87 (Butch Cassidy/
Jonathan Blair); Getty Images pp.4 (students in
canteen/Comstock), 7 (Korean children and robot
dog/Tomas van Houtryve/VII), 8 (worried football
fans/Andrea Comas), 8 (exam results/
MachineHeadz), 12 (video call/mikkelwilliam),
15 (Ashlyn Blocker/Jeff Riedel), 18 (Suspension
bridge/Konrad Wothe), 19 (Cavern diver/Karen
Doody/Stocktrek Images), 19 (Kayaking/Heath
Korvola/Aurora Open), 21 (Base jumping/Max
Dereta), 23 (Mike Perham celebrates/Oli Scarff),
24 (Boat sinking/Troy Plota), 26 (Hiking/Rich
Wheater/All Canada Photos), 27 (ATV quad runner/
pixeldigits), 42 (meteor/David Troncoso), 46 (Ewa
Wisnierska/Tim Clayton), 53 (student in training
class/Purestock), 56 (men in lift/Popperfoto),
67 (boy at airport/Jupiterimages), 74 (truffle/Tony
Gentile/Reuters), 77 (Glen James/Boston Globe),
81 (conference/Kim Kulish), 85 (teen shoplifting/
David Young-Wolff), 85 (gloved hand stealing
jewelry/Ghislain & Marie David de Lossy),
85 (employee stealing money/Fertnig), 85 (gloved
hand stealing jewelry/Ghislain & Marie David de
Lossy), 86 (muggers waiting to attack/John Carey),
87 (Billy the Kid/Underwood Archives), 92 (riots
and looting in London/Peter Macdiarmid),
92 (looters/Darren Staples), 112 (Anita Roddick at
her store/Cheryl Chenet), 114 (trading floor New
York stock exchange/Charles O'Rear), 114 (Wall
Street traders/Ed Eckstein), 115 (old Sherlock
Holmes/Sunset Boulevard); Kobal Collection
pp.6 (Twilight still/Summit Entertainment),
31 (Twilight/Summit Entertainment), 84 (Oceans
Eleven/Warner Bros), 109 (Cast Away/20th Century
Fox/Dreamworks/Duhamel, Francois); Manchester
Evening News Syndication p.13 (Zoe Avarianov);
Mary Evans Picture Library p.103 (Telharmonium);
Oxford University Press pp.5 (friends/Chris King),
16 (boy bodyboarding/Photodisc), 17 (boy with fake
spider/Haddon Davies), 26 (bungee jumping/
Imagemore), 29 (man on bike/Photodisc),
40 (snowflake/Photodisc), 41 (storm/Stockbyte),
43 (desert/Mark Phillips), 43 (tsunami/Christian
Vinces), 45 (pollution/Design Pics), 45 (teen boy/
Image Source), 47 (lightning/Digital Vision),
60 (woman buying clothes/Chris King),
62 (Istanbul/Luciano Mortula), 63 (Buckingham
Palace/Digital Vision), 65 (Florence/Photodisc),
65 (Alhambra sunset/Martin Froyda), 71 (Louvre
pyramid/images4), 92 (thief/Image Source), 98 (old
mobile/spe), 98 (flip phone/Hugh Threlfall),
98 (smart phone/Christian Delbert), 98 (smart
phone), 99 (maid opening door/BananaStock),

105 (cyclists/connel), 113 (Alcatraz Island/
Moodboard); Oxford University Press DAM
p.142 (winter travel scene/Getty; Digital Vision);
Rex Features p.24 (Fisherman/Design Pics, Inc.);
Rex Shutterstock pp.6 (The Hunger Games/Snap
Stills), 6 (Les Miserables/Universal/Everett),
6 (Skyfall/Moviestore), 6 (Iron Man Still/c.
Paramount/Everett), 6 (The Lord of the Rings/
Moviestore Collection), 7 (robot with map/Paul
Brown), 10 (lottery winner/Geoff Robinson),
30 (Skyfall/Snap Stills), 30 (Thor/Moviestore),
31 (Despicable me 2/Moviestore), 31 (How I met
Your Mother/CBS/Everett), 31 (Kylie Minogue/
Action Press), 31 (The Woman in Black/
Moviestore), 34 (Who Wants to be a Millionaire/
REX/Shutterstock), 39 (Iron Man 3/c.W.Disney/
Everett), 74 (fountain pen/REX/Shutterstock),
75 (gold trainers/Koji Yano), 75 (hair styling/
Startraks Photo), 84 (The Dark Knight Rises/
Moviestore), 84 (Robin Hood/SNAP), 91 (Somerton
beach), 101 (Mars One settlement/Mars One/Bryan
Versteeg), 108 (racegoers at Ascot/Robert Hallam),
115 (Sherlock Holmes/c.Warner Br/Everett),
121 (Johnny Depp/Broadimage), 121 (Christina
Aguilera/Startraks Photo), 142 (thief and shame
board/Alan Lewis); Shutterstock pp.8 (bored
student/wavebreakmedia), 9 (nervous woman/
pathdoc), 9 (suspicious man/pathdoc), 9 (excited
woman/ArtFamily), 9 (angry man/Ollyy),
20 (Liverpool Street station/Keith Gentry),
21 (Backpacker/In Green), 22 (Boat sails in storm/
lafoto), 24 (reef sharks/cbpix), 26 (Whitewater
rafting/VILevi), 32 (boy using laptop/Monkey
Business Images), 33 (retro TV icon/ITS STUDIO),
35 (piracy warning/alexskopje), 35 (piracy warning/
eldeiv), 36 (gamers/BlueSkyImage), 43 (forest fire/
Evgeny Dubinchuk), 43 (volcano eruption/Ammit
Jack), 45 (teen girl/CREATISTA), 48 (shopping/
PeoGeo), 48 (parade/T photography), 49 (global
warming concept/ponsulak), 51 (couple walking/
Monkey Business Images), 52 (engineer/Monkey
Business Images), 52 (hairdresser/Tyler Olson),
52 (paramedics/CandyBox Images), 52 (architect/
goodluz), 53 (female au pair/Phovoir), 53 (gardener/
Fotokostic), 54 (girl in cafe/Olga Rosi), 55 (estate
agent/Andy Dean Photography), 55 (stunt man/
Eniko Balogh), 55 (builder/Dmitry Kalinovsky),
58 (hands and lego/STUDIO GRAND OUEST),
62 (Eiffel Tower/pisaphotography), 62 (Statue of
Liberty/Katharina M), 62 (Machu Picchu/vitmark),
62 (world map/AridOcean), 63 (Hong Kong/Iakov
Kalinin), 63 (African landscape/Oleg Znamenskiy),
65 (Admiralty Bay/Pawel Kazmierczak), 66 (skier
falling over/Photobac), 66 (back of camera/Kitch
Bain), 70 (women taking selfie with telephone box/
William Perugini), 73 (waitresses/CandyBox
Images), 73 (couple at the cinema/Tyler Olson),
75 (sale concept/IhorZigor), 78 (rubbish dump/
ThavornC), 81 (cloud computing concept/
makeitdouble), 82 (orchestra/iOso), 82 (football
training/matimix), 85 (burglar/Brian A Jackson),
92 (daylight robbery/Dmitri Ma), 93 (Dublin/Pavel L
Photo and Video), 95 (modern classroom/PlusONE),
95 (computer room/RTimages), 96 (dandelion/
Przemek Klos), 98 (old mobile/elbud), 98 (smart
phone/), 99 (old friends/Monkey Business Images),
111 (European map/Jktu_21), 142 (dairy farmer/
goodluz), 142 (hotel receptionist/Kzenon), 142
(waitress/CandyBox Images).

*Sources:* www.washingtonpost.com, www.bbc.co.uk,
www.news.com.au, www.dailymail.co.uk,
www.independent.co.uk

*Illustrations by:* Andy Parker pp.4, 84, 91 (Man, note);
117, 120, 121; Mark Duffin pp.95, 97 (90 degree
glasses); Adrian Barclay pp.119, 122, 126, 132.

*Although every effort has been made to trace and contact
copyright holders before publication, this has not been
possible in some cases. We apologize for any apparent
infringement of copyright and if notified, the publisher
will be pleased to rectify any errors or omissions at the
earliest opportunity.*